FINAL DAY

SECOND EDITION

FINAL DAY

10 CHARACTERISTICS
OF THE SECOND COMING
OF JESUS CHRIST

RICHARD D. WILES

ISBN Hardback: 978-164764649-3
ISBN Paperback: 978-0-578-26081-5

Second Edition, January 2022

The Authorized King James Version of the Holy Bible is the source for all scripture quoted in this book, except where one or more other translation is noted. Italics are the author's own and added for emphasis.

Published in the United States of America by
Great Company Publishing LLC
www.GreatCompanyPublishingLLC.com

I dedicate this book to Jesus Christ, my Savior, and Redeemer. He is also my older brother, role model, hero, and dearest friend. I'm always bragging about Him because He is the best brother imaginable. My sincerest desire is for you to know Him too. Turn your heart toward home and be reunited with your Heavenly Father. He loves you and desires your presence at the big family reunion that He has planned someday. Don't let anything in this world prevent you from living with Him for eternity.

TABLE OF CONTENTS

ACKNOWLEDGMENT

NO WORTHWHILE PROJECT IS accomplished alone. The contributions of many people come together to produce something new that impacts multitudes of people who will never know about the work, sacrifice, time, effort, struggle, and investment that was necessary to make the project a success.

Firstly, I must thank Susan, my wife, for surrendering 40 consecutive weekends to permit me to devote my uninterrupted time to writing *Final Day*. I must also thank my son Jeremy who has consistently encouraged me to pursue my passion for writing more than any other person in my life. Because of Jeremy, I was motivated to make a radical change in my daily schedule for nine months to write this book and prepare it for publication.

Our daughter Karissa and son Jeremy must be thanked too for giving Susan and me ten fantastic grandchildren who are my motivation to take a firm stand for Jesus Christ and His kingdom. I desire them to remember their grandfather as a righteous man who loved God with all his heart, mind, and soul, and that he refused to compromise the integrity of the Word of God in an age of spiritual rebellion and apostasy. I hope my example encourages them to fearlessly stand upright for God and never bend or back down.

Lastly, I extend my sincere appreciation to all our outstanding team members at Flowing Streams for performing their duties during my extended absence from our office much of each day as I wrote this book. Raymond Burkhart, Jody Schlabach, and Paul Benson are among those who deserve special recognition. I also thank Paul Benson for recording the Holy Bible scriptures in the audio version of this book.

One more "thank you" goes to Gator, my Golden Retriever buddy who tirelessly forced himself to sleep next to my feet for nine months as I wrote *Final Day*. Gator and I spent most of our time in the backyard of our Florida home and moved like sundials from one shady spot to the next each day. Now that I finished the manuscript, Gator and I can swap places. I can get some rest while he finally writes his very revealing and up-close autobiography, *They Treat Me Like a Dog*.

Postscript: By the time the second edition of Final Day was published, Gator had passed away on September 25, 2021, seven weeks shy of his thirteenth birthday. I deeply miss my furry friend, but I know that, according to Job 12:10, God is holding Gator's soul until the restitution of all things. Whenever tears fill my eyes thinking about him, I tell myself, "Gator is safe. Papa is holding him."

INTRODUCTION
The True Story Behind The Writing of This Book

D O YOU BELIEVE THE universe had a first day? Do you think the universe has a final day?

Anything that has a beginning must have an end. This book is not a Bible prophecy book about the Last Days. It is a book about the last day, the final day of the cosmos, the Earth, and the age of mankind. It is about the final day before the first day of eternity.

I was physically born on August 20, 1953. My body came out of my mother's womb alive, but my soul arrived DOA: Dead on arrival. Nearly 25 years later, my soul was reborn on June 11, 1978. My pastor at that time baptized me by immersion in a nearby creek on the same day, and the Holy Spirit sealed me.

In my early years as a young Christian, I heard many inspiring sermons about the Second Coming of Jesus Christ. Christians were excited in the 1970s and 1980s about Jesus returning someday. They were also motivated to finance foreign missionary projects to evangelize lost souls on every continent and build Christian

1

television and radio stations. But, as the years passed by, I detected a cooling of the religious zeal of American Evangelical churches. Saving souls was no longer their passion. Evangelists proclaiming the coming of the Lord were replaced by life coaches teaching personal motivation, self-improvement, "empowerment," and financial success. Zionism was welcomed into many American churches and even, in some places, Kabbalah mysticism. The State of Israel replaced Jesus. The occult Star of David replaced the old, rugged Cross. Charismatic churches gradually became infested with New Age gurus, pagans, witches, and warlocks serving as self-appointed apostles, super-apostles, and prophets. What a mess. The cooling-off that started in Evangelical churches in the 1990s became a spiritual ice age in the twenty-first century.

Meanwhile, the mass popularity of *The Late Great Planet Earth* Bible prophecy book and the *Left Behind* novels and films subtly seduced Christians not to yearn for the glorious appearing of our blessed hope Jesus Christ and our resurrection from the grave. Instead, they became obsessed with escaping persecution and tribulation, transferring our faith in Jesus Christ and His finished work on the Cross to having faith in the Zionist State of Israel to save and bless us. Gradually, Christian Zionism "Replacement Theology" replaced traditional Evangelical Christianity in many American churches.

By the 1990s, selling "The Rapture" had become a thriving multibillion-dollar religious business. Pastors, prophecy teachers, and celebrity evangelists on television assured Evangelical Christian Zionists they would not experience trouble, persecution, or tribulation. The "Rapture" would take them away, and everybody else would be "left behind." Some enthusiasts even purchased "Rapture insurance" policies for their dogs and cats. Such policies guarantee that an atheist or pagan, or anybody else who will not be taken away in the Rapture, will care for the policy owner's beloved pet during the Great Tribulation.

I freely acknowledge that I do not believe in a popular doctrine known as the Rapture. Furthermore, I do not think a Jewish kingdom in Jerusalem will rule the world for one thousand years after the Lord returns. If you insist, despite my protestations, on placing me in a religious box, you can say I am a traditional, orthodox Christian who rejects chiliasm and embraces amillennialism. An amillennialist is a Christian who believes that Revelation 20 refers to Jesus Christ ruling and reigning in and through His Holy Church now, in the period between Jesus' Ascension to Heaven and Second Coming to Earth. Revelation 20's reference to a "thousand years" is a metaphor that refers to an unlimited number of years, as Psalm 50's "cattle on a thousand hills" means God owns all creatures worldwide and the hills too.

I do not belong to any denomination. Theologically, I am a mixed breed mutt who aligns mostly with Reformed Baptist churches, minus the Calvinistic doctrine of the predestination of souls. Is there such a critter as a free will amillennial Reformed Baptist who is a member of the one, holy, catholic, and apostolic Church? Well, there is at least one roaming around in Florida. I also identify with conservative Presbyterian, Anglican, Methodist, Lutheran, General Baptist, and Congregational churches. I avoid all churches that wave Israeli flags with their occult emblem and celebrate the brutal occupation of Palestine. My heart grieves for the beautiful Palestinian people, both Christians and Muslims, who have suffered so greatly since 1948. My undivided devotion and loyalty are to King Jesus, not Zionism, the enemy of my Lord and His Church.

God saved my soul in 1978. For 20 years, our family attended church congregations affiliated with the Church of God (Cleveland, TN), Assemblies of God, the Southern Baptist Convention, and several non-denominational charismatic churches along the way. I identified for many years as an all-American, flag-waving, red-white-and-blue patriotic Protestant Evangelical Christian. In other words, I was a proud member of American Babylonian Churchianity.

Today, I am no longer associated with it. I escaped the Babylonian religious plantation decades ago to pursue primitive Christianity. It took the Holy Spirit many years to deprogram my mind by eradicating doctrines, beliefs, and practices contrary to the Holy Bible and the early church. After all these years, I still struggle with religious cobwebs left behind in my mind from past indoctrinations. I passionately pursue Jesus Christ but must continually maneuver around religious stumbling blocks that litter my path.

At best, many of today's churches are lukewarm. At worst, they are apostates. Yes, I originally heard the Good News in a Pentecostal church in the late 1970s. Today, however, I would not dare enter some charismatic churches unless armed with a three-foot crucifix and a five-gallon bucket of holy water to extinguish the strange fire at the altars. What am I today? I am a follower of The Way: a disciple of Jesus Christ. I am a recipient of the victory that Jesus Christ won in a spiritual war at Calvary over two thousand years ago. I don't have to do anything to be saved other than to believe, receive, and walk in Christ's victory. I affirm the three ancient creeds of the true apostolic Church: The Apostles' Creed, the Nicene Creed, and the Athanasian Creed.

I believe that salvation requires confession of belief in Jesus as Lord and Savior and baptism in water. Jesus said, "He that believeth and is baptized shall be saved; but he that believeth not shall be damned." Baptism alone cannot save your soul. Likewise, confession of faith without baptism does not save you. People can argue with me, but I'm committed to doing things Jesus' way. He said belief and baptism. Who am I to tinker with His formula?

I also believe that Christ is present in the Lord's Supper, also known as Holy Communion, the Eucharist, and the Thanksgiving Feast. I do not believe in transubstantiation and a bloodless sacrifice on a church altar. I agree with my eastern Orthodox brethren, who say that the sacred meal is a holy mystery that human minds cannot understand. By faith, we believe that our Savior is present in the Lord's Supper to nourish our soul. In this respect, I lean toward traditional, conservative Anglican, Presbyterian, Reformed, and Methodist theology. Jesus is the Bread of Life and the Living Water who satisfies my hunger and thirst. I feast on Christ. It grieves my soul when I see churches treat the Lord's Supper as nothing more than serving crackers and grape juice every three months to remember something important that happened thousands of years ago.

I study church history, particularly the ante-Nicene and Reformation ages, and collect old Christian books containing sound doctrine. My two favorite preachers were Polycarp and Patrick of Ireland. The godly men who most profoundly impacted my walk with Christ include Charles Spurgeon, Alexander Maclaren, G. Campbell Morgan, and Philip Mauro.

I see good things in almost all Christian denominations. Most of them began with a holy fire to honestly proclaim the Gospel of the Kingdom and defend the ancient faith. Errors in doctrine crept in along the way, and lukewarm spirituality became the norm. Some became apostates, ordained homosexual clergy, endorsed same-sex marriages, abortion, and invited witches and warlocks to preach and teach in their churches. Such denominations and churches departed the true faith and can no longer be called Christian.

I would readily join a new denomination that cultivates the best confessions of faith, traditions, and characteristics of the great religious movements in Christian church history. Perhaps they could name it the United Orthodox Reformed Anglican, Presbyterian, Wesleyan Methodist, Lutheran, Primitive Freewill Six-Principle Baptist, Spirit-filled Holy Apostolic Old Catholic, Evangelical Moravian, Messianic Disciples of Christ, Assemblies of God's Missionary Baptists! Forget it. That name will not work. The outdoor church signage would be massive. City governments will never issue permits for church signs that big. The point I am making is that I find good things in almost all Christian denominations. I can find common ground and fellowship with members of most denominations and respect our differences. Regardless, my soul yearns to know and practice primitive Christianity as seen in the Acts of the Apostles and the writings of the ante-Nicene church fathers. The closer I get to original Christianity, the more alien and strange American Babylonian Churchianity looks to me.

I have been a born-again Christian since 1978. The Word of God is a lamp unto my feet. The Holy Spirit is my friend, counselor, advocate, and comforter. Throughout my journey of faith, my beloved Heavenly Father has, from time to time, spoken directly to me in dreams and visions that gave me direction and insight into matters of my life. I experienced a dream about the last days shortly before becoming a Christian. I was a dope-smoking, beer-drinking party boy when God gave me that dream in early 1978. It disturbed me so much that I went to church that same Sunday morning. Someday I will share it in another book.

Twenty years later, in 1998, the Lord spoke to me again in a vision about the final day. Years earlier, I was hired personally by Paul F. Crouch, the founder of the Trinity Broadcasting Network, to be the network's marketing director. My office was in Irving, Texas. I loved my job. I love Texas, rodeos, pickup trucks, sunsets, country music, longhorn cattle, barbeque brisket, pinto beans, and jalapeno peppers. I was happy! (Have I ever told you that I love Texas?)

I traveled around the United States of America and met with cable television executives to persuade them to sign affiliation agreements to carry TBN on their cable systems. I also developed and managed national advertising campaigns, attended national and regional trade shows, and worked with prestigious trade publications to write positive articles about TBN. Life could not have been better for me at age 44. Corporate recruiters offered me lucrative marketing management positions at other cable television networks. I was a cocky corporate marketing hotshot, and I knew it.

God, however, had a different plan than mine. My life changed suddenly. In the first weeks of March 1998, the Holy Spirit nudged me to begin a fast. I put it off by telling myself that my business schedule was too full for fasting. Airline travel, meetings, conferences, trade show expos, breakfast meetings, luncheons, and dinners with clients filled my calendar. How could I fast and do business at the same time? Couldn't the Lord see how busy I was working for Him?

By April 1998, the hint had become an urge and then a command. I finally succumbed to the Holy Spirit and began my fast in the third week of April. On the third or fourth day of the fast, the Holy Spirit interrupted my workday by beckoning me to meet Him in TBN's chapel. It was mid-afternoon. I told the office secretary I would be away from my desk for a few minutes. Little did I know how long I'd be in the chapel.

As I walked to the chapel inside TBN's International Production Center in Irving, Texas, something ominous and even foreboding descended on me. I became aware that my appointment with God would be more than just "having a little talk with Jesus." I felt a spiritual heaviness descend upon me. I remember thinking that perhaps God was about to tell me I had only a few months to live, and I must get my life's affairs in order. By the time I reached the chapel door, I was nervous. I felt like a mischievous schoolboy on his way to the school principal's office. The chapel was empty. Let me clarify that statement: There were no humans in the chapel. The room, however, was saturated with the holiness of Almighty God. Immediately, I thought about Isaiah when he was given a vision of Jesus upon His throne.

"Woe is me! For I am lost; for I am a man of unclean lips, and I dwell in the midst of a people of unclean lips; for my eyes have seen the King, the Lord of hosts!"

Isaiah 6:5

Unlike Isaiah, I did not see the Lord in the chapel. It was His holiness that was present. I felt like Adam: naked, hiding behind a tree, with God asking: "Who told you that you were naked?" I was spiritually naked in front of my Maker. Suddenly aware of my sensual and corporeal humanity, I wasn't gleeful to recognize the Holy Spirit's presence saturating the room. I trembled as a mortal human thrust into the presence of the Spirit of the eternal living God who formed me in my mother's womb, gave me a soul, breathed life into my nostrils, and kept my heart beating.

Often, I have heard Christians exclaim how much they wish Jesus would appear and speak to them. Typically, they say, "I would shout and jump up and down and dance before the Lord!" But that's not what you would do if Jesus walked into a room. I can tell you from experience. You would fall on your face, shake, and tremble in the presence of Almighty God. Most Christians have little comprehension of the overwhelming holiness of God. They will fully see it on the final day.

That day in April 1998, I entered the chapel as a 44-year-old guy in his prime who was marketing the world's largest religious television network. Yet, in the presence of the Holy Spirit, my life flashed before my eyes, and it wasn't a pretty sight. I became aware that my life was falling woefully short of the glory of God and the heavenly calling in Jesus Christ. What if it had been *my* final day? Was I satisfied with my life? I knew Christ had saved my soul, but would my works in this life survive the test of fire on the final day?

I did a lot of repenting, crying, and pleading for forgiveness. I promised God I would change. I don't recall precisely how much time passed, but I do remember the moment God forgave me. I truly felt His love restore my relationship with Him. All was well again between the Lord and me.

That's when the vision started. The velvet curtains parted to reveal a movie screen in front of me. My eyes were open, yet I was in a trance. I saw the heavenly movie screen supernaturally suspended in the air in the chapel. The movie God was showing was *Judgment Day*, starring Jesus Christ. I saw a city on fire with black billowing smoke rising into the sky. Chaos filled the streets, and terrified citizens fled the destruction. To this day, I remember the faces of refugees who escaped the burning urban sprawl.

What happened to the city? I do not know. The Heavenly vision did not reveal to me the calamity that struck the metropolis, but I perceived it was horrific. Only a remnant of the city's inhabitants could have survived to tell the story. The vacant, listless survivors I saw looked shell-shocked, as though they had come from a battlefield, and were amazed they were still living. I saw survivors walking through fields and farmland beyond the city limits. They were disheveled, and their clothing was torn and tattered. Ashes covered their faces. Many survivors were bleeding. I saw frightened mothers clinging to their infants and fathers pulling their children in wagons. One man vividly remains in my memory. He was pushing his elderly mother in a wheelbarrow.

The vision ended as quickly as it started. With tears streaming down my cheeks, I asked God to reveal what I saw in the vision. In my spirit, I heard the quiet, still voice of the Holy Spirit whisper, "This is the future of your sinful nation if the people do not repent. Tell the people to repent."

I fell to my knees and wept. I asked God for a Bible verse to confirm the vision was from Him. I opened my Bible and looked down. I was staring at Isaiah 24 while still on my knees.

Behold, the Lord will empty the earth and make it desolate, and he will twist its surface and scatter its inhabitants.

Isaiah 24:1

Isaiah's prophecy (verses 1-23) is one of the Bible's dual-fulfillment prophecies, meaning it was fulfilled once in the land of Israel and will be fulfilled again in the last days. It foretells God's judgment upon humanity's wickedness and rebellion. The "Lord will empty the Earth and make it desolate." The stark meaning is God will depopulate the planet. He will remove its inhabitants and take away its bountiful wealth. God will also twist and mutilate its surface through ruinous calamities that will disfigure the planet. So great will be the firestorm of judgment that nobody will recognize the world. The Earth will revert to its original darkness without form and void.

That's only the beginning of Isaiah's vision. There was more destruction on its way. First, however, Isaiah told us the cause of the divine judgment. The sins of its inhabitants defiled the planet. The people transgressed God's commandments, violated His statutes, and broke His everlasting covenant with them. He is no longer bound to honor it with those who have sinned against Him. And so, a curse will devour the Earth, and the people will suffer in their guilt. They will be scorched. Few will survive His judgment.

The earth mourns and withers; the world languishes and withers; the highest people of the earth languish. The earth lies defiled under its inhabitants; for they have transgressed the laws, violated the statutes, broken the everlasting covenant. Therefore a curse devours the earth, and its inhabitants suffer for their guilt; therefore the inhabitants of the earth are scorched, and few men are left.

Isaiah 24:4-6

Many Bible scholars interpret Isaiah 24 as a judgment upon ancient Israel. Arabic Christian scholars, however, interpret the "emptying" as the removal of the inhabitants of the whole world by incomprehensible disasters that befall humanity when God pours from seven bowls His wrath upon the wicked.

> **Then I heard a loud voice from the temple telling the seven angels, "Go and pour out on the earth the seven bowls of the wrath of God."**
>
> **Revelation 16:1**

Isaiah's vision matches St. John's vision in the Apocalypse. The Old Testament prophet saw the city's commercial vitality dissolve when divine judgment arrived. The city that formerly bustled with activity, commerce, and voices was silent. There was no wine, no food, no music, no singing. Only sorrow, wailing, and mourning rang out through the desolate city. St. John saw the sudden destruction of Babylon.

> **The merchants of these wares, who gained wealth from her, will stand far off, in fear of her torment, weeping and mourning aloud, "Alas, alas, for the great city that was clothed in fine linen, in purple and scarlet, adorned with gold, with jewels, and with pearls! For in a single hour all this wealth has been laid waste." And all shipmasters and seafaring men, sailors and all whose trade is on the sea, stood far off and cried out as they saw the smoke of her burning, "What city was like the great city?"**
>
> **Revelation 18:15-18**

Standing in the chapel, crying, I asked God why He had shown these things to me. Again, I heard the gentle voice of the Holy Spirit. He said, "I am calling you today to tell the people to repent." I reminded the Lord that He chastised me for sinning against Him minutes earlier. I said, "I'm not holy like you. I'm the wrong man for this task. There are other men who are holy whom You can send to tell the people to repent." The response I heard in my spirit was, "I did not call you because you are holy. I called you because you are a good repenter. When I convict you of your sins, you repent quickly. Go tell the people to repent of their sins. I will forgive them."

I returned to my office, never mentioned the chapel experience to anybody at TBN, and remained quiet for the remainder of the day. My soul was troubled by my encounter with God in the chapel. I didn't even tell my wife, son, or daughter when I went home that evening. But the following day, our daughter said to me, "Dad, Jesus spoke to me last night."

Karissa was nearly twenty-two years old when this happened in 1998. Surprised by her remark, I asked, "Did you see Jesus last night?" Karissa replied, "No, I was asleep. He came into my room and stood next to my bed and spoke to me in my sleep. I knew it was Jesus standing next to me." "What did He say?" I asked. Karissa replied: "Daughter, beginning tonight, I will speak to you about the last days through dreams and visions."

"Dad, He gave me a dream," Karissa continued with her astounding story. "You, Mom, Jeremy (our son), and I were huddled together as a family. Thousands of people surrounded us. The people revolved around our family as though they were standing upon a giant moving carousel. Dad, I must tell you one more thing. Those people in the dream were skeletons! I remember looking at their skulls and peering into their eyeball sockets. They pointed their bony fingers at you and cried in a loud voice, 'If you knew this was going to happen, why didn't you tell us?' Dad, I don't know what God is telling you to do with your life, but you better do it!"

Stunned by my daughter's dream, I told her what had happened in the TBN chapel. I also vowed to God that I would spend the rest of my life telling people to repent of their sins, telling them to believe in the name of Jesus Christ, and warning them to get ready for divine judgment to strike the planet. Nothing has been the same in my life since that day.

Over the next few months, I privately shared my vision several times with Dr. Paul F. Crouch in his office. The founder and president of TBN listened intently and respectfully but said little about it. I still wasn't sure if I was up to the task God had set before me. I even persuaded myself that God had given me the vision because Mr. Crouch was too busy building and managing TBN's global affairs, and I was supposed to relay it to him. Foolishly, I hoped that Paul Crouch would go on his international television program and tell the world to repent. I still thought I could quietly go back to work as his marketing director. After all, I was a business marketing hotshot, not a seminary-trained preacher.

It didn't work out the way I assumed. God had a different plan. Eventually, and reluctantly, I submitted to it, such that when the Holy Spirit spoke to me again in June 1998, telling me, "Write a book titled *Judgment Day*," I did as I was instructed, albeit a little too eagerly, in retrospect.

If you are a parent, have you ever instructed your children, and they immediately started the task while you were still describing the instruction? I did the same thing to God. I didn't wait for God to finish telling me His wishes. I galloped off to write the book. In my mind, I assumed He would be pleased with how fast I leaped to begin the assignment.

In hindsight, I should have waited upon the Lord in prayer and drawn closer to Him through Bible study before commencing the task. The business world loves self-motivated, aggressive men who don't need supervision, but things are done differently in God's kingdom. Success requires a careful balance between patiently waiting on the Holy Spirit to guide and your determination to complete an assignment. Such wisdom comes over time as we age and mature.

In the days after the incredible spiritual experience in TBN's chapel, I searched my human, carnal mind for a logical explanation for the things I'd seen in my vision. Cities on fire! Burning skyscrapers! Fleeing refugees! It had to mean that a catastrophic event was on the horizon. I looked around for a likely candidate. What was the scariest item in the news in 1998? Y2K, of course. Experts told us that computers would crash worldwide at midnight on December 31, 1999, when computers would roll over to the year 2000.

"Certainly," I reasoned, "this must be the explanation for the vision. God wants me to warn people to prepare for Y2K! The chaos will be our judgment." So, I set about researching the dire and ominous Y2K projections and warnings issued by reputable computer IT experts, scientists, government officials, corporate executives, bankers, and military commanders. Newspapers, magazines, online news websites, and television news channels warned that "doomsday" was coming worldwide on December 31, 1999.

The experts warned that computers worldwide would crash because they were not programmed to recognize double zeros as a date. They predicted global havoc after commerce and banking stopped functioning, and darkness covered the world when utilities ceased providing electricity.

What else did the experts predict would happen on New Year's Eve in 1999? They said air traffic control systems would go haywire, and passenger planes would crash because the pilots would lose all navigation systems in the cockpits. Pentagon generals told United States Senators that Russia's nuclear-armed ICBMs would accidentally launch from their silos and kill tens of millions of Americans. The dire warnings in 1998 and 1999 were not imagined and propagated by "conspiracy theorists." On the contrary, the most frantic and dire doomsday predictions came from highly educated experts, IT professionals, government officials, military generals, bankers, and economists.

They spread fear throughout the world. What was the motivation? We may never know the truth. Perhaps Y2K was a worldwide psychological warfare experiment. Maybe it was an elaborate scheme by Western intelligence agencies to compel people, companies, and organizations to download a Y2K remediation patch approved by the intelligence agencies. How many new computers purchased in 1999 had pre-installed backdoors that allowed government agencies to snoop on the owners over the next decade? Who knows what happened?

A nuclear war planned by NATO could be another plausible explanation for the Y2K propaganda operation. The public was fed disinformation about the alleged Y2K noncompliance of the Russian computers that controlled the country's thousands of nuclear-armed intercontinental ballistic missiles. Did NATO plot to nuke Russia by telling the world that Moscow launched missiles at midnight? Yes, it is a far-fetched explanation, but we are presently experiencing another worldwide propaganda operation: the Covid-19 pandemic. Over $300 billion was spent worldwide on remediation efforts to avoid a global meltdown. It was a costly hoax if Y2K was only a conspiracy theory. Whatever the Y2K scare's true purpose, it pales compared to the worldwide Covid-19 propaganda fear campaign.

Regardless of whatever was behind the Y2K propaganda, I wrongly concluded that the vision God gave me in April 1998 was a glimpse of the chaos that was coming on December 31, 1999. Immediately, I galloped off to write the book *Judgment Day* as instructed by the Lord, but I added something to the title. I included the year 2000 in the book's title. That was my idea! I did it by myself with no help from anybody else, including the Lord. Like many Christians, I did not wait on God for the complete instruction, and I added something to it. Whenever we do this, we produce an Ishmael. Giving birth to an Ishmael means making child support payments for years.

In August 1998, the Holy Spirit revealed that my time at TBN was over. I submitted my resignation letter to Paul Crouch. My last day as TBN's marketing director was September 8, 1998. I said goodbye to my friends and coworkers. I walked out the door and went to my vehicle in the parking lot. I took a final gaze at the majestic TBN headquarters, drove away, and never looked back.

I published *Judgment Day 2000* in October 1998. Something unusual happened one night in that month. My daughter Karissa called in the afternoon to suggest that I attend a town hall meeting about Y2K in Garland, Texas. We were living in Colleyville at the time. I told her I was too busy to drive to Garland to meet about a topic I already knew. After all, I'd written a book about it. I was a certified Y2K expert. Karissa persisted; I relented. I went to Garland and sat near the back entrance of the hotel conference room. Several hundred people were there too.

The moderator had read *Judgment Day 2000* and recognized me to my surprise. He asked me to stand up and tell the audience about the book. When I sat down, I felt a tap on my shoulder. A woman seated behind me whispered that she had to speak to me immediately. We both went to the hotel hallway. Her name is Leah. (Susan and I are still friends with Leah today.) The well-dressed woman appeared rattled. She nervously said, "I've been praying for you for two years!" I replied, "How could that be so? We are meeting for the first time now." Leah answered, "Two years ago, I had a vision of a man sitting at a desk typing a book manuscript on a computer. The title of the book was Judgment Day. You are that man in the vision! I've prayed for two years for you to write the book." That was weird, too. But it happened.

For the remainder of 1998 and the first five months of 1999, I crisscrossed America speaking to audiences in hotels, meeting halls, and churches. I told them about the vision and pleaded with them to repent of their sins. I paid my way by draining the $52,000 in our savings account, which Susan and I had set aside to purchase a home in Texas.

In addition to my public speaking engagements, many radio talk show hosts interviewed me in late 1998 and early 1999. One day in April 1999, the manager of a popular religious radio station in Dallas-Ft. Worth called while I was in a hotel during a speaking engagement in another city to ask if I had ever thought about hosting a radio show. I told him the thought never occurred to me, and I wasn't interested. He politely insisted that we should meet when I returned to the area.

We eventually met, and he offered me an hourly weekday slot at 7:30 AM. As a marketing professional, I knew that 7:30 AM was drivetime when millions of people were commuting to work in their cars and trucks. It was a coveted slot. But there was a catch: The radio station classified the available airtime as paid programming time, which meant that I had to buy the airtime from the station. It was nearly $7,000 per month, and the station's terms required cash upfront each month. In 1999, seven thousand dollars per month was a lot of money, especially for a guy no longer employed in a regular job.

I was also facing another problem. I had drained down the savings we used after I resigned from TBN. I used the money to self-publish *Judgment Day 2000*, travel expenses across the USA and even London, and our monthly living costs. There was nothing left over. There was no way I could sign a legally binding twelve-month contract and commit the last of my funds to pay only the first installment of $7,000.

God, however, had a plan. The man who hosted the Y2K meeting in Garland the previous year invited me to lunch. We met at a barbeque restaurant along Texas Highway 183, somewhere between Euless and Haltom City. My friend also invited one of his friends to join us. After finishing our meal, my friend asked me to talk about the radio talk show opportunity. His businessman friend asked me what I planned to say on the radio show. I replied that I would tell people to repent of their sins, believe in the name of Jesus Christ, and get ready for the Second Coming of Christ.

The Fort Worth businessman asked me if I would accept the radio station's offer. I answered, "I cannot afford the $7000 upfront cash the radio station requires to start broadcasting." We exchanged business cards after the lunch meeting and went our separate ways.

The next day, the businessman called and asked me to visit his office in Fort Worth. He said he would not be there, but his secretary would have something for me. Later that day, I met his secretary, and she handed me an envelope. I left the office, went to my vehicle, and opened the envelope. What was inside? A check for $7000 and a note that said, "Start the radio show."

Amazed by the miraculous appearance of the money, I promptly called the radio station manager and agreed to start a weekday radio show. Our first broadcast was on May 24, 1999. The broadcast was named *America's Hope*. My daily message was, "Jesus Christ is America's only hope."

Weeks before the launch of the radio show, our son and daughter each entered a British Airways contest. They both won! Jeremy and Karissa each received two free roundtrip tickets to Europe. In this way, God generously gave us a memorable two-week family vacation in Great Britain, France, and Switzerland before we began a new adventure, with me as a radio talk show host. Susan and I have not had many vacation days since 1999.

We returned from Europe on May 22, 1999. I vividly remember saying to God, "I am not afraid of work. Work me hard for Your kingdom." Dear reader, allow me to offer some advice: Be careful what you say to the Lord. Because He sure took me up on the offer. I have never stopped working hard for Him since. He's taken me to Africa, Europe, Asia, Central America, Latin

America, and the Caribbean, representing His kingdom. What an adventure, and what a privilege.

To my absolute surprise, *America's Hope* was an immediate success. People responded to the message of repentance. The size of our audience soared throughout the summer of 1999. In early June 1999, the Holy Spirit instructed me to say on the radio program for 90 days, "Judgment starts in America on September 11." I did not know the meaning, but I obeyed and said it many times over the next three months. Because Y2K was on its way, many radio listeners assumed it meant September 11, 1999. But the Lord never said the year, only the month and day. All He said was: "Judgment starts in America on September 11."

The radio station's owner transferred the local manager to another station in Denver, Colorado, and an acting manager assumed control of the Dallas station. Because I did not own a production studio, hosting the show required me to drive each morning in heavy rush-hour traffic to Dallas to produce it live from the radio station's studio. One morning in September 1999, the acting manager waited for me to exit the studio. She wanted to talk privately with me. I followed her to an empty office where she hesitantly gave me the bad news. The station's wealthy owner had decided to change the station's format and, therefore, was canceling all religious programming in 30 days despite having legally binding contracts.

My world collapsed. Two weeks before the cancelation notice, I confidently signed real estate agreements to purchase a house under construction and a small office building. I used a "creative financing" idea on both sellers, and it worked. Both contracts were 90-day leases starting on October 1, with the closing date on

December 28, 1999. And yet, I knew the radio cancellation was not a surprise to God. He inspired me to purchase both properties, told me what to offer, and blessed me with divine favor and success.

Indeed, God had a plan. Once again, my inner man heard God's voice gently speak, "I will stretch your faith. I will build a studio for you. I will take your ministry nationwide."

Thirty days later, *America's Hope* signed off the Dallas radio station. I earnestly sought God for direction. Sure enough, the Holy Spirit gave me another instruction: "Go on international shortwave radio and the Internet." It did not make sense to me as a media professional.

Shortwave radio broadcasting was a World War II technology losing its aging audience, and Internet audio streaming had very few listeners in 1999. I could not see how God's plan would work, but I had no choice. I was off the air and heading toward insolvency. I was sinking and needed to learn to swim quickly. I decided to swim by faith.

We moved into the small office building that we had purchased on a 90-day lease-to-buy deal. I had three months to find the money to pay for it. Likewise, I had to find the money for the house too. The office building was originally a house that a previous owner converted into a daycare center for toddlers. The smell of urine and vomit in the carpet saturated some rooms. To me, though, it was a palace because it was mine. We were excited to have a headquarters for our new upstart radio ministry.

My son Jeremy and I ripped out and replaced the old, stained carpet, painted all the rooms, and made other upgrades. Within weeks, we had an excellent facility. Jeremy and I also constructed a studio in a small room that was the size of a small walk-in closet.

We used leftover carpet to soundproof the walls. My friend Mike donated a vintage 1960s-era audio control board from an AM radio station he previously owned. Our checking account had just enough money to purchase a high-quality broadcast microphone for $500. We were in business again.

Instead of the local radio station, *America's Hope* was available internationally through the old technology of shortwave radio broadcasting and the new medium of Internet audio streaming and MP3 audio files. I was podcasting long before podcasts, a term not coined until 2004.

Our radio program found an audience on both shortwave radio and the Internet in late 1999. We benefited from the sizable audience in North America that was still listening to world news programs on the BBC's shortwave transmissions. Sufficient donations arrived each week to keep the lights on, but not much more. My immediate future appeared to be bleak, but the vision of the city on fire and my daughter's dream kept me going.

Y2K fizzled, and life went on. The remaining inventory of *Judgment Day 2000* books went to a landfill. I dusted myself off and carried on, despite the post-Y2K ridicule directed at me. Nobody blamed the experts who said doomsday would happen on December 31, 1999. The public only mocked those of us who believed the experts and reported what they said. Life is not fair.

Twenty years after writing *Judgment Day 2000*, the Holy Spirit inspired me to write another book. I drafted the chapter outline in 2018. I started writing this book in February 2019. The working title was "Ten Characteristics of the Second Coming of Jesus Christ." I knew the working title was too long, but my focus was on the Lord's return. What will happen on that day?

The official title came to me on Monday, March 25, 2019. I'd taught from this book's unfinished manuscript the previous Sunday evening at the church where I am a presbyter and teaching elder. In my sermon, I told the congregation that there had been many "day of the Lord" events in history. For example, the day of the Lord arrived suddenly and unexpectedly for the inhabitants of Sodom and Gomorrah. The day of the Lord came in 70AD when the Romans captured Jerusalem and destroyed the Jewish temple. Nineveh had a "day of the Lord" visitation 40 years after Jonah's warning. You could say Pompeii had a "day of the Lord" experience too.

The day of the Lord is a sudden and unexpected visitation by God to strike a city or nation with divine judgment after repeated prophetic warnings fail to change the hearts and behavior of its inhabitants. God repeatedly warns individuals, cities, and countries to repent, which means changing their ways. Sent by God, inspired prophets warn rebellious individuals and populations that the Lord will suddenly visit them and bring judgment upon them. Eventually, God's patience runs out, and He sends one or more calamities. The day of the Lord arrives unexpectedly because the people do not expect God to perform what His prophets say He will do to them.

After I'd delivered a sermon in March 2019, a member of our ministry team said something to me that changed this book: "Pastor Rick, as you were teaching, I was thinking that the book you are writing is about the last day of the Lord." His words resonated with my spirit. I thought about them that night. The following day, I heard the Holy Spirit say to me, "The book's title is *Final Day*."

Four weeks later, which was the third week of April 2019, another revelation came. That week was the twenty-first anniversary of my vision in TBN's chapel, during which I had seen a burning city, heard God's call to me to preach repentance, and then been stunned by my daughter's dream. That vision was what inspired me to write a book in 1998. The Lord told me to call it Judgment Day, as I explained earlier. I foolishly added the year 2000 to the title. I also erroneously focused on Y2K as the logical explanation of the vision I saw in TBN's chapel.

I was wrong about all of it. God wanted me to write a book about the one and only Judgment Day for the entire world. In the third week of April 2019, I heard the Holy Spirit speak inwardly to me, reassuring me: "You are now writing the book I desired you to write in 1998."

This book is about the final day. It will be the last "day of the Lord." I did my best to get it right this time. I hope my Heavenly Father is pleased with this book. I love Him very much.

Maranatha! O Lord, come!

CHAPTER 1

HIS SECOND COMING
SHALL BE SINGULAR

HOW MANY TIMES DOES Jesus Christ return to Earth? Once or twice? Will there be one "Second Coming" of Jesus or two?

The question sounds silly. If Jesus returns twice, the second "Second Coming" would have to be called the Third Coming of Jesus Christ. The obvious answer is: There is only one Second Coming of Jesus Christ. Why must such a ridiculous question be asked in the first place? Despite the question's absurdity, tens of millions of sincere Christians, who genuinely love the Lord, are confused about the answer.

The laws of mathematics do not operate the same way in all churches. In most traditional Christian churches worldwide, one plus one always equals two. But math is different in other churches, primarily Christian Zionist churches in the United States of America. For them, one plus one equals one because the first one does not count. Are you following along?

Which denominations, churches, and seminaries use traditional math in counting the number of times Jesus will return in the Second Advent? Generally, the list includes most conservative Lutheran, Anglican, Presbyterian, Methodist, Reformed, Congregationalist, General Baptist, Orthodox (Greek, Russian, Syrian, Eastern, and Assyrian), and Catholic churches (Roman, Melkite, Maronite, Armenian, Malabar, Syriac, Coptic, and Ethiopian). For the sake of simplicity, let's call this group Traditional Christians.

On the other side of the math divide are influential denominations, churches, and seminaries that teach one plus one equals one. This school of mathematics is Evangelical Zionism Math, or EZ Math. Religious organizations that teach EZ Math include the Southern Baptist Convention, Assemblies of God, Church of God (Cleveland, TN), Calvary Chapel, the Church of God in Prophecy, International Pentecostal Holiness Church, Dallas Theological Seminary, Moody Bible Institute, Bob Jones University, Liberty University, The Master's Seminary, and Evangel University. They are Christian Zionists because their eschatology is built on the modern State of Israel being God's Number One priority and the Church is God's little sideshow to occupy His time between the First and Second Advents of Christ.

In fairness to both sides, godly men and women who love Jesus Christ, share the Gospel with others, and faithfully await the Second Coming of the Lord are in Traditional and Christian Zionist denominations, churches, and seminaries. However, they have a significant difference of opinion on two eschatological topics of extreme importance: Does Jesus come back to Earth once or twice? Is God's Israel the Christian Church or a Zionist political state?

The core controversy revolves around a concept known as "the Rapture." The doctrine is the lynchpin that holds in place other vital parts of Evangelical Christian Zionism. Those parts include the separation of the Church and Israel, the Millennial Kingdom, and the timing of the Day of Judgment. If you remove the lynchpin, Christian Zionism theology will collapse into a heap of religious junk. That's why Evangelical Zionists become irate when somebody challenges "the Rapture" doctrine. They must guard and defend the lynchpin, or the religious Rapture industry will implode. "The Rapture" is the queen bee in Christian Zionism's hive, and from it, a lot of financial honey flows to prophecy teachers, authors, publishers, TV networks, and seminaries.

As explained by Christian Zionists, the Rapture is the next big event to happen in the fulfillment of Bible prophecies. The Rapture concept first appeared in Great Britain in the early 1800s through the teaching of John Nelson Darby, a disgruntled Anglican priest whose family owned a haunted castle in Ireland where ghosts and goblins roamed its halls. Darby's relatives were necromancers. Is it possible that John Nelson Darby received his theology from a spook?

Mr. Darby was vehemently opposed in London by Reverend Charles H. Spurgeon. What preacher would dare to make Spurgeon his fiercest critic? The fiery Reformed Baptist pastor called Darby the "Protestant Pope" because of his dogged insistence that Darby's new theology was "recovered knowledge" that God kept hidden from the worldwide Church for 1,800 years and that everybody had to accept it as biblically sound doctrine. Mr. Darby also invented dispensationalism, a theory of biblical history that claims that God assigned different administrative principles to different historical ages, otherwise known as dispensations.

Darby's unorthodox eschatology attracted few disciples in Great Britain. He made several voyages to America looking for converts but enjoyed limited success selling his novel ideas to American preachers. One person, however, who was intrigued with Darby's new systematic theology was Reverend Dwight L. Moody, the Chicago-based soul-winning evangelist. Moody's Bible school later hired Cyrus Scofield to write and edit Bible correspondence courses that taught Darbyism. After his death, Scofield appropriated Darby's ideas, and, with the help of a powerful New York City Jewish lawyer, acquired a deal with London's Oxford University Press to publish a reference Bible with footnotes inspired by Darby's doctrines.

When the first copies of the Scofield Reference Bible rolled off Oxford's printing presses in 1909, America's Evangelical and Traditional churches were still essentially unified in their beliefs about the Second Advent of Christ. The main differences were over issues such as the one thousand years mentioned in Revelation 20. Does it mean a literal Millennial Kingdom after the Lord returns, or does it figuratively mean that Christ is ruling and reigning now through His saints on Earth? Overall, the idea that Jesus would return twice was unheard of in most American churches in the nineteenth century.

Sales of the Scofield Reference Bible fueled the slow but steady growth of the Rapture sect in the United States of America during the first seven decades of the twentieth century. Oxford sold an estimated two million copies of Scofield's shoddy reference Bible in the first several years after its publication. Throughout those years, most American churches continued to preach and teach traditional Christian eschatology. However, the Rapture movement took off like a rocket in the 1970s, after Hal Lindsey and Carole C. Carlson co-authored *The Late Great Planet Earth*, which reportedly sold over 40 million copies.

A second booster rocket propelled the Rapture doctrine into orbit in the 1990s when Tim LaHaye and Jerry Jenkins co-authored the wildly successful *Left Behind* series of fictional novels and movies. The *Left Behind* book series sold an estimated 80 million copies. Today, the Rapture doctrine is settled law in tens of thousands of churches. Most Christian Zionists pastors, Bible teachers, and church members assume all Christians worldwide have always believed it. To this day, belief in the Rapture is still an American Christian Zionist concept that has little support in churches elsewhere in the world.

Are the Rapture and Second Advent the Same Event?

This chapter poses seven crucial questions to the reader: Firstly, does Jesus Christ return to Earth once or twice? Secondly, are the Rapture and the Second Coming the same or different events? Thirdly, if the Rapture and Second Coming are separate events, does not that mean Jesus Christ will return to Earth twice? Fourthly, why did Jesus neglect to tell His disciples that He would return twice? Fifthly, why did the Apostles never teach early Christians that Jesus' return would be a two-stage event spread out over seven years? Sixthly, why did the early church fathers not mention the Rapture? Seventhly, why did the Holy Spirit conceal "the Rapture" for over 1,800 years until the days of John Nelson Darby?

If questioned, both Christian Zionists and Traditional Christians would concur that the dead in Christ will rise first and quickly be followed by those alive when Jesus Christ returns. Here's where the two camps disagree: Is that event "the Rapture" or the Second Coming? Christian Zionists would reply that it is the Rapture. Traditional Christians would say it is the Second Coming. Which is it? Unless the Rapture and the Second Coming are the same events, it cannot be both.

According to the Darby-Scofield-Moody school of theology, the return of Jesus Christ will be a two-stage reentry, spread over seven years. Darby taught that the Rapture would happen first. It will be secretive because only Christians will see Jesus in the Rapture. Unsaved people will be stunned when hundreds of millions of humans vanish with no explanation for their sudden disappearance. Tim LaHaye fanned the religious nonsense with his novels and fictional films that predicted driverless automobiles would crash into other cars and buildings, commercial jetliners without pilots would plummet to the ground, and terrified fathers would return home from work to discover that their wives and children vanished.

Christian Zionism teaches that seven years of great tribulation and the rule of the Antichrist will follow the Rapture. At the end of the seven years, Jesus will return to Earth again to crush the Antichrist and establish His kingdom in Jerusalem. For Christian Zionists, it will be the official Second Coming. That's why one plus one equals one, according to EZ Math. They say the first appearance by Jesus, the so-called Rapture, does not count as a Second

Coming of the Lord, but His second visit seven years later that should be recognized as the official Second Coming. Furthermore, Christian Zionists believe nobody will be caught up in the clouds to meet Jesus in His Second Coming. In Darby's world, all saved Christians will be "raptured" before the Great Tribulation.

The Darby-Scofield-Moody seminary cafeteria menu includes a fully loaded Rapture enchilada. You cannot pick and choose the toppings but must eat the whole thing. The toppings tray comprises a wide assortment of events, prophecies, and timelines they swear must happen.

Among the most popular toppings are:

- Christians will be taken to Heaven for seven years
- the Holy Spirit will be removed from the Earth
- the time of great tribulation will last seven years
- 144,000 Jewish male virgins will preach during those seven years about a revived Davidic kingdom
- Gentiles will convert after believing the message of the Jewish male virgins
- a spotless red heifer will be born in Israel
- a third temple will be built in Jerusalem
- the Antichrist will make a peace treaty with the State of Israel that he intends to violate
- the Antichrist's armies will encircle the State of Israel
- the battle of Armageddon will be fought at Megiddo to destroy the State of Israel
- Jesus' Second Coming will be seven years after the Rapture
- Jesus will return to save the State of Israel from destruction
- Jesus will revive the Davidic Kingdom, and its worldwide headquarters will be in Jerusalem

- Gentiles will be saved during the Great Tribulation, but they will not be given glorified bodies at the Second Coming of Christ
- saved Gentiles will dwell in mortal human bodies with Adam's sin nature during the Millennial Kingdom, and they will commit sins
- animal sacrifices will be reinstated at the new third temple to atone for the sins of Gentiles who will live during the thousand-year kingdom
- saved Gentiles will give birth to children during the Millennial Kingdom
- saved Gentiles will die and be buried during the Millennial Kingdom
- Gentiles who die during the Millennial Kingdom will be resurrected at the end of the thousand years
- Satan will be released from the abyss at the end of the thousand years
- there will be a final confrontation between God and Satan at the end of the thousand years
- some Gentiles who live during the Millennial Kingdom will switch their allegiance to Satan
- the Day of Judgment will be after the thousand years
- God will not destroy the Earth but instead, merely refurbish it.

The Darby-Scofield-Moody doctrine has three big problems: Jesus never said it. The Apostles never taught it. And the universal Church never heard it for eighteen centuries.

If you ask Christian Zionists whether they believe in the Second Coming of Jesus Christ, they will unanimously respond "Yes." Likewise, if you ask Christian Zionists if they believe in "The Rapture," they will also answer "Yes." Here's their dilemma: You cannot believe Jesus Christ returns to Earth only once if you also believe in the Rapture taught by the doctrine's zealots. If Jesus Christ comes first in the Rapture and again in the Second Coming, it means He will return to Earth twice. One plus one always equals two in actual math, regardless of how the Christian Zionists count. Jesus will return one time.

Do You Believe in the Rapture Pooka?

The Darby-Scofield-Moody narrative is ludicrous and absurd, yet tens of millions of sincere church members believe it. Why? Because Darby's heterodoxy was jammed into their pastors' minds by seminary professors also indoctrinated with the radically new eschatology that appeared in the nineteenth century. The Zionist indoctrination of Christian clergy has been ongoing since the days of Cyrus Scofield. The Caiaphas Cabal found a way to enter Christ's Church and change it from the inside.

How do you persuade people who believe in an invisible secret event that it is not real? It would be akin to convincing Elwood P. Dowd, as portrayed by Hollywood acting legend Jimmy Stewart, that his mythical Celtic pooka pal Harvey wasn't a real rabbit. In the 1950 movie *Harvey*, only Elwood could see Harvey, the six-foot-three inches-tall rabbit. A pooka is a mischievous goblin in Irish folklore. Christian Zionists have an invisible pooka pal, too. His name is Rapture. You cannot see the Rapture Bunny in the Holy Bible, but his devotees passionately swear it is there. They become angry if you challenge their religious delusion. It's best to smile and say you see their pooka pal if you want the conversation to remain civil. Keep peace in your family. You never know when you will need your pooka-believing brother-in-law to repair your air conditioner on a hot summer day.

How do you convince your elderly mother, who went to church every Sunday her whole life, that the Rapture pooka is not real? Her favorite Bible prophecy teachers on religious television stations frequently talk about the Rapture. Are they all wrong, and only you are right? Mom will have a tough time deciding whom to believe if you rupture her Rapture. If Mom admits her favorite Bible prophecy teacher misled her about the Rapture, she must also question other doctrines they taught her. Most people cannot go there. When challenged with scriptural evidence, people typically continue to believe a falsehood rather than consider the possibility that trusted religious leaders, unintentionally or intentionally, misled them for years.

It may not seem a big deal when a six-year-old child believes in Santa Claus and the Easter Bunny. What do you say, however, to a 60-year-old adult who still believes in mythical beings? That's when you lovingly pat your father on his back and say, "Dad, I see the Rapture pooka too." Do not argue with them about their imaginary bunny. Guard important relationships. The important thing is that your relatives and friends have faith in Jesus Christ to save their souls and resurrect their bodies on the last day.

Sadly, many Christian Zionists privately know there is no Rapture Bunny but fear a confrontation with their church's elders if they challenge the religious delusion. Their pastors and Bible teachers are obligated to defend the honor of their denomination's cherished pooka. However, the modern world's rapid movement toward embracing the Antichrist Beast system is compelling many Christian Zionist pastors to rethink their church's eschatology. Christian Zionist pastors who do not see the Rapture pooka fear their denomination's Pharisees may angrily revoke their ministerial credentials and sabotage their ministry's future. Sooner or later, pastors and Bible teachers must courageously declare, "The Rapture doctrine is false."

Go ahead and say, "The Rapture pooka is not real." It's okay not to believe in the Rapture. Nothing terrible will happen to you, except you may be asked to leave your local Christian Zionist church. If your Southern Baptist or Calvary Chapel local church boots you out the door, relax. Many conservative Presbyterian, Methodist, Anglican, Congregational, Lutheran, and Reformed churches will gladly welcome you as a new member.

There was a day when you were a toddler and said, "Santa Claus is not real." Christmas still came each year, and plenty of gifts appeared under the Christmas tree. You grew up understanding that Mom and Dad purchased the toys. Santa Claus is not coming someday, and neither is the Rapture pooka. The odds are higher for Saint Nick to come down your chimney than the Rapture pooka to appear and take you to Heaven for seven years.

It is time to grow up in the faith and stop believing in mythical pookas. Jesus Christ is returning one time for His holy nation of Israel, meaning all Christian saints worldwide. He will not come back a second time seven years later for another load. Jesus will make one trip from Heaven to Earth. You must be at the bus stop on the corner of Believe Avenue and Baptism Boulevard. The Salvation Bus is coming one time, and its arrival will be sudden and unexpected. We must always be ready and waiting for Him to arrive for us.

Besides, Jesus doesn't need to make two trips from Heaven to Earth. He will get it all done in one trip. Jesus is amazingly capable of doing far more than we can imagine. Therefore, wrapping up the age of humankind on one day, the final day, will not cause the Lord to overexert Himself and profusely sweat. His Heavenly Father will not sigh and say, "Son, you tried to accomplish too much in one day. You traveled from Heaven to Earth in record speed and powered down the Sun, the Moon, and the stars. After turning out the lights in the universe, you resurrected all dead people, bundled the wicked to be burned, and caught up the saints to meet you in the clouds. You sat on the Great White Throne to judge the nations. You supervised the angels to organize all humanity by their respective countries and separated them into groups of goats and sheep. You judged every person who ever lived and tested in your crucible the works of the saints. If that wasn't enough for one day, you also chased down the Devil and tossed him in the lake of fire. Somehow you found time to roll up the universe like a scroll, set fire to the Earth, and burn up the elements. Before 5 PM, you created a new Earth and heavens, transported New Jerusalem from Heaven to the new Earth, packed up all your stuff in Heaven, and moved to New Jerusalem. Wow! What were you thinking? You should have stretched it out over one thousand years. Now your back hurts from overexertion. Please make an appointment with Heaven's chiropractor and have your spine adjusted in the morning."

No, my friend, Jesus will not strain His back getting it done in one day. Time will disappear when Jesus appears. The bridegroom has patiently waited for the big wedding ceremony. He will move, act, and complete His to-do list more speedily than any of us can imagine. He is God in human flesh. Stand back and watch how fast He does it on the final day.

The Great Word Switcheroo

Most business owners, corporate executives, and all lawyers know that the enforcement of business contracts can hinge on the interpretation of one word. In the Rapture versus the Second Coming debate, the interpretation also hinges on understanding the meaning of words. Words matter. Unfortunately, Christian Zionists are from Venus, while Traditional Christians are from Mars. We don't speak the same language.

Both camps in the Body of Christ agree that Jesus will snatch up the saints to meet Him in the clouds when He gloriously returns to Earth. That is not the point of contention. The contentious issue debated by both camps is when the saints shall be caught up in the air to meet Christ. Christian Zionists say there will be a secret Rapture of the saints before the time of great tribulation. Furthermore, Christian Zionists believe the Second Coming is at the end of the Great Tribulation, and nobody will be caught up in the clouds to meet Jesus at the Second Coming.

Traditional Christians say the secret Rapture theory is fictional, not biblical. They believe the saints will endure the tribulation and be caught up in the air to meet King Jesus at His Second Advent. Christian Zionists and Traditional Christians quote 1 Thessalonians 4:13-18 as scriptural evidence to support their competing beliefs. Traditional Christians interpret the verses as referring to the Second Coming of Christ. On the other hand, Christian Zionists cite the same verses as evidence of a secret Rapture seven years before the

Second Advent. Both cannot be right. Who is wrong? Christian Zionists or Traditional Christians?

> **But I would not have you to be ignorant, brethren, concerning them which are asleep, that ye sorrow not, even as others which have no hope. For if we believe that Jesus died and rose again, even so them also which sleep in Jesus will God bring with him. For this we say unto you by the word of the Lord, that we which are alive and remain unto the coming of the Lord shall not prevent them which are asleep. For the Lord himself shall descend from heaven with a shout, with the voice of the archangel, and with the trump of God: and the dead in Christ shall rise first: *then we which are alive and remain shall be caught up together with them in the clouds, to meet the Lord in the clouds: and so shall we ever be with the Lord. Wherefore comfort one another with these words.***
>
> I Thessalonians 4:13-18

The emphasis is on the word "caught," as interpreted by the King James Bible translators. The Greek word used by St. Paul is *harpazo*. The Christian Zionists replaced the Greek *harpazo* with the Latin word *rapere*. When Jesus Christ returns with a shout, the graves will open, and the bodies of departed saints will be suddenly snatched (*harpazo*) into the atmosphere to meet the triumphant King of Glory. Right behind them will be all the Christian saints who will be physically alive when Jesus appears in the sky.

There is no debate about whether the dead in Christ shall rise first. Likewise, there is no debate about the living saints joining them in the air. The issue is whether Apostle Paul referred to the only Second Coming of Jesus Christ or a mystical, invisible, secret mass intervention to relocate Christians from Earth to Heaven to escape tribulation and persecution seven years before the official Second Coming of Jesus.

The Greek-to-Latin word switcheroo is vital to grasp. The Greek word *harpazo* is a verb, not a noun. Christian Zionists, however, decided to replace *harpazo* in the original Greek manuscripts with a Latin word that is also a verb, but they made it a noun! Imagine somebody removing an English word from the United States Constitution and replacing it with a Russian word. It would not make sense. Anyway, that is what the Christian Zionists did to the New Testament's Greek manuscripts.

The Christian Zionists' preferred Latin word is *rapere*. Like harpazo, *rapere* is also a verb. The Christian Zionists, however, went one step farther. They converted a Latin verb into an English noun. They needed it to be a noun because "The Rapture" must be an event, not an action. However, the original Greek verb *harpazo*, is an action, not an event. Thus, we get "The Rapture." Do you see the Christian Zionists' subtle but devious deception?

The Greek word *harpazo* is used numerous times in the Bible, always as a verb, never as a noun. It means "to pluck, snatch, or take." The Greek verb conveys the sudden exercise of physical force to move somebody or something. The direction an object or person goes after it has been plucked or snatched is not relevant to the use of the word. It makes no difference whether a thing or person goes up, down, over, or sideways. About the Second Coming, however, the saints will be snatched up. *Harpazo* is how something happens, not what happens.

Here is where John Nelson Darby's nimble fingers pulled off his sleight of hand magic trick. Perhaps the spooks in the Darby family castle taught him how to perform this illusion. Darby and his disciples converted a Greek verb into a Latin verb and then made the Latin verb an English noun. Therefore, Christian Zionists should call their Rapture event "The Plucking" or "The Snatching."

According to Christian Zionists, "caught" comes from the Latin words *rapiemur, rapere, and raptus.* The etymology of *rapere* points to an action "to abduct, of forcibly and violently dragging or plucking off." The Latin word *raptus* means "seized." Thus, *rapere* means "to seize," and *raptus* implies something has been "seized." In ancient Roman law, *raptus* referred to property crimes such as robbery and confiscation. The Romans also used *rapere* for violent crimes such as kidnapping. The Latin word *rapere* was the source for the English word *rape.* Is Jesus Christ coming to rape the Christian Church violently? Words matter. Christian Zionists should not tinker with words in the Holy Bible to bolster their theology.

What is the English definition of *Rapture?* It is a mystical religious experience! Merriam-Webster's Dictionary defines *Rapture* as a noun that means "an expression or manifestation of ecstasy or passion; a state or experience of being carried away by overwhelming emotion; a mystical experience in which the spirit is exalted to a knowledge of divine things."

Thus, Christian Zionists teach that there will someday be a special religious event with a pronoun name: The Rapture. Based on the Latin word they chose to use, this event will be both a violent rape and an expression or manifestation of ecstasy or passion, a state of being carried away by overwhelming emotion, a mystical experience in which people's spirits know divine things. Christian Zionists do not seek to convey that message to their audiences. Still, the definition is consistent with the Latin word *rapere* that they arbitrarily inserted in the Holy Bible without God's permission. Words matter.

Let's stick with the facts: *Rapere, raptus, and Rapture* are not in the original Greek manuscripts of the New Testament Bible. The original Greek word is *harpazo*. The debate is not whether Christians will be caught up in the air to meet Jesus in the clouds. The Holy Bible tells us it will happen at the time of Jesus' arrival and presence. The debate is over John Nelson Darby's claim that Jesus will secretly snatch up Christians seven years before His official arrival.

Quite frankly, we should not be wasting time debating a ridiculous theology. It is a mystery how the cunning John Nelson Darby snookered an Evangelical preacher as smart as Dwight Moody into believing his nonsense. It was unfortunate because Dwight Moody was a good man. On the other hand, Cyrus Scofield was a money-hungry deceiving scoundrel who lied for decades about his Civil War role as a Confederate Army soldier, and his phony Doctor of Divinity degree. Nevertheless, Moody hired Scofield to write Moody's Bible school mail-order correspondence courses.

Without Darby, Scofield, and Moody, "the Rapture" hoax would not be known in churches today. The three of them did a lot of damage to the Christian faith by inserting their ludicrous ideas into the minds of millions of sincere Christians and interjecting a lot of needless confusion into the Body of Christ. The universal Church should jettison the Darby-Scofield-Moody baggage and present a unified message to a lost world of sinners.

More Magical Manipulation of Words

If the Greek *harpazo*, and not the Latin *rapere*, is the correct word for the snatching up of the saints into the air, what is the right Greek word for the Second Coming of Jesus? It is *Parousia*.

Parousia is used twenty-four times in the New Testament Bible. Six of those verses refer to the Second Coming of Jesus when the entire Body of Christ, the Church Triumphant and the Church Militant, will officially welcome and greet King Jesus in the air.

Parousia means a presence, a coming to a place, an arrival. In ancient times, it denoted the arrival and presence of royalty or some other very important person. It was customary for a town to send an official delegation to officially welcome and greet the appearance of a monarch or nobleman. The unique arrival of the VIP was called the *Parousia*. It meant that the presence of the king or queen and the full regal authority of the kingdom had arrived.

Both eschatological camps, Christian Zionists and Traditionalists, agree that the Greek word *Parousia* is the Second Coming of Jesus Christ. The confusion caused by Darby, Scofield, and Moody is over the oddball notion that the snatching (*harpazo*) of the saints is a separate event from the arrival (*Parousia*) of King Jesus. Furthermore, they argue that seven years separate the two events.

The *Parousia* is the only appearance of Jesus Christ. When Christ returns, He will gather His flock unto Himself, resurrect the dead, judge sinners, and cast them into the lake of fire. At the same time, the Lord will also burn up the Earth and the entire cosmos, create a new Earth, and move New Jerusalem to the new planet. Lastly, the Father, Son, and Holy Spirit, along with all angels, will move to New Jerusalem to dwell forever with the children of God.

It shall be a kingdom that has no end. There will not be a seven-year gap between the snatching up of the saints and the arrival of King Jesus. It is the same event.

Let's review how the Christian Zionists pulled off a slick trick that fooled tens of millions of sincere Christians. Here are the things we have learned thus far:

1. The Greek word *harpazo* means to snatch, and *harpazo* is a verb, not a noun. It is an action, not an event.

2. Christian Zionists snatched *harpazo* from the original Greek manuscripts of the Holy Bible and slyly replaced it with a Latin word that has a more aggressive definition.

3. *Rapere* is the Latin word preferred by Christian Zionists, and that it means to kidnap somebody, as in rape.

4. *Rapere* is also a verb, not a noun. It is an action, not an event.

5. However, Christian Zionists converted *rapere* into a proper noun representing the formal title of an event, not an action. Thus, they gave us "the Rapere," commonly known as "the Rapture."

Hold on! There is more Christian Zionists hocus pocus to expose. Here again, we see another sleight of hand magic trick by Christian Zionists in the way they switch words back and forth to justify their theology. Grasping the linguists' illusion is like figuring out the whereabouts of a pea as a slick magician rapidly moves it between three walnut shells.

Keep your eyes on those shuffling walnut shells! The Christian Zionists prophecy teachers are slick magicians. Like an illusionist who uses a saw to cut in half a woman in a box on the stage, the minions of John Nelson Darby, Cyrus Scofield, and Dwight Moody cut in half the Second Coming of Jesus! One event encompasses the glorious arrival of King Jesus (Parousia) and the catching up of the saints in the air to meet Him (harpazo). Christian Zionist magicians, however, cut that one event into two pieces. It was a very devious trick that fooled multitudes for over a century.

Watch closely! They split apart the snatching of the saints from the arrival and presence of King Jesus. And they cleverly declared both to be separate events separated by seven years of great tribulation. They gave the snatching up of the saints a formal name derived from a Latin word for rape. They called it "the Rapture." The Christian Zionists brazenly declared that "the Rapture" is not the Second Coming of Christ. Thus, according to Christian Zionist theology, the glorious arrival of Jesus will be seven years after "the Rapture."

Who authorized Darby, Scofield, and Moody to rape the truth? Who empowered them to cut in half the glorious arrival of Jesus Christ? Who granted ecclesiastical authority to Darby, Scofield, and Moody to replace a Greek word in the original biblical manuscripts with a Latin word, convert it from a verb to a noun, and make it an event instead of an action? Is it any wonder why so many sincere Christians are confused about the Second Coming of Christ?

An unbiased reading of 1 Thessalonians 4:13-18 clearly states that the snatching of the saints and the arrival of King Jesus shall happen simultaneously. It will be the final day, the day of the Lord. Modern Christian Zionist eschatology is nothing more than religious fables. Today's Christian Zionists should repent and return to the ancient faith.

A Silent Shout and Soundless Trumpet Blast?

Apostle Paul said the Lord himself shall come down from Heaven with a commanding shout, with the voice of an archangel, and with a blast from the trumpet of God. Will the command come from Jesus Christ or the archangel? Will God blow the trumpet or instruct an angel to blow it? The answers to those questions are open for debate. What is not debatable is the noise. Can a divine shout and trumpet blast reverberate throughout the cosmos and not fill the ears of every living creature on Earth? Will the entire human population except Christian Zionists wear earplugs on that day and not hear the noises? The Christian Zionists must think so. How else could they explain why billions of people will not hear the shout and trumpet?

A vital plank in The Rapture platform is secrecy: nobody except Christians will see nor hear Jesus in the Rapture. Belief in such secrecy repudiates everything the Holy Bible says about the glorious arrival of Jesus Christ on the final day. Ah, but Christian Zionists do not believe "the Rapture" is the glorious arrival of Jesus Christ.

Ardent proponents of the Darby-Scofield-Moody doctrines cite 1 Thessalonians 4:13-18 and 1 Corinthians 15:52 as their scriptural proof of a secret Rapture of saints before the start of great tribulation. Let's read the Bible scriptures as mentioned:

> **But I would not have you to be ignorant, brethren, concerning them which are asleep, that ye sorrow not, even as others which have no hope. For if we believe that Jesus died and rose again, even so them also which sleep in Jesus will God bring with him. For this we say unto you by the word of the Lord, that we which are alive and remain unto the coming of the Lord shall not prevent them which are asleep. *For the Lord himself shall descend from heaven with a shout, with the voice of the archangel, and with the trump of God:* and**

the dead in Christ shall rise first: then we which are alive and remain shall be caught up together with them in the clouds, to meet the Lord in the air: and so shall we ever be with the Lord. Wherefore comfort one another with these words.

1 Thessalonians 4:13-18

In a moment, in the twinkling of an eye, *at the last trump: for the trumpet shall sound,* and the dead shall be raised incorruptible, and we shall be changed.

1 Corinthians 15:52

Christian Zionists would enthusiastically swear on a stack of Scofield Reference Bibles that these scriptures are solid proof of a secret Rapture event seven years before the Second Coming of Christ. They have a dilemma. They ardently teach that "the Rapture" will be a silent event for the non-Christian world of humanity. Only Christians will hear the shout and trumpet blast. Only Christians will see Jesus in the clouds. Somehow hundreds of millions of Christians will suddenly disappear, but billions of non-Christians will not see them depart, nor hear the heavenly shout and trumpet blast. Neither will they observe the opening of millions of graves worldwide.

Can such astounding things happen silently and invisibly? Do Christian Zionists expect us to believe that nobody except them and dead saints in their graves will hear the heavenly shout and the loud and triumphant sound of the trumpet? Will the Rapture be a celestial pantomime? Apostle Paul wrote that "the trumpet shall sound." Will God's trumpet have a muffler on it? Will Jesus move His lips but only pretend to shout? You cannot have it both ways.

Which is it? Is the Rapture silent or noisy? The answer is that the so-called Rapture is an imaginary event, but the Second Coming will be an enormously loud event.

Eve-vangelicals Ate Scofield's Babylonian Fruit in Darby's Garden of Deception

The glorious Second Coming of Jesus Christ, the resurrection of the dead, and the arrival of New Jerusalem should be a source of hope and joy for all Christians. The Christian Zionists, however, have made it a topic of confusion, fear, anxiety, division, and strife. Millions of sincere Christians are confused because of one thing: The Rapture. Aha! The sneaky serpent persuaded people in the Church to change what God said. It's the oldest trick in Satan's worn-out bag of deception. He entices people to doubt, misquote, or misinterpret the Word of God. Satan is amazed the trick still works on humans after all these years since the Garden of Eden, but he knows that human nature has not changed.

Satan tempted Eve to eat the fruit of the tree of knowledge of good and evil by asking her a question: Did God say you shall not eat of every tree of the garden? Satan knew what God said about the trees in the Garden of Eden. The Devil slyly twisted God's words to interject confusion and doubt into Eve's mind. Eve herself misquoted God in her reply to Satan. She told the serpent that God said, *"Ye shall not eat of it, neither shall ye touch it, lest ye die."* But God never told Adam he could not touch the fruit. God only told him not to eat it.

God instructed Adam before God made Eve. Adam's responsibility as Eve's husband was to teach his wife the Word of God accurately. One of three things happened: (1) Adam taught God's instructions incorrectly to Eve, or (2) Eve did not listen closely to what her husband correctly said; thus, she misunderstood his words; or (3) Adam correctly taught Eve, but she consciously chose to ignore or alter her husband's instructions.

Regardless, Eve misquoted God, and Satan took advantage of her inaccuracy. He deceived her through her unwillingness to stick to the exact words God spoke to Adam. The lesson is: Do not tinker with the Word of God. Always quote it accurately.

> Now the serpent was more subtle than any beast of the field which the Lord God had made. And he said unto the woman, Yea, hath God said, Ye shall not eat of every tree of the garden? *And the woman said unto the serpent, We may eat of the fruit of the trees of the garden: but of the fruit of the tree which is in the midst of the garden, God hath said, Ye shall not eat of it, neither shall ye touch it, lest ye die.* And the serpent said unto the woman, Ye shall not surely die: for God doth know that in the day ye eat thereof, then your eyes shall be opened, and ye shall be as gods, knowing good and evil. And when the woman saw that the tree was good for food, and that it was pleasant to the eyes, and a tree to be desired to make one wise, she took of the fruit thereof, and did eat, and gave also unto her husband with her; and he did eat. And the eyes of them both were opened, and they knew that they were naked; and they sewed fig leaves together, and made themselves aprons.
>
> **Genesis 3:1-7**

This example shows us how easily we can be deceived and not even know it. Eve thought God said she could not touch the fruit, but God said she and Adam could not eat it. It was a slight variation of God's word, but the damage was significant. We must vigilantly guard our minds and lips against believing and speaking things that are not in the Holy Bible.

Eve opened her heart to be deceived by Satan because she misquoted God's instruction to her husband. She paid a steep price for not precisely knowing or by altering what God said to Adam. God evicted Adam and Eve from the Garden of Eden for disobeying His commandment. The lesson for us is clear. Follow God's instructions. Do not change the meaning of His words. Did God say Jesus would split His return into two parts separated by seven years? If He did not say it, why do Christian Zionists deceive people into believing it is true?

At the turn of the twentieth century, some of America's Evangelicals started acting like Eve-vangelicals. It wasn't much longer until Lucifer shrewdly converted the Eve-vangelicals into Deceived-vangelicals by tempting them to read the Scofield Reference Bible littered with Darby's deceptions in the footnotes. They became Deceived-vangelicals when they embraced Zionism.

Adam's wife sincerely believed that God said she could not touch the fruit of the tree of knowledge of good and evil, or she consciously changed God's instructions. Like Eve, Christian Zionists sincerely believe the Holy Bible says there will be a secret Rapture of Christians, or they are knowingly deceiving others to make them think there will be a secret Rapture of saints. Eve was sincerely wrong, and so too are the Deceived-vangelicals. They ought to meditate on why and how Eve lost her place in the Garden of Eden.

How did Lucifer cleverly convert Evangelicals into Deceived-vangelicals? It was a long time in the making. The deception came primarily through five things devised and popularized by Darby and his legions: Firstly, they switched the Greek word *harpazo* (to snatch) for the Latin word *rapere* (to violently grab). Secondly, they split the Second Coming of Christ into two parts, separated by seven years. Thirdly, they separated Israel from the Church. Fourthly, they redefined Israel by eliminating the definition of God's people who obey Him by faith. They changed it into meaning people who share a similar ethnicity and race. They willfully ignore the historical fact that Abraham, the father of our faith, was not a Jew, and neither was his son Isaac and grandson Jacob. His faith, not his DNA, made Abraham righteous. Fifthly, they said the Church is a temporary parenthesis in time, a time-out in God's bigger plan for Jewish Israel. Furthermore, the Christian Zionists believe God made the Church for Gentiles, not Jews.

The serpent deceived Eve, and so too today's Christian Zionists. They foolishly believe the Rapture pooka is real. Deceived themselves, they go about deceiving others too. Some Evangelicals morphed into "Deceived-vangelicals" by enthusiastically eating and sharing the big lies that were dangling from Cyrus Scofield's Tree of Babylonian Knowledge in John Nelson Darby's Garden of Deception.

Is the Blessed Hope an Event or a Person?

The promised return of Jesus Christ and the full manifestation of His Kingdom, the *Parousia*, should be the happy hope of all brethren in Christ. Apostle Paul admonished disciples of Jesus Christ to live soberly in this world while awaiting the arrival of Jesus Christ. In his Second Epistle to Titus, the beloved saint wrote:

For the grace of God that bringeth salvation hath appeared to all men, teaching us that, denying ungodliness and worldly lusts, we should live soberly, righteously, and godly, in this present world; *looking for that blessed hope, and the glorious appearing of the great God and our Savior Jesus Christ;* who gave himself for us, that he might redeem us from all iniquity, and purify unto himself a peculiar people, zealous of good works. These things speak, and exhort, and rebuke with all authority. Let no man despise thee.

Titus 2:11-15

The thoughts and actions of early church brethren regarding the Second Coming of the Messiah were rooted in four pillars of faith: belief, expectancy, readiness, and fruitfulness.

- They believed Jesus Christ would return to Earth
- They earnestly lived in a state of expectancy, never knowing what hour or day He would appear
- They sought to be spiritually ready for the Second Coming of the Messiah
- They diligently worked to be busy, productive, and fruitful for their Master's kingdom.

Apostle Paul encouraged the saints to be "looking for that blessed hope, and the glorious appearing of the great God and our Savior Jesus Christ." What is the blessed hope? Is it an event? Christian Zionists claim that the "blessed hope" is their mythical Rapture pooka: The evacuation of God's "Heavenly People" from Earth to safety in Heaven during a time of great tribulation that they say will last seven years.

Instead of asking *what is* the blessed hope, perhaps we should ask: *Who* is our blessed hope? Our blessed hope is a person, not an event. It is not an escape to Heaven, nor is it Heaven itself. The blessed hope is the ultimate hope of all saints in all nations throughout all the ages. Our hope is the appearance of King Jesus in all His glory and the full manifestation of His kingdom that shall have no end. Christian Zionists eagerly look forward to the Rapture, an event that evacuates them from Earth to Heaven. Yet, our blessed hope is not us going to Heaven. It is Heaven coming to us.

...looking for that blessed hope, and the glorious appearing of the great God and our Savior Jesus Christ...

Titus 2:13

The arrival of Jesus, along with His kingly presence for eternity, is our blessed hope. Men and women of faith in the Old Testament and New Testament held onto their hope of the promised arrival of the Messiah. Old Testament patriarchs were not looking for land. They were yearning for the promised Messiah to deliver them from the curse of death brought upon humankind by Adam's sin. New Testament apostles never spoke a word about the Jews returning to Israel someday to reclaim their land. Instead, they told both Jews and Gentiles to look for that city whose builder and maker is God.

Ever since the Ascension of Jesus to Heaven, traditional orthodox Christians have eagerly waited for the glorious appearance of our blessed hope, Jesus Christ, and the ultimate fulfillment of God's promises to faithful Israel: the opening of all graves, the resurrection of the dead, the Church caught up in the air to meet the Lord in the clouds, the glorification of our human bodies, the consummation of all things, the judgment of all humankind, the testing of our works, the destruction of the old Earth, the creation of new heavens and a new Earth, the arrival of New Jerusalem, and the restitution of all things to their proper order. The Rapture is not our blessed hope. Our blessed hope is Jesus Christ in all His glory.

Jesus Prayed God Would Not Take Us Out of the World

Jesus repeatedly warned that His return to Earth would be sudden and unexpected and that His disciples must always be ready. Jesus never promised His disciples an easy exit from Earth during a time of wars and rumors of wars, violence, upheaval, famine, calamities, and persecution. He also never mentioned a two-stage return to Earth, meaning a secret evacuation of saints before the time of great tribulation, followed seven years later by a full-scale Second Coming.

He did promise never to leave nor forsake us. Instead of asking His Heavenly Father to evacuate His disciples from Earth to avoid persecution and significant troubles, He prayed to God not to take His flock out of the world but to protect them from the evil in this world.

> **I pray not that thou shouldest take them out of the world, but that thou shouldest keep them from the evil.**
>
> **John 17:15**

Prior to His crucifixion, Jesus prayed to His Heavenly Father for His disciples, whom He would soon leave. The English Standard Version of John 17:15 says, "I do not ask that *you take* them out of the world, but that you keep them from the evil one." The Greek word for "you take" is "ares." It means "to raise, lift up, take away, remove." Christian Zionists teach that Jesus will take you out of the world before the evil Antichrist appears. Thus, they teach the opposite thing the Lord prayed for His disciples.

They promise Christians that Jesus will appear in a secret Rapture event to "raise, lift up, take away, and remove" them from global trouble. You may be thinking, "The Parousia does the same thing. Saints will be caught up in the air to meet Jesus." Yes, that is true, but Jesus will not take Christians somewhere to hide them from the Devil for seven years. The Parousia is the arrival and presence of Jesus Christ forever. It is not a search and rescue mission. The saints of God will not be the people in great danger. It will be the wicked who will face terrible trouble that will have no end. The Christian Zionists have it backward. It will not be Christian saints looking for a hidey-hole. It will be the wicked who will crawl in caves and beg the rocks to crush them.

Every man and woman who confesses Jesus Christ as Lord has a work in this life to complete for their Savior. Anglican theologian and bishop Charles Ellicott wrote, "The Christian ideal is not freedom from work, but strength to do it; not freedom from temptation, but power to overcome it; not freedom from suffering, but joy in an abiding sense of the Father's love; not absence from the world, but grace to make the world better for our presence; not holy lives driven from the world, and living apart from it, but holy lives spent in the world and leavening it."

Jesus Christ never promised His disciples that He would rescue them from persecution and tribulation. Instead, He promised never to leave nor forsake them. Throughout the ages, followers of The

Way have suffered persecution, rejection, violence, hardship, and death for their devotion to Jesus Christ. The world's hatred of Christians will continue and intensify until the final day. Enemies of the Cross shall kill some of us. The world will despise all saints. Still, many spiritually weak people who confess Christianity will fall away and betray devout Christians.

Then shall they deliver you up to be afflicted, and shall kill you: and ye shall be hated of all nations for my name's sake. And then shall many be offended, and shall betray one another, and shall hate one another.

Matthew 24:9-10

Nevertheless, Christ's Church shall prevail until the end. Satan's disciples shall wage warfare against the Church in every nation. Hell's gates, however, will not be strong enough to stand against the power of the blood-bought Church of God. A loyal and royal remnant of saints will endure to the end preaching the Gospel of the Kingdom until they see Jesus in the sky, beckoning them to come up and join Him.

This bold and mighty End Time army will not preach the Gospel of prosperity, the Gospel of personal motivation, the Gospel of social justice, nor the Gospel of Zionism. God's end time army will proclaim throughout the world the Gospel of the Kingdom for a witness to all nations and as evidence to be presented on the final day that the inhabitants of each country heard the message of salvation through faith in Jesus Christ.

But he that shall endure unto the end, the same shall be saved.

Matthew 24:13

Days of Noah 2.0

Noah's example is another confirmation that Christian saints shall go through the time of great tribulation. Jesus compared His Second Coming to the days of Noah. Millions of men and women woke up at sunrise, unaware they would be dead by sunset. It was their final day. The Creator visited His Creation, and everything changed. Sudden death was the new normal for everybody and everything that lived on the ground.

An unimaginable sea of water swept them into eternity. The water level overtopped mountains by the fortieth day of rain. Jesus said people were eating and drinking and getting married until the day Noah entered the ark. That day was their final day. Jesus said the flood came and took them all away. When Jesus returns, it will be the final day for the entire human race except for those people whose names are in the Book of Life.

> **But as the days of Noah were, so shall also the coming of the Son of man be. For as in the days that were before the flood they were eating and drinking, marrying and giving in marriage, until the day that Noah entered into the Ark, and knew not until the flood came, and took them all away; so shall also the coming of the Son of man be.**
>
> **Matthew 24:37-39**

Christian Zionists do not see it that way. They cite Noah's protection during the Great Flood as proof of a secret pre-tribulation Rapture of saints from a time of worldwide persecution. Please pardon the pun, but their argument does not hold water. Firstly, God did not physically remove Noah and his family from the deluge of water. He preserved them in the great flood. Their entrance into the ark assured their safety. The ark had a single door, not multiple openings. Likewise, Jesus is the single door by whom we must enter to be saved. They are not many paths to God.

In the New Testament age, water baptism is our ark. Apostle Peter said so in the third chapter of his first epistle to the saints. In the days of Noah, the ark preserved the righteous from death by sparing them from burial in water. For us, it is the opposite. God bestows upon us eternal life when we believe in the name of Jesus Christ, confess His name, and we are buried with Christ in water. Apostle Paul wrote that "we are buried with him by baptism into death: that like as Christ was raised up from the dead by the glory of the Father, even so we also should walk in newness of life."

In the New Covenant age, water baptism preserves the souls who believe in and confess the name of Jesus Christ as Lord and Savior. In Mark 16:16, Jesus said those who believe in Him and are baptized into His holy Church shall be saved, but people who do not believe shall be damned, meaning that baptism only, without confession, does not save anybody.

Secondly, Christian Zionists who see Noah's Ark as a type of Rapture are missing an important fact. God did not whisk away Noah and his family from the planet. They were not taken to Heaven for 40 days. Instead, they safely hid in the ark throughout the entirety of the worldwide calamity. There was no magical escape from the flood, but there was divine protection until the storm ended. Noah and his family safely remained on the Earth protected by God as a worldwide flood raged outside the ark. Christian Zionists would bet the family farm on the certainty they will be gone when tribulation arrives.

Thirdly, the vast underground reservoirs broke open on the surface of the Earth, a heavy downpour fell from the black clouds immediately after Noah and his family entered the ark. God warned Noah a week earlier that the flood would begin in seven days. Noah devoted those seven days to his final preparation for the deluge. Noah entered the ark at the end of the seven days, and God locked the door. The rain fell when the door closed. Immediately, the sky dropped massive amounts of rain for 40 days, and the Earth's crust burst open to release underground oceans.

In the six hundredth year of Noah's life, in the second month, the seventeenth day of the month, the same day were all the fountains of the great deep broken up, and the windows of heaven were opened. And the rain was upon the Earth forty days and forty nights. In the selfsame day entered Noah, and Shem, and Ham, and Japheth, the sons of Noah, and Noah's wife, and the three wives of his sons with them, into the Ark; they, and every beast after his kind, and all the cattle after their kind, and every creeping thing that creepeth upon the Earth after his kind, and every fowl after his kind, every bird of every sort. And they went in unto Noah into the Ark, two and two of all flesh, wherein is the breath of life. And they that went in, went in male and female of all flesh, as God had commanded him: and the Lord shut him in.

Genesis 7:11-16

The Great Flood was the end of the world for everybody on Earth except eight people. For the wicked, their final day arrived. Noah and his family, however, remained on Earth protected by

God in an ark that safely floated in a worldwide flood. God did not rapture Noah off the planet for 40 days. He covered and preserved him from the judgment He poured out upon the wicked. The Great Tribulation will be Satan's wrath against Christ's disciples. The day of the Lord will be God's wrath against Satan's disciples.

God will unleash His wrath upon the wicked on the final day. Baptized saints, sealed by the Holy Spirit, will be suddenly caught up into the air to meet our triumphant King Jesus on that day. His wrath will quickly overwhelm wicked people and unbelievers on Earth. The time-maker will abolish time when He comes from Heaven to our dimension of time, space, and matter. There will be no further need to measure the duration in which all things happen. Therefore, the final day will be as brief or lengthy as the King decrees it.

If, however, time clocks still work on the final day, there will be less than a mere millisecond between the snatching up (harpazo) of Christians into the air and the ignition of the fireball below that will engulf the world. As it was in the days of Noah, the wicked will not know what hit them. Their true horror will be that they will fry but not die. Their flame-broiled punishment will last forever. Nobody, including God, will hear their screams. He will wipe their memories from His mind.

For as in the days that were before the flood they were eating and drinking, marrying and giving in marriage, until the day that Noe entered into the Ark, and knew not until the flood came, and took them all away; so shall also the coming of the Son of man be. Then shall two be in the field; the one shall be taken, and the other left. Two women

shall be grinding at the mill; the one shall be taken, and the other left. Watch therefore: for ye know not what hour your Lord doth come.

Matthew 24:38-42

Noah's Great Flood was God's first Great Reset of human civilization. The wicked were swept away by water. The next time they will be swept away by the flames of God's wrath. The flood began when Noah entered the ark. When Jesus arrives on clouds of glory, the flood of fire will commence on Earth when the saints enter the clouds. There will not be a seven-year gap between the harpazo and the Parousia. The snatching up of the saints is synonymous with the arrival of the King.

The Antichrist's relentless and ruthless persecution of Christians will compel Almighty God to cut short the days of tribulation. Satan will inflict unimaginable affliction and distress upon the saints. It will be dreadful beyond description. Satan's feverish hatred of Christians will test the saints' ability to resist and endure. Therefore, the Father will dispatch His Son to depart Heaven and rapidly travel to Earth to end the devilish war against the Church.

For in those days shall be affliction, such as was not from the beginning of the creation which God created unto this time, neither shall be. And except that the Lord had shortened those days, no flesh should be saved: but for the elect's sake, whom he hath chosen, he hath shortened the days.

Mark 13:19-20

Jesus told us when He would arrive to deliver His saints from Satan's violent oppression. His Parousia (arrival, presence) shall be "in those days, after that tribulation." The sequence of events is easy to understand. Jesus said the lights would go out in the cosmos *after that tribulation*, the powers that are in heaven shall be shaken, the Son of Man shall come in the clouds with great power and glory, and He shall dispatch angels to gather the saints from every part of the Earth. The only return of Jesus Christ shall be "in those days, after that tribulation." Where is the secret Rapture in the Holy Bible? Was it written in invisible ink?

> *But in those days, after that tribulation,* the sun shall be darkened, and the moon shall not give her light, and the stars of heaven shall fall, and the powers that are in heaven shall be shaken. And then shall they see the Son of man coming in the clouds with great power and glory. *And then shall he send his angels, and shall gather together his elect from the four winds, from the uttermost part of the Earth to the uttermost part of heaven.*
>
> Mark 13:24-27

Thief in the Night

Christian Zionists are quick to admonish everybody that Jesus will return to Earth "as a thief in the night." In their theology, "the thief in the night" and "the Rapture" are synonymous. They teach that Jesus will come suddenly as a thief in the night and take away Christians in "the Rapture." Traditionalists teach that the day of the Lord will come upon mankind as a thief in the night. Once again, we must ask: Which is it? A secret Rapture or His grand and glorious Second Coming? Will the thief make two appearances?

Jesus used the thief simile to represent both Himself and "that day." St. Peter and St. Paul compared the day of the Lord to a thief coming in the night, yet Jesus used the thief analogy to speak of Himself. There's no conflict. Jesus Christ and His Parousia are synonymous. Wherever Jesus goes, His Parousia travels with Him. It is His regal presence.

Christian Zionists' imaginary secret event only distracts Christians from the magnificence of that day which will arrive suddenly. That day is the glorious arrival of the King and His royal presence. Nothing else will matter on that day. He will be the only star of the show. That day is His day.

Apostle Paul told the Thessalonian saints that the day of the Lord would come as a thief in the night when the world was saying "peace and safety."

But the times and the seasons, brethren, ye have no need that I write unto you. For yourselves know perfectly that the day of the Lord so cometh as a thief in the night. For when they shall say, Peace and safety; then sudden destruction cometh upon them, as travail upon a woman with child; and they shall not escape.

1 Thessalonians 5:1-3

What happens when the day the Lord catches the world by surprise? Paul said sudden destruction would come upon them. If sudden destruction accompanies the Christian Zionists' much-ballyhooed pre-tribulation "Rapture" event, either today's Christian Zionists are confused, or St. Paul was confused. Christian Zionists need to get their story straight. Does the world continue for seven more years after "the Rapture," or does sudden destruction come upon the wicked? Which is it? What about the Christian Zionists' Millennial Kingdom? How could a Jewish kingdom rule the world for one thousand years after the Second Coming of Christ if the world experiences sudden destruction? Something is not right with this picture. Where is the sudden destruction?

If you dismiss the Rapture story as a Masonic-inspired religious fable, then clearly, St. Paul meant the Second Coming of Jesus Christ would arrive like a thief in the night that will be swiftly followed by sudden destruction. The great apostle's reference to "the day of the Lord" can mean nothing less than the day when Jesus Christ returns to Earth one time to end His Father's controversy with the nations permanently. The day of the Lord is God's appointed time to take vengeance upon the wicked for the crucifixion of His Son, their rejection of the Kingdom of God, and their persecution of His saints. It will be Judgment Day.

Paul knew there was no reason for him to teach the Thessalonian Christians about times and seasons because they knew perfectly that the day of the Lord would arrive like a thief in the night. How did they know perfectly? Most likely, Paul wrote the letter within twenty years after the crucifixion of the Lord. All believed the same doctrine as given to the Apostles by Jesus Christ only two decades earlier. When St. Paul wrote that all Christians knew perfectly about the Second Coming of the Lord, he validated that saints in every church knew what Jesus Christ said about His return. There were not two camps among them, Christian Zionists, and Traditionalists.

All churches were orthodox and catholic, meaning all saints believed the Apostles' Doctrine. There were no denominations. No Roman Catholic Church. No Greek Orthodox Church. No Anglican Church. No Southern Baptist Convention. No Assemblies of God Church. No Calvary Chapel. The Church was one, but local congregations existed in many cities and towns guided by presbyters and overseen by bishops.

All saints fully understood what St. Paul meant when he taught about the day of the Lord. There was no need for Thessalonian Christians to ask Paul to clarify his remarks. Was he talking about "the Rapture" or the Second Coming of Jesus? Of course, Apostle Paul taught only the Second Coming of the Lord. Poor Paul. John Nelson Darby was not there to enlighten the apostle.

It was an absolute certainty among the saints that the Son of God would come unexpectedly under cover of darkness and that sudden destruction would accompany His arrival. Where did they get that idea? All apostles taught it. The saints heard from the apostles' mouths the exact words the Apostles' ears heard from their Master's lips.

There possibly were members among the Thessalonian congregation who personally heard Jesus Christ teach. The apostles repeated to the saints the words they heard Jesus speak. Jesus said in Matthew 24:43, "But know this, that if the goodman of the house had known in what watch the thief would come, he would have watched, and would not have suffered his house to be broken up." The Apostles quoted Jesus and expounded on the deeper meaning of His words. Therefore, the saints knew perfectly that the thief in the night and the day of the Lord were synonymous.

They also knew perfectly the day of the Lord would not overtake the saints as a thief. Why? Because they did not live in a state of spiritual darkness. Their peaceful assurance originated from the religious education they received from St. Paul, who taught them the words of Jesus, not Darby, Scofield, and Moody.

But ye, brethren, are not in darkness, that that day should overtake you as a thief. Ye are all the children of light, and the children of the day: we are not of the night, nor of darkness.

1 Thessalonians 5:4-5

A paraphrase of Apostle Paul's words could read: "Dear brethren, you already know about the times and God's appointments, so there is no need for me to write to you about these things. You know that the day of the Lord will take sinners by surprise because they are living in darkness. That day will come upon the wicked like a thief in the night because they live in spiritual darkness. It shall not overtake you by surprise because you are children of the light."

Where did Paul get the idea that disciples of Jesus are children of light? Jesus taught His disciples, "Ye are the light of the world." Consequently, Thessalonian Christians, along with saints in many other cities, fully understood the meaning of St. Paul's letter that said the thief would not overtake them. Why not? Because Christians are children of the light. And what characteristics define children of the light? They are hopeful, cheerful, bold, brave, honest, and pure. Children of the light must not permit the sin and lusts of this world to stain their souls and bodies.

People who live in God's light are not ignorant about spiritual matters, especially that awful day when God will judge the wicked and all people who refused to believe in the name of Jesus. The Lord's arrival as a thief in the night will catch them unprepared for the day when the present order of the cosmos shall come to a sudden end.

St. Paul's message is easy to understand. Those who dwell in darkness, the ungodly and unbelieving, will be overtaken when the day of the Lord suddenly appears without warning. Those who live in the light, the disciples of Jesus Christ, will not be overtaken because Jesus told them to watch and be ready for His return. The Church of God will not be surprised by Jesus' return. However, the day and hour of His return will surprise us. His big surprise shall happen once, not twice.

St. Peter echoed the words of Jesus and Apostle Paul about the day of the Lord. He, too, said it should overtake the wicked as a thief in the night. The apostles often heard Jesus declare it. Apostle Peter elaborated on what will happen on that day when the Lord comes as a thief in the night. Everything will melt and disappear.

But the day of the Lord will come as a thief in the night; in the which the heavens shall pass away with a great noise, and the elements shall melt with fervent heat, the Earth also and the works that are therein shall be burned up.

2 Peter 3:10

Where did Apostle Peter get the idea that the Earth and cosmos shall burn up? He heard Jesus say, "Heaven and earth shall pass away, but my words shall not pass away." Peter said the fire that engulfs the Earth will produce a great noise. The noise will likely not be the roar of flames but instead the rolling up of the cosmos as a scroll. Humanity's show will be over. The Creator will unveil a new theater and stage designed and built for eternity. He will grant admission only to the children of the light.

Spiritual preparation and readiness for a sudden reentry of the Son of Man into humankind's existence was a standard message in Jesus' teachings, especially in His parables. In the Apocalypse, Jesus told us to be ready because His return to Earth would occur in an hour we would not think was likely. He admonished us to hold fast to the things He taught; and repent, be watchful, and keep our garments clean and holy, lest we walk naked in shame when He returns.

What will happen on the final day? Without warning, Jesus Christ will suddenly burst into humanity's dimension of time, space, and matter. His kingly presence will disrupt the entire cosmos. Every eye will see Him. Every unsaved man and woman outside the Church will instantly know their jig is up, and the game is over; the end of the world has finally arrived. A secretive pre-tribulation Rapture of saints is impossible.

The Second Coming of Jesus is the Parousia. The catching up of the saints happens when His presence occurs. They are the same event. His singular Second Coming shall immediately usher in His regal presence and the full manifestation of His kingdom. His appearance will automatically open all graves. Every man, woman, and child who ever lived, going back to Adam and Eve, will come out of their graves, the seas, or whatever place holds their bones. No burial place will be deep enough to keep the dead in their graves when the One who is truth and life enters our world.

All dead humans, saints and sinners alike, will come out of their burial places. Reaper angels with soul sickles will harvest the wicked and unbelievers and bundle them. The Spirit of the Lord will reconnect their evil souls to their sinful bodies. Lacking the seal of Christ, they will be hauled away to the lake of fire.

Likewise, the Spirit of the Lord shall unite the righteous bodies of departed saints with their justified spirits who arrive with their

Lord. Immediately after that, Jesus will command the saints alive on Earth to come up in the air to meet Him in the clouds of glory. He will transform their mortal bodies during the brief flight.

His Second Coming shall be singular. Almighty God offered Jesus Christ once to bear the sins of many. He shall appear once a second time for those who are looking for Him.

> "...so Christ was *once offered to bear the sins of many*; and unto them that look for him shall *he appear the second time without sin unto salvation.*"
>
> Hebrews 9:28

The Second Coming of Jesus Christ on the final day shall be:
- Singular

CHAPTER 2

HIS SECOND COMING SHALL BE SUDDEN AND UNEXPECTED

HAVE YOU EVER TAKEN a long journey on a highway across several states or provinces? You drive endless hours knowing that many more miles are ahead. You chat with fellow travelers in the vehicle, listen to music or an informative podcast, or enjoy the scenery as the miles pass by your window.

Before satellite-based radio navigation systems (GPS), travelers not very long ago relied on paper highway maps to show them the way to their destination. Today, drivers listen to automated voices instructing them where to go and prompting them to turn onto another road or street. The digital voices even tell them when they have arrived at their destination. (Presently, our society is quickly moving toward autonomous-driven vehicles that will eliminate the need for human drivers who follow GPS navigation.) How would you travel from one place to another if global positioning satellites failed because of an electromagnetic storm or attack? Do you own a highway map? Do you even remember how to use one? Do you have a compass? Can you read it?

Back in the day, drivers without GPS also relied on highway signs. There was no need to be super-alert when your destination was a hundred miles away. However, as you got closer, it was necessary to sit up in your seat and pay close attention to the highway signs. A series of highway signs in succession alerted you to the distance to your destination. One hundred miles. Fifty miles. Twenty-five miles. Fifteen miles. Ten miles. Five miles. One mile. Next exit!

Notice that the closer you get to the exit, the more signs appear to alert you to get ready for your desired destination. The next highway sign is fifty miles ahead when you are one-hundred miles from your destination. By the time you are ten miles away, the following road sign is only five miles ahead. It shouts, "Your destination is very close. Prepare to exit!" Shorter spaces between highway signs mean you are quickly approaching the end of the journey. Failure to pay attention to the highway signs or the GPS navigation voice could make you bypass the exit.

So too will be the coming of our Lord Jesus Christ. We must watch for the signs of His glorious appearing. The closer we approach our exit from this world, the faster the road signs will appear along the way. Devout Christians walking closely with God, fellowshipping with the Holy Spirit, studying the Holy Bible, and closely monitoring world events and trends will not be surprised by Jesus' sudden arrival. Indeed, they will be eagerly anticipating Him! The Lord's return will be sudden but not unexpected for alert Christians. It's like a friend who calls to say he is coming to your house soon. Suddenly, your doorbell rings, and there stands your friend waiting to enter. You knew he was coming soon, but you're still amazed at how quickly he arrived! Your friend's arrival is sudden but not unexpected. He told you he was coming quickly. It will be different for lost souls and spiritually dull church members. Jesus' arrival will be sudden and unexpected. He will arrive suddenly when they least expect it. That day will come as a thief in the night for people living in spiritual darkness.

Great Flood is a Stark Reminder of Sudden Destruction

One of the highway signs Jesus told us to anticipate is the world returning to its wicked, rebellious state as in the days of Noah before the Great Flood. Lascivious sexual behavior, debauchery, homosexuality, sorcery, thievery, lying, violence, and wanton bloodshed had become the norm in human society, like today's Chicago, New York City, Manila, and Bueno Aires. Adam's fall in the Garden of Eden produced a harvest of wickedness, sin, rebellion, and bloodshed. Humankind's compulsion to sin grieved God so much that He regretted the day He made Adam.

And God saw that the wickedness of man was great in the earth, and that every imagination of the thoughts of his heart was only evil continually. And it repented the Lord that he had made man on the earth, and it grieved him at his heart. And the Lord said, I will destroy man whom I have created from the face of the earth; both man, and

beast, and the creeping thing, and the fowls of the air; for it repenteth me that I have made them. But Noah found grace in the eyes of the Lord.

Genesis 6:5-8

Jesus recounted to His disciples what went down that day, more than 2,300 years earlier. He would know. Jesus was there to supervise the Great Flood. He said people were partying, getting drunk, feasting, and getting married right up to the day Noah stepped into the ark. It was just another day in Sin City. Humans lived in a state of unrestrained and rampant sinfulness for over a thousand years after Adam's fall in the Garden. Rebellion against God became a way of life. The "garden story" was old news; people had moved on. Humans no longer feared the God who evicted their ancestors from the Garden of Eden. Indeed, humans no longer thought about God. He was irrelevant to their daily lives.

Then it happened. Rebellious humanity didn't see it coming. Bam! God re-entered humanity's dimensions of time, space, and matter. He made a big statement to humans who arrogantly rebelled against their Divine Maker. The Great Flood story is not a parable. It is not an ancient fable, nor is it folklore. It is history. Cynics ask, "Where is the evidence of a worldwide flood?" Have they ever seen the Pacific or Atlantic oceans? How do they think that much water got there? Do they know about Pavlopetri, Greece, and Heracleion, Egypt? Why are those ancient cities still submerged underwater? Why have archeologists discovered numerous dinosaur mass burial sites around the world? Could it be that dinosaurs were swept away by massive walls of water in a sudden worldwide flood?

Moses, the human author of the Book of Genesis, told us when the deluge started. In Genesis 7:11, the Hebrew patriarch wrote, "In the six hundredth year of Noah's life, in the second month, the seventeenth day of the month, the same day were all the fountains of the great deep broken up, and the windows of heaven were opened."

Noah preached God's warning for over one hundred years, but only his family believed him. Unbeknownst to Planet Earth's lustful, violent inhabitants, the Judge of the Universe rendered a verdict in Heaven's Court. His gavel came down mightily with a guilty verdict. The Judge decreed the punishment was death by drowning. Angels did not notify Earth's inhabitants that they had been found guilty in Heaven's court. Nor did they inform the worldwide human population of its appointment with sudden death. In God's kingdom, the guilty have no rights. The Lord had no obligation to tell them the date of their execution because Noah warned the people for over a century, but they mocked the preacher of righteousness. Suddenly it was God's turn to mock the mockers.

> **The earth also was corrupt before God, and the earth was filled with violence. And God looked upon the earth, and, behold, it was corrupt; for all flesh had corrupted his way upon the earth. And God said unto Noah, The end of all flesh is come before me; for the earth is filled with violence through them; and, behold, I will destroy them with the earth.**
>
> **Genesis 6:11-13**

Noah's Great Flood is a powerful lesson for all of us today. The worldwide calamity reminds us that God's patience with humanity's sin and rebellion will be exhausted again, Heaven's court will render a guilty verdict, and God will set the date of humanity's execution but not inform Earth's population. Execution Day will arrive suddenly and unexpectedly. Jesus told us the Great Flood and the day of the Lord are similar. "Just as it was in the days of Noah, so will it be in the days of the Son of Man," the Lord told His disciples. People in Noah's age lived each day without awareness that something was seriously amiss between them and their Creator. They were "eating and drinking and marrying and being given in marriage" until Noah entered the vessel.

What happened next? The ark's door was shut, but Noah did not do it. There is an essential sentence in Genesis 7 that we must note concerning the Second Coming of Christ. The sixteenth verse says, "And the Lord shut him in." When all the animals and his family had entered the boat, Noah went inside too. God personally shut the door and sealed Noah safely in the ark.

Divine judgment swept over the planet, but Noah and his family were kept from it even while they were in it. Jesus did not secretly appear and take Noah and his family to Heaven for forty days to escape trouble on Earth. Noah was not removed from the place of punishment but was safely sealed and preserved by God while He poured His wrath upon the rest of humanity.

No Hankies in Heaven

Another flood will suddenly and unexpectedly cover the Earth. The future deluge will be a flood of fire. Jesus told His disciples that when He returns to Earth, people will be gleefully sinning and rebelling against God as they did in the days of Noah. It was business as usual until Noah entered the ark. They did not know it was their last day when God sealed Noah inside the ship. Never-ending atmospheric rivers drenched them from above and underground seas below burst through the planet's crust and the rushing water crested ever higher by the hour until it covered the mountains of Ararat, the Alps, and the Rockies. The deluge came suddenly and unexpectedly. Sinners did not see it coming because their eyes were blinded by sin and lust.

Jesus said, "the flood came and destroyed them all." In the same manner, the final day's flood will come suddenly and unexpectedly. A deluge of fire will engulf the planet, and its flames will be higher than the tallest mountains. Satan conveniently neglected to inform humanity that sin is a highly combustible substance. When Jesus lights a match on the final day, this sin-soaked planet and its inhabitants will burst into ferocious flames. Anybody not sealed inside the ark of baptism will perish that day.

One thing is sure: The global fire will erupt suddenly and unexpectedly. Sinners will not hear fire alarms warning them to flee the planet. No stairwells will miraculously appear to allow people to exit the burning world. And no heroic firefighters will extinguish the raging inferno on every continent and the seas. Yes, the oceans will be on fire too. Even fire will be on fire. The elements will dissolve in the fervent heat, and fire is one of Earth's elements. Thus, Heaven's fire will burn up the Earth's fire.

The wicked and unsaved will not receive text messages on their mobile devices alerting them of impending global combustion. The truth is God has repeatedly warned them to repent, but they would not listen nor respond. Indeed, the antichrist spirit of this world is increasing its efforts to censor and silence the voices of righteous men and women crying out to lost souls to repent, believe in the name of Jesus, and be baptized in water. Censors may hinder the saints, but Christ will turn the censors into cinders when angelic reapers suddenly separate the wheat and tares, the sheep and goats.

The harvest of souls will be sudden, swift, and final. Souls found outside the Church will not have permission to speak before the Great Judge to plead their defense and make excuses for their behavior. They will arrive shackled with "Guilty on Arrival" stamped on their foreheads. Angelic bailiffs will escort the prisoners to the Great Throne of Judgment. The purpose of their brief appearance before God will be to receive the punishment they chose while living on Earth: eternal damnation in the lake of fire. Perhaps a large sign in Heaven's Court will warn, "No repenting allowed." Repentance is for today. Your tears will not move God's heart on the final day. Now is the time for remorse and weeping over your sins. There are no hankies in Heaven.

Doctor Jesus' Health Advice: Beware Three Snares

There is a fascinating but greatly overlooked passage in the Holy Bible about the Second Coming of Christ. Modern Bible prophecy teachers love to talk about the mysteries in the Book of the Revelation of Jesus Christ, but they run away from expounding on Jesus' plain talk about three deadly snares. His blunt warning is not mysterious. It is easy to understand, but it doesn't motivate prophecy junkies to buy books and courses to know more.

Nevertheless, Jesus strongly advised us to "take heed to yourselves" regarding the three traps that could trip us up on the final day. Indeed, one would assume that the deadly traps must be the top three of the seven deadly sins: pride, greed, and lust. Not so, but it does include Number Five on the Big Seven Sins. We are talking about gluttony.

Curiously, only St. Luke was inspired to record Jesus' warning that we must each conquer these three sins before we die, or He returns on the final day. It should not be surprising that it was St. Luke. Apostle Paul called Luke his "beloved physician." Luke was Paul's doctor who traveled alongside him. Doctor Luke knew that his patients' poor eating habits caused many illnesses.

More than the other three Gospel writers, St. Luke ministered to the saints' spiritual, emotional, and physical needs. Only Dr. Luke recorded Jesus saying, "Physician, heal thyself" and "They that are whole need not a physician, but they that are sick." Consequently, because Luke was a doctor, his ears perked up when Jesus mentioned three bad habits that lead to poor physical and mental health.

> **And take heed to yourselves, lest at any time your hearts be overcharged with surfeiting, and drunkenness, and cares of this life, and so that day come upon you unawares. For as a snare shall it come on all them that dwell on the face of the whole earth. Watch ye therefore, and pray always, that ye may be accounted worthy to escape all these things that shall come to pass, and to stand before the Son of man.**
>
> **Luke 21:34-36**

Jesus embedded the warning inside His extended response to the disciples' questions about the temple's destruction, the sign of His coming, and the end of the age. Most Holy Bible students are well acquainted with the twenty-fourth and twenty-fifth chapters of the Gospel According to St. Matthew. Those two famous chapters contain Jesus' lengthy reply to the three questions asked by the disciples. Neither St. Matthew nor St. Mark included the words recorded by Dr. Luke.

The Lord talked in length about the last days. He mentioned wars and insurrections; earthquakes, famines, and plagues; great signs, persecution; signs in the Sun, Moon, and stars; roaring seas; fainting people; and the powers of the heaven shaken. Suddenly, out of the blue, Jesus tossed in gluttony, drunkenness, and preoccupation with daily living. Where did that come from? What do our eating and drinking, and daily habits have to do with the Second Coming of Christ the King? Did Dr. Luke not know where else to insert Jesus' quote? Why stick it in Jesus' talk about the end of the world?

It wasn't a typographical error in the Gospel. Upon conclusion of His answer to the disciples' questions about the last days, Jesus told His listeners, "And take heed to yourselves..." What does that mean? "Take heed" means to "be on guard." It also means "make sure you don't let this happen." In today's parlance, Jesus would say to us, "Heads up! The following message is a strong warning. Please pay attention to what I'm saying to you."

Jesus identified the three traps that all Believers must avoid at all costs: surfeiting, drunkenness, and the cares of this life. Let's start with surfeiting. What is it? The Authorized King James Version of the Holy Bible translators used the old English word "surfeiting," which means "excessiveness." Primarily, it refers to gluttony in food and drink. A person prone to surfeiting is a man or woman who overindulges in food and beverages. They eat far too much food and drink far more beverages than are necessary. The physical desires of their bodies overrule their minds and souls. They excessively eat and drink to satisfy an emotional emptiness, pain, weakness, need, craving, or lust. Jesus said it is a sin Christians must conquer before they die or before His Second Coming. Hopefully, Heaven will not impose a weight limit for Christians to be taken up in the air to meet the Lord in the clouds.

Next is drunkenness. It is surfeiting's twin sin. Both originate from a lack of self-discipline over physical and emotional cravings and lusts for satisfaction. Devout Christians may sincerely differ on whether they are permitted to drink beer and wine, but there can be no toleration of drunkenness among disciples of Jesus Christ. Drunkenness is forbidden. There is nothing to debate.

The warning against intoxication also applies to marijuana and all mind-altering drugs. But what about antidepressants and pain medications? How many Christians are stumbling through life addicted to pills to lessen depression? How many Christians are addicted to pain medications? Do they not know that pharmakeia is witchcraft and sorcery? Disciples of Christ should not blur their minds with alcohol or drugs. The Lord is coming back, and we must be sober and ready for His return. You cannot be vigilant if you are not sober. The Lord expects us to be sober when we exit this life or when He returns.

But the end of all things is at hand: be ye therefore sober, and watch unto prayer.

I Peter 4:7

The third trap is the cares of life. Obsession with daily living and worrying are familiar themes in Jesus' sermons. In the Great Manifesto, Jesus told the people gathered on the Mount not to worry about food, clothing, and housing. His Parable of the Sower said the seed falling among the thorns refers to people who hear God's Word, but the cares of this world and the deceitfulness of riches choke out God's Word and make it unfruitful. As Mary sat next to Jesus' feet, listening to Him teach about the kingdom, her sister Martha fretted in the kitchen as she hurried to prepare a meal for a whole house of unexpected guests. Jesus lovingly admonished her, "Martha, Martha, thou art careful and troubled about many things...." Few people in the history of the world ever experienced the blessing given to Martha: a divine visitation of God in her home. The Son of God was in Martha's house personally teaching the principles of the Kingdom, and the only thing on Martha's mind was mashed potatoes!

One or more of the snares can entrap sincere Christians without their awareness. How do they hinder our spiritual preparations for the final day? They make us intoxicated with the world. They dull our senses. We become befuddled with carbohydrates, sugar, wine, entertainment, social media, politics, sports, business, financial investments, and a host of other attractive distractions. A life devoid of an intimate relationship with God, Bible study, the Lord's Supper, church attendance, prayer, fasting, and fellowship with brethren will inevitably become insensitive to and unaware of spiritual things, signs of the times, and even to the condition of their souls. Eventually, complacency in the present world will replace passion for the next one.

Jesus said we must "take heed" so that our hearts are not over-taken by gluttony, liquor, drugs, pharmaceuticals, making a living, amusements, entertainment, or day-to-day living. Why? Because "that day" will come upon you like a trap. "That day" is the final day.

It shall come suddenly and unexpectedly. "That day" will capture billions of souls like animals in traps.

For as a snare shall it come on all them that dwell on the face of the whole earth.

Luke 21:35

What must we do? Jesus said we must always be watchful and prayerful in our daily lives. Why? He desires us to possess the strength to prevail over the horrendous things that will undoubtedly come to pass at the end of the age. We must also stand before the Son of Man, meaning the judgment seat of Christ. Apostle Paul wrote to the brethren in Corinth, "we must all appear before the judgment seat of Christ; that everyone may receive the things done in his body, according to that he hath done, whether it be good or bad."

The day of the Lord, the final day, will explode upon humankind suddenly and unexpectedly. As a hunter suddenly cast his net over a flock of birds on the ground, so too will angels cast the Lord's net over the world's people. If the birds had been watchful, they would have escaped the trap. So too, we must be vigilant.

Jesus commanded all past, present, and future disciples:

1. Take heed to yourselves.
2. Do not become addicted to the pleasures of this world.
3. Always be ready for that day when the calamities prophesied in the Holy Bible come upon rebellious humankind.

Always be prepared for the hour your soul separates from your body. We must live chaste and holy lives daily in a state of humility, obedience, expectancy, and hope. Carnally minded people cannot rightfully expect to possess eternal security. Our spirit must rest each hour in the sure knowledge that no sins are separating us from God.

Neither death nor His Second Coming should catch us in acts of sin, drunkenness, gluttony, sexual immorality, or in pursuing the sensual pleasures of this world with no thoughts spared for God, judgment, and the eternal destination of our soul. King Solomon said a wise man thinks much of death, while the fool thinks only of having a good time. He also said the day of death is better than the day of birth.

Therefore be ye also ready: for in such an hour as ye think not the Son of man cometh.

Matthew 24:44

Make Ready a People Prepared for the Lord

The New Testament Bible is mainly about being ready for the final day, but you wouldn't know it by listening to many of the sermons preached these days. There is a troubling lack of urgency in many modern churches about the Lord's return. The clergy and congregations don't seem eager for Christ to return soon. They act like they are content to live longer without Him. Tragically, that day will catch billions of souls unprepared for a sudden global calamity, divine judgment, and eternal punishment for the wicked, unbelievers, and those not prepared.

If you asked Christians to describe the primary mission of John the Baptist, most would reply, "To baptize people." Yes, John the Baptist baptized multitudes in the Jordan River. However, baptisms were not his primary mission. His purpose was, according to Luke 1:17, "to make ready a people prepared for the Lord." Not everybody! His assignment was to "make ready a people." And for what was this specific group of people made ready? They were to be "prepared for the Lord." And how did John make them ready and prepared? He preached repentance, baptism, and straight living!

In those days came John the Baptist, preaching in the wilderness of Judaea, and saying, Repent ye: for the kingdom of heaven is at hand. For this is he that was spoken of by the prophet Esaias, saying, The voice of one crying in the wilderness, Prepare ye the way of the Lord, make his paths straight.

Matthew 3:1-3

Early Christians were known initially as "people of The Way." What was the way, and whose way was it? They followed "the way of Jesus." He instructed the Apostles to teach people to walk the straight and narrow path through life in this sinful, wicked, lustful, carnal, vile, greedy, violent, bloody, and selfish world. His disciples can only keep their souls unsullied by contact with this filthy world by walking His way.

Repentance is a daily necessity. Indeed, it is an hourly one. Millions of traditional orthodox Christians around the world pray the Jesus Prayer throughout each day: "Lord Jesus Christ, Son of God, have mercy on me, a sinner." Unbeknownst to most members of Christian Zionist churches, each Sunday, millions of traditional orthodox Christians also sing the Kyrie Eleison: "Lord have mercy." *Eleison* is the Greek word for "have mercy" in many church liturgies. It shares the same Greek root word, which means oil from an oil tree. In the Book of Genesis, Noah released birds from the ark to seek land. A dove brought Noah a twig from an olive tree. Thousands of years later, the image of a dove holding an olive tree twig in its beak is still a symbol of mercy, forgiveness, peace, and love. The way of the Lord is mercy, forgiveness, peace, love, and holiness.

God sent John the Baptist "to make ready a people prepared for the Lord." He made them ready for the Lord by showing them "The Way." After the resurrection of Jesus Christ, His disciples were called people of "The Way." His way has not changed. It is the same today. If the Holy Bible instructs us to prepare ourselves for His second appearance on Earth, we must first prepare His way. The true Church on Earth should be in a perpetual state of repentance, mercy, forgiveness, peace, love, and holiness. Be ready! "That day" will come suddenly when you least expect it.

Entrance Denied

Religiosity is not synonymous with spiritual readiness. Jesus directed many sermons to religious people, not heathens. His talks and parables often warned religious folks that they must always be ready for the day of the Lord. If Jesus expects us to expect the unexpected, it would be wise for all of us to examine our hearts daily for signs of spiritual sluggishness.

The parable of the five foolish virgins represents religious people who are spiritually dull, lazy, complacent, and preoccupied with this world. The bridegroom's expected arrival came at an unexpected hour in the parable. All ten bridesmaids believed the bridegroom would arrive for the wedding, but his unexpected delay tripped up five of them.

Then shall the kingdom of heaven be likened unto ten virgins, which took their lamps, and went forth to meet the bridegroom. And five of them were wise, and five were foolish. They that were foolish took their lamps, and took no oil with them: But the wise took oil in their vessels with their lamps. While the bridegroom tarried, they all slumbered and slept. And at midnight there was a cry made, Behold, the bridegroom cometh; go ye out to meet him. Then all those virgins arose, and trimmed their lamps. And the foolish said unto the wise, Give us of your oil; for our lamps are gone out. But the wise answered, saying, Not so; lest there be not enough for us and you: but go ye rather to them that sell, and buy for yourselves. And while they went to buy, the bridegroom came; and they that were ready went in with him to the marriage: and the door was shut. Afterward came also the other virgins, saying, Lord, Lord, open to us. But he answered and said, Verily I say unto you, I know you not. Watch therefore, for ye know neither the day nor the hour wherein the Son of man cometh.

Matthew 25:1-13

In Matthew 24, Jesus gave us the sign of His Second Coming and the end of the age. Sitting on the Mount of Olives, He prophesied the future demolition of the Jewish temple in Jerusalem. Jesus gave the saints warning that they would suffer intense persecution. He promised that God would cut short the days of tribulation for the sake of the elect. He said the Sun, the Moon, and stars shall go dark. Jesus taught His disciples the Parable of the Fig Tree. He also warned that human civilization would be like it was in the days of

Noah. Jesus compared His Second Coming to a thief's unexpected arrival in the night. Lastly, He said wise disciples would be busy serving the right food at the proper time when He returns.

After His detailed description of the final day, Jesus' next spoken word, which marks the beginning of Matthew 25, is "then." Then what? "Then shall the Kingdom of Heaven be likened." Likened means "it shall resemble." Thus, the Parable of the Ten Virgins teaches us that when Jesus returns to judge humanity, it will resemble the bridegroom's father instructing the bridesmaids to be ready any time for his son to arrive for the grand wedding ceremony.

The bridegroom in this parable is Jesus. The event is the marriage of Jesus with His bride, but the parable does not identify the bride. Neither the bridesmaids nor the guests can also be the bride. St. John wrote in the twenty-first chapter of the Revelation of Jesus Christ that New Jerusalem is the bride. The bridegroom was not betrothed to marry the ten bridesmaids in the parable. Bridesmaids don't get married to the bridegroom. The bride marries the bridegroom.

Likewise, Jesus also did not identify the bride in another parable about the final day. In the Parable of the Wedding Banquet, the story's focus was on the spiritual fitness of the guests. In contrast, the Parable of the Ten Virgins theme was about the bridesmaids' readiness for the bridegroom's sudden arrival at an unexpected hour.

Wedding customs in old Eastern cultures usually required marriages to occur at night. Young men, known as the friends of the bridegroom, attended to the bridegroom at his father's house. Likewise, young virgin women, known as bridesmaids, attended to the bride at her father's house. Typically, the custom was that the bridegroom should go where the bride was waiting and take her to the wedding ceremony at his father's house. When the bridegroom's arrival was soon, somebody would shout that he was on his way. The bridesmaids would meet him and accompany the couple with lit lamps to the wedding ceremony venue. When they entered the house of the bridegroom's father, the doorkeeper shut the door, and the wedding ceremony commenced.

However, the parable's imagery implies that the wedding ceremony was not held at the bridegroom's house. Theologians differ in their interpretations of this deviation from Eastern custom. Did the bridegroom arrive from a great distance with his bride? Or did the bridegroom travel a long way to fetch her? Regardless of which interpretation is correct, the bridegroom's father expected the ten virgins to wait for the bridegroom's arrival so that the wedding ceremony could begin.

The ten virgins represent the whole body of people who confess belief in the Christian faith as divided into two groups: wise and foolish. Unlike actors in other parables, Jesus did not classify the ten virgins as good or bad, righteous or evil, prudent or careless. All were virgins, yet five were foolish. All were friends of the bride and equipped with lamps and oil. Five had extra oil, but the other five had the bare minimum oil supply. The amount of oil possessed by each of the ten virgins resulted from individual choices made by each young woman during the daylight hours.

All ten virgins, wise and foolish, went forth to meet the bridegroom, whom all expected to arrive for the wedding ceremony. "Went forth" implies that all ten virgins took the initiative to act in their responsibilities.

Both wise and foolish bridesmaids knew four things about the bridegroom. They knew his identity and that he was coming from a far distance to marry his bride. They also knew that somebody would alert them by shouting that the bridegroom was on his way. And they knew it was their duty to escort the bridegroom with lit lamps to the wedding ceremony location. All ten bridesmaids also shared three other things:

1. They were unanimous in their desire to attend the grand marriage event.
2. Official invitations were sent to all ten bridesmaids.
3. None of the ten virgins knew they were in two separate groups, wise and foolish.

None of the five foolish virgins gazed into a mirror that day and sighed, "I am a fool." And none of the five wise virgins looked into a mirror and sighed, "I am wise." The foolish, however, deceived themselves because they thought they were wise.

What factor separated the ten virgins? The five foolish virgins went forth to meet the incoming bridegroom with their lit lamps but no extra oil. The five wise virgins did the same but also carried vessels, meaning containers filled with oil. The sin of the five foolish virgins was not wickedness, fornication, unfaithfulness, or apostasy. Their sin was neglecting adequate preparation for the bridegroom's sudden arrival at an unexpected late hour. They paid a severe price for their neglect of duty.

The parable says in verse five, "While the bridegroom tarried, they all slumbered and slept." There are three things in this verse to see: Firstly, the bridegroom delayed his arrival for an unknown reason. Secondly, all ten virgins got sleepy. Thirdly, all ten virgins fell asleep while the bridegroom attended to some other matters that prevented him from arriving earlier.

While all ten bridesmaids were deep asleep, a shout was heard at midnight, "The bridegroom is coming! Go out to meet him." The cry was the defining moment when the two classes of bridesmaids became obvious. Until then, they were one group. Let's look at three things they had in common before the loud shout announced that that the bridegroom was on his way:

1. The bride's or bridegroom's parents officially designated all ten virgins as the wedding's bridesmaids.
2. All ten young women had lamps to light their way.
3. All ten women arose at the sound of the shout and trimmed their lanterns.

The trimming of the lamps was the defining moment. Until then, both groups of virgins looked the same. None appeared to be foolish before they trimmed their wicks. Only when circumstances compelled them to trim their lamps at midnight did the separation of the virgins into two camps become visible. The line that divided them into two camps was their supply of oil.

Oil lamps require daily care. The wick draws oil up from the storage reservoir. A trimmed wick is more economical than an untrimmed wick and can burn for hours to provide light. However, an untrimmed wick creates a flame that is dim and smoky. It burns faster, thus consuming the available oil quicker than a trimmed wick that provides a brighter flame. The rapid consumption of the oil results from an untrimmed wick having more of its length burning.

Upon trimming their lamps at midnight, the five foolish virgins suddenly realized they were in trouble. All ten lamps had burned for hours while they slept. All ten lamp reservoirs were nearly empty. The five wise virgins, however, were not perturbed by their lamp's flickering flames. They brought vessels filled with oil. They calmly refilled the reservoir tanks in their lantern. They knew their flames would burn brightly again.

The foolish virgins brought no extra oil. It had never occurred to them that the bridegroom would delay his arrival. They counted on an early arrival. The foolish virgins had enough oil for the arrival time they anticipated, but not an unexpected late arrival. The bridegroom's change of plans caught them by surprise.

As young siblings commonly do, the foolish virgins begged the wise virgins to share their oil. The wise women resoundingly rejected their unreasonable request. They explained that sharing could result in none of them having sufficient oil to complete the journey.

The five wise bridesmaids reasoned that five was better than none making it there on time. They instructed the other young women to buy oil. However, it was midnight, and the oil merchant was in bed in the apartment above his shop. They had no other option other than to walk back to town, knock on the merchant's door until he woke up, convince him to sell oil in early morning hours, fill their lamp reservoirs, and hurriedly walk to catch up with the wise virgins who had departed for the wedding. The lack of preparation cost them valuable time at a time they could least afford not to be ready for the bridegroom's late arrival.

There was an unhappy ending for the foolish virgins. They missed the grandest wedding ever. Even worse, the bridegroom ignored them when they repeatedly knocked on the door and begged to enter the wedding party. Insulted by their late arrival, the bridegroom acted like he never knew them. But the parable ended happily for the five wise virgins. Jesus said that those ready went in with him to the marriage, and the door was shut.

"Wise" in this parable means trustworthy stewards who are prudent and intelligent. They were sagely aware that the time of the bridegroom's arrival was uncertain. The careless, foolish virgins may have heard many people in the village say, "He's coming soon!" The bridegroom never told anybody, however, that he would come soon. He said, "Behold, I come quickly." Soon means the near future, the time between the present and the anticipated event. Quickly means the velocity that somebody or something travels between two points.

Jesus never told us He would come soon. He said He would come quickly. We do not know the hour nor the day of His Second Coming. What we do know is that when He departs Heaven, He will arrive here quickly. Human minds cannot comprehend the rate of speed Jesus will travel on His trip from Heaven to Earth. It will be instantaneous.

All ten bridesmaids had lamps with oil, but only five made sure nothing would prevent them from attending. Five entered the wedding ceremony on time with the smiling bridegroom. The other five stumbled in the darkness and missed both the bridegroom and the wedding. Adding insult to injury, he snubbed them at the door when they arrived late and pleaded to take their place in the ceremony.

Preparation Requires an Investment

Jesus taught other parables that contained similar warnings about the necessity of preparation and readiness for His sudden arrival at an hour nobody expects. The Parable of the Faithful and Unfaithful Servants also teaches us the absolute necessity of being ready for the Lord's return at an unexpected hour. In that parable, Jesus taught those wise servants would always dress for action, have their lamps lit, and prepare for their master to return *from* the wedding banquet so that they may open the door for him as soon as he knocks. Once again, He compared the master's late arrival to a thief coming in the night.

> Let your loins be girded about, and *your* lights burning; and ye yourselves like unto men that wait for their lord, when he will return from the wedding; that when he cometh and knocketh, they may open unto him immediately. Blessed *are* those servants, whom the lord when he cometh shall find watching: verily I say unto you, that he shall gird himself, and make them to sit down to meat, and will come forth and serve them. And if he shall come in the second watch, or come in the third watch, and find *them* so, blessed are those servants. And this know, that if the goodman of the house had known what hour the thief would come, he would have watched, and not have suffered his house to be broken through. Be ye therefore ready also: for the Son of man cometh at an hour when ye think not.
>
> **Luke 12:35-40**

The unfaithful servant made a deadly assumption. In Luke 12:45, the servant said in his heart, "My master has delayed his coming." What is the difference between the Parable of the Ten Virgins and the Parable of the Watchful Servant? The foolish bridesmaids did not anticipate the bridegroom's delay and late arrival. In the other parable, the assumption was the opposite. The unfaithful servant did not expect his master's early arrival. In both parables, the central figure attended a wedding ceremony. One arrived late before the ceremony, and the other arrived early after the ceremony. The faulty assumptions in both parables dearly cost the actors. Five bridesmaids who desired and expected to attend the wedding made an erroneous assumption the bridegroom would arrive early.

The foolish virgins assumed the bridegroom would arrive soon; therefore, they made no effort to be ready for his late arrival at midnight. However, the unfaithful servant gambled his soul away on a false hope that he had more time to live his best life now. In his case, the unfaithful servant assumed he could get his life's affairs in order hours before his master arrived. Both suffered dire consequences for their failure to be ready for the sudden arrival of a VIP at an unexpected hour.

What do the lamps and oil represent in the Parable of the Ten Bridesmaids? Psalm 119:105 says, "Thy word is a lamp unto my feet, and a light unto my path." Therefore, the lamp in the parable is the Word of God. His holy Word shines the light for our feet to travel through life. Without the light from His Word, we will stumble in the world's darkness. The oil is God's grace supplied to us from the Holy Spirit as we read and study the Holy Bible, hear the Word of God preached and taught, fellowship with the Lord, and frequently attend the Lord's Supper in holy communion with Him.

The five foolish virgins represent people who profess Christianity yet exert minimal effort and resources to sit at the feet of the Master and learn His ways. Discipleship demands discipline, devotion, and dedication. True disciples know that discipleship does not come easy or quickly. You cannot obtain it overnight. Discipleship comes with a price.

Discipleship requires countless hours of reading, studying, meditating, and praying until your soul is saturated with the Word of God and remains saturated throughout your life. True disciples know that you cannot fake it until you make it. The Word of God is in you, or it isn't.

The Holy Spirit bestows grace to those who desire Jesus Christ. Pursuit is proof of desire. Men and women who desire Christ with all their hearts will pursue Him. To those who seek Him, the Holy Spirit will reward them with abundant grace from Heaven. There are many Wordless Christians who never or seldom read and study the Holy Bible. It is impossible to separate Jesus Christ and the Word of God. They are the same. Jesus is the Word, and the Word is Jesus.

In the beginning was the Word, and the Word was with God, and the Word was God. The same was in the beginning with God. All things were made by him; and without him was not anything made that was made. In him was life; and the life was the light of men. And the light shineth in darkness; and the darkness comprehended it not.

John 1:1-5

Jesus said if you love Him, you will keep His commandments. What are His commandments? They are His words. He said if you abide in Him, and His words abide in you, you shall ask whatever you desire, and God the Father shall give you what you ask Him. Jesus did not say, "If you abide in Me, and I abide in you." He said, "and my words abide in you." What is His promise when we abide in Him, and His words abide in us? "Ye shall ask what ye will, and it shall be done unto you."

The five foolish virgins were late for the wedding because they had not prepared for the journey that came upon them suddenly and unexpectedly at a late hour. They had some oil, but not enough oil. When the final day arrives, there will be many church members with some of God's Word in their hearts and minds, but not enough for the midnight journey. Instead of the Word of God, the Lord will find that their minds are cluttered with useless information: sports scores, news, information, investments, deals, money, conspiracy theories, politics, recipes, gossip, TV sitcoms, pornography, horoscopes, social media banter, and everything else they readily consumed each day.

Today, we see a foolish mentality among Christian Zionists who don't prepare for difficult days of tribulation because they expect "The Rapture" to take them to Heaven at any minute. The lesson is that people can outwardly profess belief in Christ but not inwardly possess Christ. They live today on yesterday's grace. They received a dose of grace years ago and foolishly assume it is sufficient for tomorrow. They make little effort to replenish their supply of God's grace through prayer and meditation, the study of the Word of God, frequent dining at the Lord's Supper, good works, and witnessing their faith to lost souls.

"But the wise took oil in their vessels with their lamps." Wise saints walk in the Spirit each day, thus receiving a fresh refueling of grace. There is no indication in the parable that the foolish virgins even owned vessels to store extra oil. The lack of storage containers indicates how little value they placed on preparation for the unexpected. They are like modern drivers who travel when their fuel gauges warn that their gasoline tanks are nearly empty. If you know that you must regularly refill your automobile's fuel tank, how much more should you know that you must replenish your soul with heavenly grace?

Just as driving a car with a nearly empty fuel tank is dangerous for your engine's health and your safety, so too is resting on yesterday's grace. You do not know in the morning what will happen by nighttime. Will you have garnered sufficient grace to get through it? If tragedy strikes you today, does your soul possess an abundant supply of grace to light your lamp at the midnight hour? The foolish virgins did not prepare for the bridegroom's unexpected delay nor his sudden arrival at midnight. Their lamps burned out at an hour they could not afford to be without light.

A burning lamp requires oil and fire. The Word of God is our lamp, and God's grace is our oil. The fire that ignites the grace to produce light is the Holy Spirit. The wise virgins conscientiously acquired an abundant supply of oil, meaning God's grace. The foolish virgins were satisfied with yesterday's oil supply and neglected their duty to replenish their inventory. The wise virgins acted differently. They instinctively knew they could not rely on yesterday's oil inventory for sudden and unexpected circumstances today.

What is the moral of the story? Always remain ready. Be prepared for things to happen suddenly and unexpectedly. Have enough of the Word of God in your life for the Holy Spirit to ignite a flame that generates light for your journey through life. If you stumble in the darkness, it will be your fault, and you may miss what God desires to give you. Being shut out of the grand wedding ceremony will be your most tremendous loss. Eternity will last a long time with no breaks.

They All Slumbered and Slept

All ten virgins expected the bridegroom to arrive. All went forth to meet him. The bridegroom, however, was delayed in his expected arrival. The delay represents the time between the Ascension and the Second Coming of Jesus Christ. During the bridegroom's unexplained and unexpected delay, all ten brides-maids became slumbered and slept. It means they became weary and exhausted in their journey and needed rest. Slumbering and sleeping in this parable represent aging and death.

All confessors of Christ, both wheat and tares, must lie down in their respective graves and sleep. We all await the resurrection when the bridegroom shall arrive after traveling a great distance for the wedding ceremony. Wise and foolish Christians shall both sleep in their graves until the shout is heard, "The Bridegroom is coming. Go out to meet Him."

All graves shall open, but not all bodies will be caught up in the air to meet Jesus Christ in the clouds. Some of the bodies that come out of their graves will stretch forth their arms to Jesus, but He will look the other way and not recognize them. Their bodies shall fall back to Earth, unable to rise into the atmosphere with the wise saints who will receive glorified bodies when their eyes see Jesus.

It was nighttime the first time Jesus came to Earth as God in human flesh. Born in a Bethlehem manger, an unusually bright star hovered above Palestine that night. Joyful angels sang songs of glad tidings to mankind. It will be different the second time He comes to Earth as God in human flesh. His illuminated sign in the sky shall replace the Bethlehem star to alert all wise men and women that the King is coming.

The parable's reference to midnight refers to the state of Christ's Church when He returns. Isaiah prophesied that darkness shall cover the Earth, and gross darkness shall cover the people. Apostasy, lukewarmness, and lack of zeal for God's kingdom will characterize much of Christendom in the runup to the day of the Lord.

Despite most of Christendom falling away from the truth, a mighty remnant Church will boldly hold up high and enthusiastically wave the banner of Christ. In a world that will become increasingly hostile to the name of Jesus, His faithful saints will appear as insignificant people on Earth. A sizable portion of the world's population would prefer to rid the planet of the pesky Christ-lovers. Figuratively, the end time saints who refuse to compromise as the final day approaches are members of the churches in Smyrna and Philadelphia. The wicked Synagogue of Satan will cruelly persecute both churches.

The foolish virgins discounted the possibility that the bridegroom's arrival could be as late as midnight, the darkest hour. Consequently, their lamps went dark too. They stumbled in the darkness, unable to see the path to the wedding house. An extra effort earlier in the day would have prevented the costly error at midnight that resulted in being denied entrance to the wedding event.

Keep Thy Heart with All Diligence

Disciples of Christ will need all the spiritual oil they can carry in the last days. Your Heavenly Father has one way to illuminate your journey through this life. It is the Holy Bible. The Holy Spirit will bestow grace to you in proportion to your hunger for God's Word. You must passionately pursue His grace. There is a price to pay for discipleship. The abundance of your heart is the evidence of what you desire and seek.

Proverbs 4:23 says, "Keep thy heart with all diligence; for out of it are the issues of life." What overflows from your heart today? Is it the Word of God, or is it the world's trash talk? Is it knowledge of Christ and His kingdom, or knowledge of news, sports, entertainment, movies, politics, fashion, social media, financial investments, business, food, sex, liquor, parties, or education? Your heart is not empty but full of something. You invested time, money, resources, and energy in pursuing and acquiring something. What did you spend a lifetime chasing and getting? Will it get you to the wedding on time?

When the final day arrives, you will either be alive or sleeping in your grave. Either way, you must possess a sufficient supply of the oil of grace to complete your journey, meaning gaining entrance to the grand wedding ceremony on the final day. There will be no time to search for grace when the final day suddenly and unexpectedly explodes upon the world. You will either have it or not. Your opportunity to acquire more grace ceases with your last breath. Sadly, many departed church members from ages ago will wake up on the final day only to discover that their lamps burned out as they slept in their graves, to their shock and dismay. Suddenly awakened by the loud angelic shout that the bridegroom is coming, they will have nowhere to acquire extra grace to produce the light they need to arrive with Jesus at the wedding event.

For those who kept their lamps trimmed and lit throughout life, God promised that He "shall arise upon thee, and His glory shall be upon thee."

> **Arise, shine; for thy light is come, and the glory of the Lord is risen upon thee. For, behold, the darkness shall cover the earth, and gross darkness the people: but the Lord shall arise upon thee, and his glory shall be seen upon thee.**
>
> **Isaiah 60:1-2**

Your journey will be in the Son's brightness if you passionately pursue Jesus Christ at all costs. However, the outcome will be different for those who confessed faith in Jesus but wasted time on the foolishness of this world. They will stumble in the darkness and discover that the door is closed in their faces. The grand wedding ceremony will commence without them. There will be no other way to enter.

Slothful Servants Banished to Hell

In the Parable of the Faithful and Unfaithful Servants, we see the exact instructions again: Be dressed. Be ready. Keep your lamp lit. However, this parable differs from the Parable of the Ten Bridesmaids. The young women had an order to be prepared to go to the wedding. Jesus reversed the order of the instruction in the other parable. The master of the house ordered his servants to be ready for his return from the wedding. The master commanded the servants to be dressed in readiness and have their lamps lit so that they may immediately open the door when he knocks. Instead of the servants serving the master, just the opposite happened. The master served the faithful servants at his table. He blessed them because they were ready for his return. In this manner, Jesus' message to us today is the need to be dressed, ready for action, and prepared for His sudden and unexpected arrival.

What about the lazy servants who were not ready? The slothful servant foolishly surmised that his master would delay his return from the wedding. He reasoned, "I have a lot more time to do what I want to do, not what my master instructed me to do. I will complete his instructions later." What happened to the lazy, disobedient servant who was not ready? It was not pretty. His master beat him.

Then Peter said unto him, Lord, speakest thou this parable unto us, or even to all? And the Lord said, Who then is that faithful and wise steward, whom his lord shall make ruler over his household, to give them their portion of meat in due season? Blessed is that servant, whom his lord when he cometh shall find so doing. Of a truth I say unto you, that he will make him ruler over all that he hath. But and if that servant say in his heart, My lord delayeth his coming; and shall begin to beat the menservants and maidens, and to eat and drink, and to be drunken; the lord of that servant will come in a day when he looketh not for him, and at an hour when he is not aware, and will cut him in sunder, and will appoint him his portion with the unbelievers. And that servant, which knew his lord's will, and prepared not himself, neither did according to his will, shall be beaten with many stripes. But he that knew not, and did commit things worthy of stripes, shall be beaten with few stripes. For unto whomsoever much is given, of him shall be much required: and to whom men have committed much, of him they will ask the more.

Luke 12:41-48

In St. Mark's Gospel of our Lord, Jesus taught His disciples the same principles about His return: take heed, stay alert, fulfill your appointed assignment, be ready.

Take ye heed, watch and pray: for ye know not when the time is. For the Son of man is as a man taking a far journey, who left his house, and gave authority to his servants, and to every man his work, and commanded the porter to watch. Watch ye therefore: for ye know not when the master of the house cometh, at even, or at midnight, or at the cockcrowing, or in the morning: lest coming suddenly he find you sleeping.

Mark 13:33-36

Living a life of spiritual readiness doesn't mean spending your days in dread and fear that you will not be ready to meet Jesus upon His return. It doesn't mean forgoing your career development, education, business, or raising a family, nor does it mean losing out on time spent with friends and relatives, traveling, or recreation. God desires us to love Him, our neighbors, and life. He does not, however, want us to love the world. The daily challenge to all Christians is to be in the world but not of the world.

Spiritual readiness means living each hour of each day in an attitude of humility, submission, awe, and respect for Almighty God, knowing that each of us must give an account someday for all that we have done and said in this world. It means we know that life is like a vapor that suddenly vanishes. Yes, we should be fully engaged in the affairs of life and not neglect our family, local church, career, education, health, recreation, and rest. We must do all things for the glory of God.

Dress for Action

If Jesus commanded us to always dress for readiness, does the Holy Bible tells us our wardrobe? Yes, it does. It is a suit of armor. We must wear it continually because a partially clothed knight is a wounded or dead knight. Satan will aim his poisonous darts at the parts of your soul not fully clothed with righteousness, salvation, truth, peace, faith, and the sword of the Spirit. When dressed in the armor of God, we can withstand Satan on any day.

Jesus said you must be constantly ready, dressed in the armor of God and our path illuminated by the Word of God. Failure to obey His instructions could result in the forfeiture of your invitation to the grand wedding. Be alert, ready, and dressed wearing the armor of God. Have your lamp lit. And store extra grace to keep your lamp lit for a treacherous journey at midnight. We do not know when Jesus shall suddenly and unexpectedly burst into our dimension of time, space, and matter.

But of that day and hour knoweth no man, no, not the angels of heaven, but my Father only.

Matthew 24:36

Thieves Don't Schedule Appointments

The day of the Lord shall surprise the unprepared as a thief in the night. How does a thief appear? Suddenly and unexpectedly! Thieves plunder homes after midnight when the owners are in a deep sleep and not prepared to readily react to a violent home invasion. Thieves don't schedule appointments to rob a home or business. Robbers don't send letters, emails, or text messages announcing their anticipated arrival time to ransack your house. The homeowner and police would be waiting for them to arrive. For the same reason, Jesus will not notify anybody of the day and hour He will burst through the world's front door and violently ransack humanity's house.

Jesus didn't say it once. He didn't say it only twice. He repeatedly taught His disciples to pay attention, stay alert, be ready, and keep their lamps lit. Likewise, the Apostles repeated the Lord's warning to be prepared and to anticipate His return constantly. Why is this vital instruction flippantly ignored by many people who profess to be followers of Jesus Christ?

Imagine a military base where soldiers lounge on lawn chairs outside their barracks and scatter their uniforms on the floor inside. How would an army general react if he conducted a surprise inspection of their readiness for combat? He would be furious that his troops ignored his command to be on alert and ready for action at any minute. He would tell the lazy soldiers, "You are not qualified to wear the uniform of this government."

Lollygagging Lot Almost Lost It

Whereas Jesus said His second coming would be as the days of Noah, He also compared it to the days of Lot. Sodom and Gomorrah had sunk into shameless debauchery. Their sins were so grotesque that there was no way to save the inhabitants. They crossed the line and became reprobates.

Lot was an essential leader in Sodom. He "sat at the gate," meaning he was a city elder, perhaps a city councilman. How did Abraham's nephew end up living in sinful, decadent Sodom? He chose to live there. When Uncle Abram gave Lot the first choice in deciding where he would live, Lot chose to dwell in the cities of the plain. The flickering lights and the distant sounds of laughter emanating from those cities were like magnets drawing Lot their way. It was akin to a traveler walking through the Nevada desert at night and seeing the lights of Las Vegas glowing in the darkness. Lot pitched his tent toward Sodom.

There was something in Lot's soul that was attracted to Sodom and yearned to live there. Yet, Apostle Peter said Lot was a righteous man who was greatly distressed by the lawless licentiousness of Sodom's citizens. According to St. Peter, Sodom's immorality and lawlessness tormented Lot.

God chose to destroy all the inhabitants except Lot and his family. He sent two angels to notify Lot that Sodom and Gomorrah were on the shortlist to be razed and permanently reduced to ashes. Lot's proximity to Sodom's sins had dulled his spiritual senses. He was in danger but didn't perceive it. Even when the angels told him face-to-face that God would soon destroy the cities, Lot didn't respond with an alarming sense of urgency. Instead, he took his time getting ready for the destruction the angels said was coming. He deceived himself into thinking he had more time. The normalcy bias prevented Lot from promptly acting on the angels' warning. Even though God sent notification to Lot that sudden destruction would soon strike his hometown, Lot chose to rationalize what the angels meant.

The Bible doesn't tell us how long or why Lot delayed his flight from Sodom, but we can only imagine what he did after receiving an angelic notification of the cities' death sentence. Perhaps he went to his garage and casually sorted through the tools he wanted to take along. Whatever he did, it was stupid. Fire from Heaven was on its way, but the warning had lighted no fire underneath Lot's feet to get out of town. His lack of urgency required another angelic visitation. On the second visit, the angels physically escorted Lot and his wife and daughters out of Sodom in the nick of time. Lot's two sons-in-law, however, were seared in Sodom. They mocked Lot's talk about angels warning him to flee the city. Likewise, his wife's body left Sodom, but her heart remained there. Consequently, she was solidified into a pillar of salt when she longingly looked back at the wicked city.

Jesus mentioned the days of Lot in His teachings about the final day. He compared it to the days of Noah. In Lot's era, they ate, drank, bought and sold, planted, and built structures. Jesus said fire and brimstone rained upon Sodom on the same day Lot departed the wicked city. The Lord said it would happen the same way on the final day.

> **Likewise also as it was in the days of Lot; they did eat, they drank, they bought, they sold, they planted, they builded; but the same day that Lot went out of Sodom it rained fire and brimstone from heaven, and destroyed them all. Even thus shall it be in the day when the Son of man is revealed.**
>
> **Luke 17:28-30**

Once again, the words of Jesus refute the pre-tribulation Rapture doctrine taught by Christian Zionists. According to them, Christians will be secretly removed in the Rapture, followed by seven years of tribulation. They say Jesus will return at the end of the seven years. The Christian Zionists also teach that God will not destroy the world when Jesus returns but will set up a worldwide Jewish-centric kingdom with its headquarters in Jerusalem. Is that what Jesus said? He said fire and brimstone would rain down on the world when He removes the saints from the Earth. "Even thus shall it be in the day when the Son of man is revealed."

What part of "rained fire and brimstone from heaven, and destroyed them all" do Christian Zionists not understand? Jesus said His return would resemble the destruction of Sodom and Gomorrah. What does that mean? It means Jesus will suddenly and unexpectedly return one time to rescue His disciples from Satan's wrath. The moment they leave Earth's surface, fire and brimstone will rain down on the planet and destroy everybody and everything. Christians will go up as the fire comes down. There will not be a long gap between the catching away of the saints and the fiery destruction of the wicked and the planet. Jesus will arrive like Indiana Jones in the Temple of Doom, just in time to rescue His faithful friends. Will you have faith in Him to do it when darkness covers the world?

The Second Coming of Jesus shall be a single event that shall suddenly and unexpectedly burst upon an unsuspecting human population on Earth. God's chosen people, the Church, will be fireproof. Angels shall evacuate them. However, fire and brimstone from Heaven shall rain upon the wicked. Angels will bundle them like firewood. For Christian saints who keep the commandments of Jesus Christ, His Second Coming shall be an instantaneous divine deliverance from a world rotted by sin and racked by unimaginable global persecution, tyranny, wars, and calamities.

It will be a different story for the rebellious. For anyone found lurking outside the ark of baptism when the fiery flood comes down from Heaven, the Lord's Second Coming shall bring instantaneous judgment and eternal damnation. Christ shall sentence to the lake of fire the wicked Synagogue of Satan for constantly persecuting the Church in Smyrna and Philadelphia. All liars shall also find their place in the lake of fire. Hell's flames will also pull into its fiery pit homosexuals, heterosexual adulterers and fornicators, and others who are sexually immoral, impure, and lewd. Idolaters and sorcerers shall perish suddenly, along with people who stir up strife, hatred, discord, rage, jealousy, selfishness, envy, and heresies. Joining them in the lake of fire will also be murderers, drunkards, gluttons, and carousers.

Faster than lightning, Jesus shall come suddenly and unexpectedly. He will fight against His enemies using the Word of God in His mouth as a mighty sword of justice. He told us always to be ready. We must stay awake and be alert. We must be dressed for action and keep our lamps lit. We must also be diligent until our Master returns so that He finds us faithful. After His return, He will reverse roles and serve us at His table.

The Second Coming of Jesus Christ on the final day shall be:

- Singular
- Sudden and unexpected.

CHAPTER 3

HIS SECOND COMING
SHALL BE ATMOSPHERIC

THERE'S AN EARLY NINETEENTH-CENTURY idiom that says: "What goes up, must come down." Of course, it refers to the law of gravity. When speaking of the Second Coming of Jesus Christ, we could say, "Who went up, must come down."

Essentially, that's what the angels said to the men who watched the resurrected Messiah lift off from Earth and soared into the sky like a SpaceX rocket blasting off from Cape Canaveral.

This book's author currently lives approximately 95 miles south of Florida's Cape Canaveral. One of the benefits of living along Florida's Treasure Coast (in addition to perpetual sunshine, beautiful beaches, palm trees, great fishing, wide rivers, turtles, tropical flowers, fresh citrus juices, dolphins, pelicans, and the annual aroma of orange blossoms in the air) is the excitement of watching rockets blast off from Cape Canaveral and streak across the sky.

Nighttime rocket launches are the best to experience. Wow! A magnificent fireball lights up the sky. People come out of their homes to watch it. Drivers pull their vehicles off the road and stand along highways and roads to observe the spectacular glowing object moving through the sky.

Whether daytime or nighttime, the first stage of the launch is fantastic. The rocket is visible for only a few minutes. As it climbs higher into the atmosphere, spectators stretch their necks and refocus their eyes to follow the rocket that quickly disappears behind the clouds. After a few minutes, the rocket is gone, and the excitement is over. There's nothing left to do but post photos on social media to let your friends know you saw the space launch. Invisible to the people on Earth, the rocket continues to soar upward on its way to outer space to accomplish its mission long after the people below stop watching it.

That's the way it was one day approximately 2,000 years ago. The resurrected Son of Man lifted off from "Cape Bethany." A cloud received Him after He soared into the daytime sky. The cloud whisked Him to a heavenly dimension from which He came to save us. In short, Jesus went home after accomplishing His mission on Earth. He arrived home as a conquering hero holding the keys of hell and death in His hands. His Father gave Him the Kingdom of Heaven and proclaimed Jesus as its king.

Weeks earlier, the wicked and sinister Jewish rulers persuaded the cruel Romans to satisfy the Jews' bloodlust by having Jesus whipped, flogged, beaten, tortured, and crucified. The Jewish religious leaders rejected their Messiah despite the adoration of thousands of Jews who believed Jesus was their promised Savior. He was buried, descended to the place of the dead, resurrected

Himself from the grave, and appeared to many disciples over 40 days. During the 40-day interlude between His resurrection and ascension back to Heaven, Jesus imparted to the apostles the whole Gospel of the Kingdom of God. It is known as the Apostles' Doctrine, the bedrock of the Church.

Jesus finished His work on Earth. He said it on the Cross. "It is finished." He didn't mean, "I'm dying. It's over." His statement implied that the Old Covenant between God and the Jews was over. A New Covenant had commenced. Anybody may now become a member of God's chosen people. "It is finished" also meant that His sacrifice on the Cross finished Satan's death grip on humanity and that He completed the redemption of humanity.

With His work on Earth completed, Jesus was ready to return home. The Holy Spirit would assume responsibility for the proclamation of the Gospel and act on Earth as the presiding governor of the Kingdom of Heaven. His disciples came together with Jesus to question Him about something fundamental to them. They asked Him if He planned to restore Israel's political and military kingdom.

When Jesus walked in Palestine, the Davidic kingdom had been out of business for many centuries. His Jewish disciples' focus was on reclaiming real estate and political power. They yearned for a revived Israel to be the dominant nation in the region once again. Unbelievable! After walking side-by-side with Jesus for three years, hearing Him teach about the Kingdom of Heaven, and witnessing signs, wonders, and miracles, these good Jewish men still wanted political power and land. They rationalized in their minds that God sent Jesus to get the job done.

Nothing has changed in over 2,000 years. Today's Zionist zealots are still obsessed with land and political power. They don't see the Kingdom of God because you must be born again through faith in Jesus Christ to see it. Thus, the veil remains over their eyes. Sadly, today's Christian Zionists are reassuring unsaved Jews that God indeed desires them to own all ancient Greater Israel and wield political power.

When His disciples eagerly asked Jesus, "Are we going to get back our land?" Jesus told them it was none of their business.

> **When they therefore were come together, they asked of him, saying, Lord, wilt thou at this time restore again the kingdom to Israel? And he said unto them, *It is not for you to know the times or the seasons,* which the Father hath put in his own power.**
>
> Acts 1:6-7

After informing them that restoring the nation of Israel was none of their concern, Jesus told them to get ready for two things: The Holy Spirit would supernaturally energize them, and they would go, go, go! These guys needed to pack their bags and put on walking shoes. There wouldn't be time to hang out in Jerusalem. Besides, the non-believing Jews would make their lives miserable anyway. Fast-changing circumstances would soon compel them to escape deadly persecution from their fellow Jews who rejected Jesus Christ as their promised Messiah. They would have to leave their homes and go into all the world.

> **But ye shall receive power, after that the Holy Ghost is come upon you: and ye shall be witnesses unto me both in Jerusalem, and in all Judaea, and in Samaria, and unto the uttermost part of the earth.**
>
> Acts 1:8

Three things awaited them: First, Jew-on-Jew violence would erupt when the Jewish Sanhedrin and synagogue rulers cracked down on the growing Jewish sect that believed Jesus Christ had, indeed, risen from the dead and was their promised Messiah. Second, the Roman army would surround Jerusalem, destroy the temple, and slaughter the Jewish inhabitants. Third, God would take the kingdom away from the Jews and give it to another nation of people who would praise Him. That other nation is the Church, composed of people of every race and nation.

In other words, Jesus said to His disciples, "Boys, you have no idea what's coming because of your identification with me. Forget about a Jewish kingdom on Earth. Get busy preaching the Kingdom of God. Leave town and go as far as you can go. Preach the Gospel. Baptize believers. Make disciples. Cast out devils. Heal the sick. I'll be back later."

As soon as Jesus told them the Holy Spirit's power would come upon them, and they would be witnesses for Him around the world, the resurrected Savior lifted off the ground. He soared higher and higher. Amazed as they gazed, the disciples' eyes were fixated on their marvelous and majestic Messiah as He vanished into the atmosphere. A cloud received Jesus, and He was gone.

"Whoa! Dude, what just happened?" could have been the first words blurted from Peter's mouth. Nobody recorded it. But if anybody said it, you know it was Peter.

The Same Jesus Shall Return

Two angels suddenly appeared and asked the incredulous men a question. "Hey guys, why stand there gawking up into the sky?" Furthermore, the angels informed the disciples that the "same Jesus" would return from Heaven. The "same Jesus" means the God-Man who departed the Earth in a resurrected human body will be the same God-Man who returns to Earth in a glorified human body. This "same Jesus" will also come back the "same way" that He left: In a cloud in the sky! The Second Coming of Christ shall be atmospheric.

> **"And when he had spoken these things, while they beheld, he was taken up; *and a cloud received him* out of their sight. And while they looked steadfastly toward heaven as he went up, behold, two men stood by them in white apparel; which also said, Ye men of Galilee, why stand ye gazing up into heaven?** *this same Jesus, which is taken up from you into heaven, shall so come in like manner as ye have seen him go into heaven.*
>
> Acts 1:9-11

Who is coming again? "This same Jesus!" The angels' words are a great promise of hope for humankind. The triumphant and victorious Jesus who went up will be the same Jesus who comes down. He will not be a facsimile, replica, clone, impersonator, imitation, lookalike, double, stand-in, mirror image, remake, virtual avatar, or holographic image. The Second Coming of Jesus Christ shall not be a metaphysical phenomenon nor a mystical religious experience. He will not appear in virtual reality. His appearance shall be authentic. The King who returns will be the only begotten Son of God who came to Earth as God in human flesh, was crucified, died, buried, and resurrected from the dead! He will be the real deal.

Without a doubt, the Second Coming of Jesus Christ will be an atmospheric event. A Heaven-sent cloud whisked Jesus away after the Resurrection. Likewise, He will return to our atmosphere someday in clouds of glory. He left on a cloud and shall return in clouds. Whoever goes up must come down. Jesus shall come down. He shall come down with fire.

The Biblical Significance of Clouds

Clouds have significance in the Bible. They are often associated with the glory of God. The Hebrew word for "cloud" means "covering." Throughout the Bible, the Hebrew word for "cloud" represents the divine presence of Almighty God. When God led the Hebrew people out of Egypt, His divine presence was in a cloud by day and fire by night.

> *And the Lord went before them by day in a pillar of a cloud,* to lead them the way; and by night in a pillar of fire, to give them light; to go by day and night.
>
> Exodus 13:21

Moses met God in a cloud on Mount Sinai. God told Moses to "come up to Me into the mount." He promised to give Moses "tables of stone, and a law, and commandments" that He expected Moses to teach to the Hebrews. Moses ascended the mountain and encountered Almighty God at the summit. God's glory encased the mountain in a cloud.

> And Moses went up into the mount, *and a cloud covered the mount.* And the glory of the Lord abode upon mount Sinai, *and the cloud covered it six days: and the seventh day he called unto Moses out of the midst of the cloud.* And the sight of the glory of the Lord was like devouring fire on the top of the mount in the eyes of the children of

Israel. *And Moses went into the midst of the cloud,* and gat him up into the mount: and Moses was in the mount forty days and forty nights.

Exodus 24:15-18

When Moses left the mountaintop to return to base camp, he was horrified when he discovered the Hebrews dancing around a golden calf idol they made while he met the Creator of the universe. In a fit of fury, Moses tossed the stone tablets and broke them into pieces at the foot of the mountain. God responded by scheduling a morning mountaintop meeting with Moses. Almighty God arrived at the meeting in a cloud.

And the Lord descended in the cloud, and stood with him there, and proclaimed the name of the Lord.

Exodus 34:5

In the Book of Leviticus, God's presence over the mercy seat was in the form of a cloud.

And the Lord spake unto Moses after the death of the two sons of Aaron, when they offered before the Lord, and died; and the Lord said unto Moses, Speak unto Aaron thy brother, that he come not at all times into the holy place within the veil before the mercy seat, which is upon the Ark; that he die not: *for I will appear in the cloud upon the mercy seat.*

Leviticus 16:1-2

King David beautifully described in the eighteenth Psalm the awesomeness of Almighty God. David praised his Maker as his rock, fortress, deliverer, strength, buckler, the horn of his salvation, and high tower in whom he trusted. In distress, David called upon the Lord. He cried unto his God, and the Lord heard his plea for help. The Earth shook and trembled, and the foundation of the hills moved and was shaken because God was angry. Smoke came out of God's nostrils, and fire came out of His mouth. God bowed the heavens and came down. He came down hidden in the clouds to rescue David.

God surprised David's enemies by riding upon a cherub and concealing His arrival to Earth enshrouded in thick clouds. It was "lights out" for David's enemies when God caught them off guard and utterly surprised them. He came suddenly and unexpectedly in the atmosphere, hidden in clouds, to rescue His beloved servant, David.

> **And he rode upon a cherub, and did fly: yea, he did fly upon the wings of the wind. He made darkness his secret place; *his pavilion round about him were dark waters and thick clouds of the skies.***
>
> **Psalm 18:10-11**

Clouds are God's canopy. He wears them like a royal robe. If you've ever wondered what the Day of the Lord will look like, read Psalm 97. Surely it will be astounding to behold.

> **The Lord reigneth; let the earth rejoice; let the multitude of isles be glad thereof. *Clouds and darkness are round about him*: righteousness and judgment are the habitation of his throne. A fire goeth before him, and burneth up his enemies round about. His lightnings enlightened the world: the earth saw, and trembled.**
>
> **Psalm 97:1-4**

Jesus Shall Travel Like Lightning

Jesus' glorious appearance shall also be like lightning. Jesus said, "For as the lightning cometh out of the east, and shineth even unto the west; so shall also the coming of the Son of man be."

How does lightning appear in the sky? Lightning appears and moves swiftly across the sky suddenly. Its brilliance illuminates the sky with dazzling flashes of light. Lightning is furious and destructive. It humbles humans because it represents the power that humankind cannot control. It sets on fire whatever it strikes.

Such shall be the coming of the Son of man when He appears suddenly and unexpectedly in the atmosphere. He shall move swiftly across the sky. Dazzling flashes of light from His glory will illuminate the sky above every continent. Glorious and mighty, Jesus' sudden and unexpected appearance in the clouds will humble every human because He represents the power that humanity cannot control. The Lord will set the world on fire.

As lightning flashes across the sky, so too will Jesus' arrival flash from east to west. Have you ever noticed that Orthodox churches face east? Do you know why? Orthodox churches are built facing eastward because it is an ancient tradition grounded on the sure knowledge that Jesus' Second Advent shall be like lightning coming out of the east and shining unto the west. Likewise, Orthodox Christians pray facing eastward as their symbolic way of reminding themselves that our great hope is the Second Coming of our Lord and Savior and that He shall first appear eastward in the atmosphere.

His appearance was linked previously with the eastern sky. How were the magi led to Bethlehem at the first Advent of Jesus? When the wise men met with King Herod, they told him they came from the east and saw the Messiah's star in the east.

In Old Covenant times, the prophet Ezekiel saw the glory of the Lord when facing east. Ezekiel 43:4 says, "And the glory of the Lord came into the house by the way of the gate whose prospect is toward the east."

Old Covenant prophet Daniel saw the Son of Man arriving in the atmosphere. God gave Daniel visions at night about the final day. In Daniel 7:13, the prophet said, "I saw in the night visions, and, behold, one like the Son of man came with the clouds of heaven, and came to the Ancient of days, and they brought him near before him."

Whom did Daniel see in the visions? He saw one with a human man's physical shape and likeness but gloriously clothed in super-human majesty like God. The Son of Man is Jesus. The Ancient of Days is God the Father. "They" are angels. Daniel saw the Son of Man arriving with the clouds of Heaven. The prophet saw the grand finale of the human saga, and it was atmospheric. Daniel saw the final day when the Last Adam would undo the damage done by the First Adam. He saw the consummation of all things and the restoration of all things. Daniel saw humanity restored without Adam's sinful nature. He prophetically foresaw the day when the seed of the woman crushes the seed of the serpent. And Daniel saw the day when God the Father, the Son, and Holy Spirit make their abode in New Jerusalem and live with the saints forever. Daniel saw the final day.

He Shall Come in the Clouds

Likewise, Jeremiah had a prophetic glimpse of the final day. In the fourth chapter of the Book of Jeremiah, the prophet saw

Jesus "come up as clouds" with His chariots like a whirlwind and his horses were swifter than flying eagles.

Numerous Bible scriptures affirm that the Second Coming of Jesus shall be an atmospheric event in the clouds. Jesus told the snarling Sanhedrin magistrates that they would see Him someday "coming in the clouds of heaven." When His disciples asked about the sign of His coming and the end of the age, Jesus said they shall "see the Son of man coming in the clouds with great power and glory." He assured the disciples that He would dispatch angels to gather His elect from the four winds and from the farthest part of the Earth to the most distant part of heaven.

Old Testament prophet Daniel saw Jesus in a night vision. Daniel saw somebody who "was one like a Son of Man coming with the clouds of heaven." The conquering hero presented himself to the Ancient of Days, who gave the victor "dominion, and glory and a kingdom, that all peoples, nations, and languages should serve him."

Daniel proclaimed that the Son of Man's "dominion is an everlasting dominion, which shall not pass away, and His kingdom that which shall not be destroyed." Jesus shall come in the clouds with great power and glory to execute judicial vengeance upon Jerusalem, Mystery Babylon, the harlot, the great city, and Sodom and Egypt. Why? Because Jerusalem is the city that killed the prophets and crucified the Savior.

In his vision on the Isle of Patmos, St. John the Revelator wrote, "Behold, He cometh with clouds; and every eye shall see Him, and they also which pierce him, and all kindreds of the Earth shall wail because of Him." Apostle John did not write, "Jesus shall come with clouds." Instead, he wrote, "Behold, He cometh with clouds...."

Whenever the Holy Bible says, "He cometh," the scriptures refer to the glorious arrival of the King of Kings. Clouds represent God's glory and majesty. The preparation for the second arrival of Jesus on Earth began when Jesus ascended to Heaven. The preparation has been underway for over two thousand years and will continue until His regal appearance and kingly presence arrives on Earth. Thus, "He cometh with clouds."

Nothing could instill more terror in the hearts and minds of wicked, rebellious men and women than the sight of the Son of God coming in the glorious clouds of heaven. Saved souls shall rejoice because their salvation is secured. Why would the innocent tremble at the sight of their Savior coming with clouds of glory? The wicked, however, shall be filled with dread because their consciences will condemn them as guilty and deserving punishment. It's no wonder that all the tribes of the Earth shall wail and mourn by beating their breasts when they see Him coming with clouds, fully knowing the prospect of their doom. They will cry on that day because they will finally admit that they despised the Son of God, pierced, and crucified the Savior of the world. They will realize they rightfully deserve to be cast into the lake of fire.

What people will behold that day shall be God accompanied by clouds and coming to judge humanity. The presiding judge is the One, in the words of the psalmist, "who makes the clouds His chariot." Old Testament prophet Jeremiah said, "Look! He shall come up as clouds, and his chariots shall be as a whirlwind." Clouds of glory shall accompany the Great Judge to judge hostile antichrist Jews and wicked heathen Gentiles and establish His government over everybody and everything.

Meeting in the Air

The clouds will represent something extraordinary for the saints. They herald the magnificent union of the Body of Christ with the Head of the Church. It is "in the clouds" where the two shall meet and be united forever.

Apostle Paul revealed the meeting in the air to Christians in Thessalonica. He desired that they not be ignorant about departed saints who are asleep in Christ. By saying he did not want them to be uninformed about the matter, St. Paul underscored the importance of the message he was about to deliver to them concerning the dead in Christ. The Apostle implied that ignoring the momentous implications of his statement could have far-reaching consequences.

But I would not have you to be ignorant, brethren, concerning them which are asleep, that ye sorrow not, even as others which have no hope. For if we believe that Jesus died and rose again, even so them also which sleep in Jesus will God bring with him. For this we say unto you by the word of the Lord, that we which are alive and remain unto the coming of the Lord shall not prevent them which are asleep. For the Lord himself shall descend from heaven with a shout, with the voice of the archangel, and with the trump of God: and the dead in Christ shall rise first: then we which are alive and remain shall be caught up together with them in the clouds, to meet the Lord in the air: and so shall we ever be with the Lord.

1 Thessalonians 4:13-17

Apostle Paul desired that the saints know the truth about the death of their physical bodies. We must not have sorrow, said

Paul, because if we believe that Jesus died and rose again, we must also assuredly know that Jesus will bring with Him the spirits of the saints who are asleep. St. Paul assured the Church there is no justification for prolonged grief and no reason to be stressed and worried about their dead relatives and friends who died in the Lord. Grief, sorrow, and stress over the deaths of family members and friends are for the unsaved, not the Church. Spiritually lost people have no hope. Paul said, "For if we believe that Jesus died and rose again...." His choice of words "for if" implies that Paul knew the saints firmly believed in the resurrection of the saints on the final day. There was no need to teach the doctrine further because it was a settled matter in the churches.

The Apostle assured the Thessalonian Christians that their departed saints would be there on that grand and glorious day. Their bodies will come out of their graves and be in the forefront of the vast fleet of flying saints who ascend through the atmosphere to meet the triumphant King Jesus in the clouds officially. The final day's fleet of flying saints are the people whom Isaiah inquired about their identity, "Who are these who fly as a cloud and as the doves to their roosts?"

If we have faith and confidence in the resurrection of Jesus Christ, we can assuredly have faith and confidence that Jesus will bring with Him on the final day the spirits of those departed saints who "sleep in Jesus." The glorious arrival of King Jesus will guarantee that their dead bodies will be transformed into glorified bodies when they come out of their graves.

Sleep, Jesus' gentle euphemism for death, was also used in the Old Testament. Prophet Daniel was told by an angel about the final day, the day of the Lord. He told Daniel that the angel

Michael "shall stand up" and "there shall be a time of trouble such as never was since there was a nation even to that time." The angel said, "many of those who sleep in the dust of the Earth shall awaken, some to everlasting life, but others to shame and everlasting contempt."

All the saints laid to sleep through Jesus, meaning they died in full communion still with Christ, will be led by Him along the same path that Jesus traveled at Calvary. He is the door by which we enter physical death. He descended to the place of the dead. Jesus gently holds our hand as we sink into our place of rest while we await the resurrection of all saints. He will not permit us to be alone and afraid during the transition from this world to our time of sleep. Our Savior leads us on the same path that culminates in the resurrection of our physical bodies on the final day. When we die, Jesus' light illuminates our way made dark by death.

Just as Jesus meets us at the time of our physical death and gently escorts us to our new position of rest, so too will Jesus meet us on the final day to lead us to the resurrection He experienced on the third day of His death. Thus, God brings our disembodied spirits with Jesus on the final day. Our Heavenly Father shall complete for us the life cycle that Jesus experienced as the Son of Man: physical birth, life, death, entrance into the place of the dead, resurrection, eternal life in full fellowship with the Heavenly Father. His violent death makes our death a gentle sleep. His glorious resurrection makes our sleep a mighty awakening. In the twinkling of an eye, the dead in Christ will enter new glorified bodies that will never die. We shall live then because He lives now.

Paul took his message to another level of authority. He said, "For this we say unto you by the word of the Lord...." He was speaking not only for himself but for all apostles. "We say" implies that all the apostles had received the word of the Lord that Paul was ready to impart to the saints in Thessalonica. We do not know how, when, and where the apostles received this word of the Lord. Paul's choice of words implied that it came to the apostles directly through divine revelation. Did Jesus personally teach it to the apostles during the forty days between the Resurrection and Ascension? Did an angel impart the knowledge? Or did the apostles each receive visions? Again, we do not know. What we do know is that St. Paul emphatically stated that what he was about to teach the saints came directly from Heaven. There could be no debate or discussion about the doctrine. It came from God. And what was this word that came directly from God? The divine message contained eight points:

1. The saints alive when Jesus returns shall not prevent the saints who are asleep from receiving the promise
2. Jesus shall descend from Heaven with a shout
3. All shall hear the voice of the archangel
4. God's trumpet shall sound
5. The dead in Christ shall rise first
6. Those alive at the Second Coming shall be caught up together with the risen saints in the clouds
7. Both groups of saints will meet the Lord in the air
8. They shall forever be with the Lord.

The word of the Lord, the revelation from Heaven to the apostles, said that we which are alive and remain unto the coming of the Lord should not prevent them which are asleep. "Alive and remain" literally means "those who are left over." Furthermore, "shall not prevent" means to "go before" or "get the start of." In other words,

St. Paul said Heaven authorized him to inform the Church that the living saints will not get a head start on the departed saints on the final day. It will be just the opposite. The resurrected saints will go up first, and then those saints leftover will follow them in the air to meet Jesus in the clouds.

The divine message also revealed a trumpet blast and shout would startle the universe! Everybody will hear it. The trumpet is the signal of the imminent arrival of the divine presence. God's trumpet blast shall silence all other sounds on Earth. A hush shall cover the world. Commanded by God to sound the trumpet, angels shall notify the entire human population, dead and alive, that a significant change is about to happen. It shall herald the greatest reset of human civilization. The trumpet blast shall announce that the consummation of all things has commenced, the end of the world has finally arrived.

All graves, not some, but all shall open. Jesus said we must not marvel at this thought: "For the hour is coming in which all who are in the graves will hear His voice." Jesus said the dead would come out of their graves, both good and evil. Each group would experience a resurrection of their dead bodies. Righteous men and women shall receive the resurrection of life, but wicked men and women shall receive the opposite. They will receive the resurrection of judgment, meaning eternal punishment in the lake of fire. Some will awake to everlasting life, but others to shame and everlasting contempt.

The graves of every human who ever lived from the beginning of time shall instantly pop open. Adam's grave shall open. Eve's grave, too, along with the graves of Cain and Abel. Noah's grave shall open. The graves of Genghis Khan, all of Egypt's pharaohs,

Adolf Hitler, Vladimir Lenin, and Fidel Castro shall burst open too. The burial places of Mozart, Rembrandt, Picasso, da Vinci, Michelangelo, and van Gogh shall pop open. Every grave! The saved and the unsaved. The righteous and the wicked. The famous and the unknown. The proud and the humble. The rich and the poor. From Adam to the last human buried seconds before God's trumpet blares its first note, everybody will hear the wake-up call. What a scene it shall be on the final day. Sheer terror or indescribable joy will greet the awakened dead depending on their spiritual fate on Resurrection Day.

The trumpet blast will signal angelic reapers that the time has come to gather and bundle the wicked and unbelievers and prepare them for perpetual burning in the lake of fire. The bodies of the dead in Christ will also come forth from their graves. They will transition from physical death to eternal life by rising from their graves, dwelling in new incorruptible bodies.

Immediately after that, those alive in Christ will likewise undergo an instantaneous change in their nature. It shall happen faster than a blink of an eye. The living shall see the resurrection of the dead. The resurrected dead shall see the transformation of the living. Christ will clothe both groups with white garments. Both will be snatched up into the air to meet King Jesus, who shall arrive in clouds of glory.

They're all coming out of their graves on the final day, but not all are going up. The righteous shall go up. Everybody saved by faith in Jesus Christ and baptized in water in the name of the Father, the Son, and the Holy Spirit shall depart the Earth in the same manner Jesus left His disciples after the Resurrection. A worldwide meeting of the Church shall convene in the air. Hallelujah! Glory

129

to God. Angels will not escort them to Heaven. Instead, Christ will bring Heaven to them. The Creator shall create a new Earth to receive New Jerusalem, which will come down from Heaven. Our Heavenly Father will change His mailing address from Heaven to New Jerusalem.

It will be a different story for the unsaved and wicked. They will be bundled and burned. Sinners will fry. Saints will fly.

Whoever goes up must come down. The first Christians gazed upward toward Heaven when Jesus left Earth. The last Christians shall be gazing upward toward Heaven when Jesus returns to Earth. They will go up when He comes down.

The Second Coming of Jesus Christ on the final day shall be:

- Singular
- Sudden and unexpected.
- Atmospheric

CHAPTER 4

HIS SECOND COMING
SHALL BE VISIBLE

THE HOLY BIBLE TEACHES that everybody on Earth will see the Second Coming of Jesus Christ. The first chapter of the Apocalypse says, "Behold, He is coming with clouds, and every eye will see Him, even they who pierced Him. And all the tribes of the Earth will mourn because of Him." How could that happen? Presently, there are over seven billion people alive on Earth. How could seven billion people see the same thing happening at the same time?

In the heyday of religious broadcasting via satellites, prominent Christian pastors, bible prophecy teachers, and religious broadcasting executives often said global television broadcasting was the explanation. They surmised that the Second Coming of Jesus would be televised worldwide in real-time. Broadcast TV stations and satellites, however, are quickly fading away into communication technology's yesteryear. Internet streaming is currently the up-and-coming technology for media content delivery systems. That, too, will change someday in the future.

Regardless, all three video communication technologies—broadcasting, satellite, and streaming—would require television news networks to fix their cameras on an incoming object in the sky. Jesus would have to slow his descent considerably as he approached the Earth. Control room operators in the studios of television news networks will need sufficient time to zoom cameras in and follow His entry into our atmosphere, like a UFO landing in New York City's Central Park.

Using media technology to explain how everybody on the planet could see Jesus when He returns also mandates that all seven billion people are awake and watching television or a mobile device at the same time. Forget this idea! It won't be on TV or your mobile smartphone.

How will everybody see Jesus returning to Earth? The answer is quite simple. Jesus Christ will be the only object lit up in the entire universe. You will not be able to miss Him. He will be the grand star of the show. Every human and animal will be staring in great wonderment at the marvelous and glorious arrival of the King of Kings and Lord of Lords.

Why will Jesus be the only object glowing in the universe? That's easy to explain too. Shortly before Jesus' grand entrance, His Heavenly Father will authorize angels to cut off the electricity to the whole universe by powering down the Sun, the Moon, and stars. Lights will go out everywhere! Isaiah said darkness shall cover the Earth, and gross darkness shall cover the people. The prophet saw the darkness of sorrow that will encompass the planet in the last days, the culmination of millenniums of sinfulness, rebellion, idolatry, sorcery, bloodshed, lewdness, and all other iniquities against God. Humankind's rapid descent into darkness will culminate in a universal blackout.

Jesus told us precisely when the universe will go dark. The lights will go out immediately after the days of great tribulation and before the appearance of the sign of the Son of Man. If you accept Jesus Christ as an expert witness qualified to talk about the end of the world, then you must receive His timeline of events.

> **Immediately after the tribulation of those days shall the sun be darkened, and the moon shall not give her light, and the stars shall fall from heaven, and the powers of the heavens shall be shaken: and then shall appear the sign of the Son of man in heaven: and then shall all the tribes of the earth mourn, *and they shall see the Son of man coming in the clouds of heaven with power and great glory.* And he shall send his angels with a great sound of a trumpet, and they shall gather together his elect from the four winds, from one end of heaven to the other.**
>
> Matthew 24:29:31

Every eye on Earth includes animals too. Frog eyes, hippopotamus eyes, eagle eyes, puppy eyes, caterpillar eyes, cat eyes, fish eyes, and all other creatures with eyes shall see Jesus Christ arrive in the clouds of heaven with power and great glory because the universe will be dark. The King of Kings shall be the only glowing object in the sky. The animals shall praise their Creator, who shall come to deliver them from humanity's madness and to destroy those who destroy the Earth. Every creature shall rejoice except the wicked, rebellious sinners, and unbelievers.

Old Testament Prophet Isaiah Saw the Final Day

Old Testament prophet Isaiah saw the final day. He prophesied about the revelation God gave him. He cried out to the rebellious, stubborn Israelites that the stars shall go dark.

For the stars of heaven and the constellations thereof shall not give their light: the sun shall be darkened in his going forth, and the moon shall not cause her light to shine.

Isaiah 13:10

What day did Isaiah see in his spirit? He saw the final day. It was not unusual that God gave an Old Testament prophet a divine revelation of the Second Coming of Jesus Christ. God has spoken to humanity about the final day ever since Adam and Eve submitted to Satan shortly after the first day. Methuselah preached righteousness, as also did his grandson Noah. All the Jewish prophets foretold the arrival of the Messiah and the final day. Thank God for the first-century Jews who believed in the name of Jesus as the Messiah. All of us should be eternally grateful for them, and we should honor their memory and legacy as saints and martyrs of the Church. They did receive the Kingdom! And they will inherit the ultimate promised land on the final day. Because of them, God graciously grafted Gentiles into Israel, the Church of God.

Thousands of years ago, Isaiah said fallen humanity would howl when the final day arrives because it will mean their destruction. Extreme terror will overtake all sinners. Their hands will weaken, their hearts melt, and painful pangs and sinking sorrows shall grip them. The sudden, unexpected end of the world will fill their bodies with excruciating pains like a pregnant woman in childbirth.

They will stare at each other in ghastly bewilderment, and their faces shall turn beet-red like they are on fire. When the final day bursts upon unrepentant sinners, it shall be cruel with God's wrath and fierce anger. He will empty the Earth and punish all sinners who rejected Jesus Christ.

> **Howl ye; for the day of the Lord is at hand; it shall come as a destruction from the Almighty. Therefore shall all hands be faint, and every man's heart shall melt: and they shall be afraid: pangs and sorrows shall take hold of them; they shall be in pain as a woman that travaileth: they shall be amazed one at another; their faces shall be as flames. Behold, the day of the Lord cometh, cruel both with wrath and fierce anger, to lay the land desolate: and he shall destroy the sinners thereof out of it.**
>
> Isaiah 13:6-9

In the sixtieth chapter of the Book of Isaiah, the prophet cried out to Israel, the Church, to rise and shine in a darkened world. Isaiah preached, "For, behold, the darkness shall cover the Earth, and gross darkness the people..." What was the darkness seen by Isaiah that shall cover the Earth? It is the darkness of sin, the darkness of violence, the darkness of hatred, the darkness of lust, the darkness of immorality, the darkness of poverty, the darkness of greed, the darkness of sorrow, the darkness of disease, the darkness of hopelessness and despair, and the darkness of death.

Indeed, Isaiah foretold that "gross darkness" shall cover the people of Earth. His choice of words implies that the planet's inhabitants would be entrapped beneath a worldwide foul-smelling, sulfurous, smokey cloud cover so thick and dark that no natural light could penetrate it. In the runup to the final day, the only light that can and shall overpower the darkness will be supernatural light emanating from the Son-lit Church of God, faithful Israel. Every anointed sermon and inspirational hymn punctures holes in Satan's dark canopy to allow light to reach humankind.

> **Arise, shine; for thy light is come, and the glory of the Lord is risen upon thee. For, behold, the darkness shall cover the earth, and gross darkness the people: but the Lord shall arise upon thee, and his glory shall be seen upon thee.**
>
> Isaiah 60:1-2

Isaiah's prophecy is a divine summons from Almighty God to the worldwide Body of Christ. Because sin, wickedness, and rebellion have darkened the world, Christ commands His Church to arise and shine. Isaiah said that the Lord shall arise upon them when the Church shines, and His glory shall be seen upon the saints. Gentiles will be attracted to the light shining from the Church and will attract kings to the Christians' rising brightness.

> **....but the Lord shall arise upon thee, and his glory shall be seen upon thee, and the Gentiles shall come to thy light, and kings to the brightness of thy rising.**
>
> Isaiah 60: 2-3

Jesus teaches His disciples that we are the light of the world. We are like a brightly lit city on a hill that cannot be hid from passersby. He said His disciples shall not walk in darkness but shall have the light of life. If disciples of Christ can shine, we also must shine before a world of lost souls trapped in gross darkness. If we walk with Jesus Christ in this life, we shall have the light. If we have the light of Christ, we will shine in a dark world. If we shine in a dark world, we shall attract lost souls seeking to escape from Satan's heavy veil of darkness that covers the globe.

When the final day arrives, it will be easy for the angelic reapers to know the sinners and the saints. Darkness will drape sinners. God's glory will make sinners twinkle like fireflies in a farm pasture on a moonless summer night.

It gets even better! By the fourteenth verse of chapter 60, Isaiah reveals the gem God has planned for His children. It is New Jerusalem, the Bride of Christ! The offspring of the people who persecuted Christians shall bow on bended knees before the saints of God. All who despised Christians shall bow down at the feet of the saints they hated. The sons of past oppressors gripped with shame over their ancestors' persecution of the Church shall pay homage to Christ's Church and call it "the city of the Lord."

The sons also of them that afflicted thee shall come bending unto thee; and all they that despised thee shall bow themselves down at the soles of thy feet; and they shall call thee, The city of the Lord, The Zion of the Holy One of Israel.

Isaiah 60:14

Christians will not dwell in old Jerusalem for one thousand years after the Second Coming of Jesus. Old Jerusalem, which the Holy Bible identifies as the harlot Babylon, shall be split three ways by a massive earthquake before the final day. The ancient city, which God also labeled Sodom and Egypt, will later be incinerated by Jesus Christ when He sets fire to the entire planet to make room for the new Earth and its shining capital city New Jerusalem.

137

John the Revelator borrowed a page from Isaiah. In his vision on the island of Patmos, John saw New Jerusalem coming down from Heaven. The city did not need the Sun, the Moon, and stars. Apostle John said God would be the light of the glorious city.

And the city had no need of the sun, neither of the moon, to shine in it: for the glory of God did lighten it, and the Lamb is the light thereof.

Revelation 21:23

Let's rewind the prophetic time machine to the days of Isaiah. The Old Testament prophet saw the same thing that the New Testament prophet John saw in his vision. How could they match up? How could the Jewish Old Testament prophecy match the Christian New Testament prophecy? Is it possible that the same Spirit inspired both men and directed their hands to write holy scriptures? Almighty God has been telling humanity the same story for millennia. He's searching for men and women who believe what He has spoken. Indeed, God desires His children to believe Him! Do you know any mother or father who does not want their sons and daughters to believe and trust them? Look at what Isaiah saw. It matches John's vision on Patmos.

The sun shall be no more thy light by day; neither for brightness shall the moon give light unto thee: but the Lord shall be unto thee an everlasting light, and thy God thy glory. Thy sun shall no more go down; neither shall thy moon withdraw itself: for the Lord shall be thine everlasting light, and the days of thy mourning shall be ended.

Isaiah 60:19-20

Every Eye Shall See Jesus

The days of our mourning shall end following the time of great tribulation. Jesus shall gather the saints unto Him in the sky, the angels will bundle and burn all sinners, and the old planet will be torched and incinerated. God will speak into existence a new planet and heaven. New Jerusalem shall come down from Heaven. God will pack up His stuff in Heaven and move to New Jerusalem to live with his children in a new Garden of Eden.

The Sun, the Moon, and the stars will become obsolete and vanish. There will be no need for them when Jesus returns. Their sudden extinguishment will be why every eye shall see Him on the final day.

> Behold, he cometh with clouds; *and every eye shall see him,* and they also which pierced him: and all kindreds of the earth shall wail because of him. Even so, Amen.
>
> **Revelation 1:7**

"Every eye shall see Him" refers to more than the people alive on Earth when Jesus returns. It includes every human who ever lived. They too shall be present to see the Messiah's glorious arrival. Billions of people who previously lived and died will be standing alongside the living. It will be elbowroom worldwide. Multitudes will bump into each other because the lights will be out in the universe. Is it any wonder why men's hearts will fail them for fear and for looking after those things coming on the Earth?

John began his statement by saying, "behold." It means, "look, see!" See what? See the coming of Jesus! How is He coming? He is arriving with clouds. Clouds represent God's great glory. John said everybody would see Jesus arriving with clouds, but he deliberately singled out a specific group of people: the people who pierced the Lord at Calvary.

The Jews and Romans who crucified Jesus shall see Him and wail. Specifically, who shall see Jesus when He returns? Roman governor Pontius Pilate will crawl out of his grave and be compelled by God to watch the arrival of the God-Man he executed to please the Jews. The Roman soldiers who whipped and beat Jesus will pop out of their old graves, too, along with the Roman soldiers who nailed Him to the Cross and tossed dice to win His robe.

Caiaphas will see Him too. All the chief priests and elders of the people who took counsel against Jesus to put Him to death will emerge from their musty tombs. God will compel Caiaphas and his Sanhedrin cohorts to behold the King of the Jews arriving with clouds of great glory. Judas will see the Savior of the world whom he betrayed with a kiss. Murderous Barabbas will watch the glorious arrival of the Messiah who died for him. Every Jew who shouted, "crucify him!" will see the return of Jesus. All the Jews, and their descendants, who arrogantly said, "His blood be on us, and on our children," shall witness the spectacular descent of the Son of God. Standing by their opened graves will be every defiant, unrepentant Jew who killed God's prophets and hindered and plotted against the work of the one, holy, catholic, and apostolic Church of Christ. On the final day, all who opposed Christ and His Church will stand next to their opened graves to behold the One they hated. His blood shall be upon them as they demanded.

When Pilate saw that he could prevail nothing, but that rather a tumult was made, he took water, and washed his hands before the multitude, saying, I am innocent of the

blood of this just person: see ye to it. Then answered all the people, and said, His blood be on us, and on our children.

Matthew 27:24-25

Can anybody fathom the utter horror and shock that will be upon their faces? For centuries, they have tossed and turned in their tormented graves. Suddenly their dark tomb of internment will open. They will climb out of their graves, crypts, vaults, caves, and even from the seafloor. Everything will be dark except one bright object in the sky. Jesus! The man they mocked and crucified will be hovering over them in the sky as the triumphant and victorious King who has returned to settle matters His way.

Old Testament prophet Zechariah saw the same thing New Testament apostle John observed about the Lord's return. They both saw the future when Christ returned to Earth. In their respective heavenly visions, each prophet saw the Jews who pierced Jesus' body.

All Who Pierced Jesus' Side Shall See Him

Zechariah made it clear he was talking about the Jews because he said the people are the "inhabitants of Jerusalem." Zechariah said the Jews would look upon Jesus when He returns and mourn in bitter sorrow. God will compel them to look upon the God-Man whom their Jewish ancestors crucified and watched gleefully as the Roman soldier pierced His side with a spear. Joining them that day will be all unsaved Jews who metaphorically pierced Jesus Christ by rejecting Him as their Messiah. They should have mourned in sorrow for their sins and repented before the final day. It will be too late when everybody sees Him. Their mourning shall be in vain.

And I will pour upon the house of David, and upon the inhabitants of Jerusalem, the spirit of grace and of supplications: and they shall look upon me whom they have pierced, and they shall mourn for him, as one mourneth for his only son, and shall be in bitterness for him, as one that is in bitterness for his firstborn.

Zechariah 12:10

How do we know that Pontius Pilat, Caiaphas, and all the other criminals complicit in the crucifixion of the Son of God will stand on the final day to witness the glorious return of the Messiah whom they murdered? Here's the proof: St. John the Theologian said we should not marvel at the amazing truth that every grave will open in the hour of Jesus' coming. All dead humans since Adam and Eve will come out of their graves when they hear His glorious voice. More than saints will come out of their graves on the final day. Sinners, too, will awaken from their long sleep. Resurrection Day is for everybody! Christ will resurrect the saints to eternal life with Him. Likewise, Jesus Christ will resurrect the wicked to eternal life without Him. Saints and sinners alike will live forever in new bodies that never die. Christian saints will live forever in New Jerusalem. Unsaved sinners will live forever in the lake of fire, begging to die. Nobody will hear their pleas.

Marvel not at this: for the hour is coming, *in the which all that are in the graves shall hear his voice,* and shall come forth; *they that have done good,* unto the resurrection of life; *and they that have done evil,* unto the resurrection of damnation.

John 5:28-29

And, behold, I come quickly; and *my reward is with me, to give every man according as his work shall be.*

Revelation 22:12

The divine shout and trumpet blast on the final day will jostle the sleeping souls of every human who ever lived since the days of Adam and Eve. Nobody will be able to sleep in their graves with all the noise and commotion above their graves. Out of their graves, they shall arise. The first thing their awakened eyes shall behold will be Jesus Christ coming with clouds of great glory. For sinners, the second thing they will see will be a giant angel with fiery eyes pointing his finger at them, saying, "You're mine. Follow me. You're going to the everlasting lake of fire."

Their time out of the graves will be brief. It will be like a peep breaking out of an eggshell and immediately snatched away by a menacing predator. If you are a peep coming out of your eggshell, and the first thing you see is a hungry coyote licking its lips, you instantly know it's going to be a bad hair day. Get over it and accept your fate. It will quickly devour you.

That's the way it will be on the final day when all graves open. Unsaved sinners and the wicked may have enough time to say, "What's up with this?" Who knows? Perhaps God will grant them enough time to stretch their legs and arms after a long snooze in their graves. The awakened wicked will quickly discern that the world is utterly dark and terrorized, screaming people are running into each other, desperate to run away from the One called Faithful and True. Christ will majestically hover above them in the sky riding upon a white stallion and leading a vast army of warrior angels.

Old Testament and New Testament scriptures both confirm that the arrival of Jesus Christ shall be visible to the entire human population on Earth, including the living and the newly awakened dead. It will significantly impact the Jews and Romans who participated in and supported the crucifixion of Jesus Christ by piercing His hands, feet, and side. Their wailing shall be utterly in vain. The Jews and Romans will not be the only people wailing on the final day. Every unrepentant sinner who has pierced the tender heart of the Lord shall also wail and mourn on that dreadful day of the Lord.

When everybody sees Jesus, it will be too late to repent. Therefore, they will wail in remembrance and sorrow of their sins and their refusal to repent and believe in the name of Jesus Christ when they had the opportunity to do it but refused to act. Nothing will fill the world with greater despair and alarm than the arrival of the Judge of the Universe to pronounce judgment and sentencing upon unrepentant sinners, the wicked, and the rebellious.

The Church Triumphant Shall See Jesus

There is good news for Christians. All Christians who ever lived shall see Jesus too! Every devout Christian who loves Jesus Christ desires to be among the chosen generation alive on the final day to witness the glorious appearance of our blessed hope Jesus Christ. Many God-fearing men and women went to their graves not seeing the Second Coming in their lifetimes. It does not matter because everybody will be there when He returns on the final day. Departed saints will emerge from their graves to join the living saints on that beautiful day.

The formerly dead and the presently living will be united on the final day to behold the arrival of King Jesus. The Church

Militant will join with the Church Triumphant. The whole Church extending back to the first generations of humans, including Methuselah and Noah, will join Old Testament prophets and New Testament apostles and martyrs. Every saved saint from every era will be standing alongside the living on the final day. It will be a giant Family Day celebration!

All the mad monarchs and treacherous tyrants throughout world history will be standing there to observe the arrival of King Jesus. Nimrod, Pontius Pilate, Herod the Great, Nero, Julius Caesar, Nebuchadnezzar, Genghis Khan, Tamerlane the Great, Vlad the Impaler, Henry VI, Mary, Queen of Scots, Ivan the Terrible, Rudolf II, Napoleon, George III, Carlota of Mexico, Adolf Hitler, Benito Mussolini, Ze'ev Jabotinsky, Menachem Begin, Muammar Gaddafi, and Saddam Hussein will watch the arrival of Jesus Christ. Standing with them will be their bloody cohorts who helped carry out their wicked orders, alongside their victims who will cry out for final justice.

Righteous kings and queens will also come out of their graves. The Spirit of the Lord will bring King David, King Arthur, and Queen Victoria from their ancient burial places to observe the grand finale of the age of mankind. Gathered with them will be their kingdoms' inhabitants.

St. Jude quoted pre-Flood prophet Enoch who said, "Behold, the Lord cometh with ten thousand of his saints...." Behold means "be sure to see" or "do not miss this!" The Greek word is an exclamatory word telling the hearer that an observable event will happen, and the hearer or reader should make sure they see it. If you heard a person point up to the sky and shout, "Look! See it!" you would immediately look up to see what was there. Therefore, Enoch said, "Look! See him! The Lord is coming."

According to Jude, Methuselah's father told us why we must see the Lord's visible return to Earth, along with ten thousand of his angels. Jesus and the angels will arrive to execute judgment upon all the Earth's unsaved inhabitants. They will also convince all ungodly people of the evil deeds they committed in their human bodies and their harsh words against Jesus Christ.

And Enoch also, the seventh from Adam, prophesied of these, saying, Behold, the Lord cometh with ten thousands of his saints, to execute judgment upon all, and to convince all that are ungodly among them of all their ungodly deeds which they have ungodly committed, and of all their hard speeches which ungodly sinners have spoken against him.

Jude:14-15

Immediately After Those Days

The universal visibility of the Lord's Second Coming refutes the fallacy of the secret Rapture doctrine as taught by present-day Christian Zionist disciples of John Nelson Darby. They insist that Jesus will return twice: Firstly, they say, He will come in a secret Rapture of Christian saints before the start of great tribulation. Secondly, they teach that Jesus will return seven years later in the Second Coming. Christian Zionist theology has a significant problem. It contradicts the Holy Bible scriptures as recorded by St. Matthew, St. Mark, and St. Luke.

Those three apostles heard Jesus teach about the end of the age. The Holy Spirit inspired each apostle to write what he heard Jesus say about His return. All three versions are amazingly similar. The scene was Jerusalem. Jesus had denounced the scribes and

Pharisees and lamented over Jerusalem minutes before He talked to his disciples about the end of the world. The disciples heard Jesus lambast the corrupt Jewish rulers. He called them hypocrites, whitewashed tombs, sons of murderers, and vipers. It was Jesus' last visit to the temple during His days on Earth.

As Jesus walked away from the temple, His disciples implored Him to look again at the splendor of the temple buildings. The disciples believed that God sent Jesus to establish a kingdom. Still, like today's Zionists, they imagined that God would once again restore the ancient Davidic kingdom with renewed political, military, financial, and religious power. Zionists today still yearn to achieve necessary control over the Middle Eastern geography that formerly was ruled by King David. The modern Zionist concept is known as Greater Israel.

St. Mark told us that one of the disciples said to Jesus, "Master, see what manner of stones and what buildings are here!" Jesus, however, was not impressed by the temple's magnificence. Minutes earlier, Jesus had exclaimed to the astonished Jewish rulers, "Behold, your house is left unto you desolate." His disciples were perplexed. Why did Jesus wish to see the temple brought down into desolation? After all, if Jesus was the Messiah, did He not plan to lead an insurrection to restore the temple to its original glory by reviving the ancient Davidic kingdom?

Jesus' answer shocked the disciples. He informed the men that not one stone of those grandiose buildings would be left standing upon another stone. In other words, the Son of God notified His disciples that He would demolish the temple someday. The destruction would be so devastating that Jerusalem's future invaders would not even allow one building stone to remain resting in its place upon another stone. That's why we know that today's Old City in the modern State of Israel is not the original city. It is a city built by Roman Emperor Hadrian in the second century. He named his pagan city Aelia Capitolina in 135AD. Archeologists continue to dig up parts of the original Jerusalem, but modern residents and tourists walk the streets of Emperor's Haiden's Roman city, not ancient Jerusalem. If today's Old City is ancient Jerusalem, it means Jesus lied. He did not lie because He cannot lie. Today's Zionists are not telling the truth about Jerusalem. Neither is the Roman Catholic Church telling the truth about the Via Dolorosa. Pagan Hadrian did not reconstruct the streets where Jesus carried the Cross to Calvary. Instead, he constructed temples for Roman gods. Today's Via Dolorosa is for tourists.

Indeed, Jerusalem and the temple had a "day of the Lord" visitation from Heaven in 70AD. The resurrected Christ led Roman army general Titus to Jerusalem to utterly destroy the city and temple. The devastating dismantling of Jerusalem and its famous shrine signified God's final separation from Judaism. God has never looked back and regretted it.

Departing the temple, Jesus and His disciples climbed the nearby Mount of Olives. Sitting atop the tall hill overlooking Jerusalem, the disciples asked Jesus three questions: When shall these things be? What will be the sign of your coming? What will be the sign of the end of the age?

Their first question was regarding Jesus' prophecy that the temple would be destroyed. Their second and third questions were closely connected because Jesus' return would coincide with the end of the age of mankind. The entire reply to the disciples' three questions spans the twenty-fourth and twenty-fifth chapters of the Gospel According to St. Matthew, the thirteenth chapter of the Gospel According to St. Mark, and the twenty-first chapter of the Gospel According to St. Luke. Jesus' reply to the questions included His warning that there would be wars and rumors of wars, persecution against the Church, earthquakes, famines, pestilences, and great tribulation.

Let's focus on the scriptures in all three narratives of the Gospel about a future time immediately after the years of great tribulation. Remember that the following scriptures are part of Jesus' lengthy answer to the second and third questions: What will be the sign of your coming? What will be the sign of the end of the age? He previously answered the first question about the destruction of the Jewish temple. That prophecy was fulfilled in 70AD when Titus destroyed Jerusalem. We still await the fulfillment of His prophecies about His return to Earth and the end of the age. St. Matthew recorded Jesus saying:

> **Immediately after the tribulation of those days shall the sun be darkened, and the moon shall not give her light, and the stars shall fall from heaven, and the powers of the heavens shall be shaken: and then shall appear the sign of the Son of man in heaven: and then shall all the tribes of the earth mourn, and they shall see the Son of man coming in the clouds of heaven with power and great glory. And he shall send his angels with a great sound of a trumpet, and they shall gather together his elect from the four winds, from one end of heaven to the other.**
>
> **Matthew 24: 29-31**

Here is the sequence of events based on what Matthew heard Jesus say:

- Immediately after the tribulation of those days.
- The Sun shall be darkened.
- The Moon shall not give its light.
- The stars shall fall from heaven.
- The powers of the heavens shall be shaken.
- The sign of the Son of Man shall appear in heaven.
- All the tribes of the Earth shall mourn.
- They shall see the Son of Man coming in the clouds of heaven with power and great glory.
- He shall send His angels with a great sound of a trumpet.
- The angels shall gather Christ's elect from the four winds, from one end of heaven to the other.

Now let's compare St. Matthew's account of the end of the age with the words that St. Mark heard Jesus say.

But in those days, after that tribulation, the sun shall be darkened, and the moon shall not give her light, and the stars of heaven shall fall, and the powers that are in heaven shall be shaken. And then shall they see the Son of man coming in the clouds with great power and glory. And then shall he send his angels, and shall gather together his elect from the four winds, from the uttermost part of the earth to the uttermost part of heaven.

Mark 13:24-27

Here is the sequence of events based on what Apostle Mark heard Jesus say.

- In those days after that tribulation...
- The Sun shall be darkened.

- The Moon shall not give her light.
- The stars of heaven shall fall.
- The powers that are in heaven shall be shaken.
- Then shall they see the Son of Man coming in the clouds with great power and glory.
- Then shall Jesus send His angels and gather His elect from the four winds, from the uttermost part of the earth to the uttermost part of heaven.

Do the accounts given by Apostles Matthew and Mark concur with Apostle Luke? Let's read St. Luke's version of the end of the age.

> **And there shall be signs in the sun, and in the moon, and in the stars; and upon the earth distress of nations, with perplexity; the sea and the waves roaring; men's hearts failing them for fear, and for looking after those things which are coming on the earth: for the powers of heaven shall be shaken. And then shall they see the Son of man coming in a cloud with power and great glory. And when these things begin to come to pass, then look up, and lift up your heads; for your redemption draweth nigh.**
>
> **Luke 21:25-28**

Here is the sequence of events as recorded by St. Luke:
- There will be signs in the Sun, the Moon, and stars.
- There will be the distress of nations, and the inhabitants will be perplexed, meaning puzzled, bewildered, mentally confused
- Oceans will be turbulent, with high waves roaring.

151

- Uncontrollable fear will cause many heart attacks when people see strange, unusual, catastrophic events on Earth and in the sky.
- The powers of heaven shall be shaken.
- Then people shall see the Son of Man coming in a cloud with power and great glory.
- When these things start happening, the saints must look up and lift their heads because their redemption from the world will be close.

Did you notice anything missing in Jesus' reply to the disciples' questions? He said not a word about returning to Earth twice. His disciples asked Him about three specific things: When shall the temple be destroyed? What shall be the sign of your coming? What shall be the sign of the end of the age?

There was never a better opportunity for Jesus to reveal to His disciples the mystery of the secret Rapture event before the start of great tribulation. Did He forget to tell them? Perhaps He winked at the guys and whispered, "Don't tell anybody this secret. I don't want it written in the Bible someday, but I will return twice. The first visit will be called the secret pre-tribulation Rapture. I will return seven years later to save the future State of Israel from being destroyed by the opponents of Zionism. For now, we must keep this plan a secret. Eighteen hundred years from now, a child will be born in Ireland. His parents will name him John Nelson Darby. After he grows up and moves out of his parents' haunted castle, my Spirit will reveal this secret plan to him. At first, few people will believe that he received recovered knowledge from Me about the end of the world. Someday there will be a country called America, and there will be churches called Christian Zionists. I will inspire a conman who went to jail for fraud to print Darby's recovered knowledge in a special reference Bible. And someday, there will be the Dallas Theological Seminary and the Moody Bible Institute to teach people the recovered knowledge my Spirit will give to Darby and Cyrus Scofield. After the deaths of Darby and Scofield, their recovered knowledge will gain popularity. Eventually, my secret plan will become very popular in America. Prophecy teachers will write books about it, and filmmakers will make movies too. Most Christian Zionists in America will believe the secret plan. Only when my secret plan successfully achieves market saturation in America will you know that the end is near."

No, my friend, Jesus did not whisper those words. There are no hidden mysteries in the Holy Bible. Jesus did not conceal His plan about the end of the age. He told us all we needed to know.

There is remarkable uniformity in all three records of the Gospel about the Second Coming of our Lord. Let's merge them. Here is the combined sequence of events:

- In those days, immediately after the tribulation.
- There will be signs in the Sun, the Moon, and stars.
- The Sun shall be darkened.
- The Moon will not give its light.
- There will be the distress of nations, and the inhabitants will be perplexed.
- Oceans will be turbulent, with high waves roaring.
- Uncontrollable fear will cause many heart attacks when people see strange, unusual, catastrophic events on Earth and in the sky.

- The powers of heaven shall be shaken.
- The sign of the Son of Man shall appear in heaven.
- All the tribes of the Earth shall mourn.
- They shall see the Son of Man coming in the clouds of heaven with power and great glory.
- He shall send His angels with a great sound of a trumpet.
- When these things start happening, the saints must look up and lift their heads because their redemption from this world will be near.
- The angels shall gather Christ's elect from the four winds, from one end of heaven to the other.

Who or what is our redemption? Our Redeemer is Jesus Christ. When shall Jesus draw near? When "these things" begin to come to pass. What things? Signs in the Sun, the Moon, and the stars; and the distress of nations, with perplexity; the sea and the waves roaring; men's hearts failing them for fear; and when the powers of heaven are shaken. That is the moment we must look up and lift our heads toward the sky. We should expect to see our Redeemer arriving in all His glory.

If you believe the Christian Zionist narrative, Christians will be air-lifted out of harm's way before the first item on the list: "in those days immediately after the tribulation." Why did Jesus not say "The Rapture" will remove Christians in the days *immediately before the tribulation?* Did He miss the planning meeting in Heaven before He was born in Bethlehem? Did He not receive the memo? Did the Ancient of Days suffer memory loss and forget to inform Jesus? Was the secret Rapture plan written on a piece of paper that Jesus left in His pocket when John baptized Him in the Jordan

River? Or did the Apostles omit it from the Holy Bible because they thought Jesus was only joking about a secret rapture?

Any level-headed person would conclude that "The Rapture" is not in the Holy Bible because Jesus never said it. Why are we having this conversation about something that is not real? Because Christian Zionists duped millions of Christians into believing the Rapture is real. They are quickly running out of time to get this right. Christ is coming. And He's coming much sooner than most Christians think.

There's nothing hidden, concealed, or mystical about the order of things on the final day. You do not need a seminary-educated prophecy expert with a complicated prophecy timeline chart to explain it, nor a rabbi with a book of mysteries. Simply read the Holy Bible and believe it. If you are confused, it is because the doctrines of men have permeated your mind. Ask your Heavenly Father to remove the cognitive cobwebs.

The Words That Made Caiaphas Furious

Jesus made a mysterious statement during His sham trial convened late at night by Jerusalem's Jewish religious leaders who entered a conspiracy to murder the Son of God. They failed to extract from Jesus' lips statements they could use to justify a court conviction and execution. The Law of Moses required a minimum of two witnesses before imposing the death penalty on a defendant. Therefore, their bloodlust demanded they find several attestants to justify the murder they plotted to commit legally.

Two liars were found and rushed to the court hearing where the high priest, elders, and members of the Jewish council were interrogating Jesus, whom they accused of blasphemy. The two false accusers stepped forward and swore they heard Jesus make a terroristic threat to physically destroy the Jewish temple and rebuild it in three days. Perhaps Jesus' recent second cleansing of the temple stirred up in the minds of the two witnesses the promise spoken by Jesus after He cleansed the temple the first time three years earlier. He said, "Destroy this temple, and in three days, I will raise it up."

What they heard was Jesus referring to His own body as the temple of God and His promise that His body would be resurrected three days after His crucifixion. Nevertheless, the testimony the two men gave the court was their misinterpretation of what Jesus said. Eager to convict Jesus, the religious rulers seized the men's words in their desperate search to acquire the crucial evidence needed for a death penalty conviction.

However, their false testimony was not the proverbial "smoking gun" that the prosecutors needed to persuade a court to find the defendant guilty of a crime worthy of death. Caiaphas, the Jewish high priest, stood up and demanded an explanation from Jesus. The Messiah said nothing. Angered by Jesus' silence, the Jewish high priest adjured Jesus to tell the Jewish tribunal whether He was the Christ, the Son of God. Caiaphas cunningly phrased his next question to force Jesus to affirm or deny His divinity. If Jesus denied He was the Son of God, they would have convicted Him of being an imposter who deceived the public into thinking He was the Messiah. Should Jesus have claimed to be divine, His admission would have been all the evidence needed for a death penalty conviction. Either way, the court was determined to find Jesus guilty and worthy of death.

Jesus responded with the most amazing reply. He did not retreat and cower in the face of such deep hostility. Instead, Jesus doubled down with an excellent response. He told Caiaphas and his assembled conspirators they would see Him again someday.

Now the chief priests, and elders, and all the council, sought false witness against Jesus, to put him to death; but found none: yea, though many false witnesses came, yet found they none. At the last came two false witnesses, and said, This fellow said, I am able to destroy the temple of God, and to build it in three days. And the high priest arose, and said unto him, Answerest thou nothing? what is it which these witness against thee? But Jesus held his peace. And the high priest answered and said unto him, I adjure thee by the living God, that thou tell us whether thou be the Christ, the Son of God. Jesus saith unto him, Thou hast said: nevertheless *I say unto you, Hereafter shall ye see the Son of man sitting on the right hand of power, and coming in the clouds of heaven.*

Matthew 26:59-64

Jesus could no longer remain silent when asked if He was the Christ, the Son of God. If Jesus remained silent, His accusers would have interpreted it as a denial of His divinity. Jesus affirmed His divinity by essentially saying, "That's what people are saying about me." In other words, "That's the word on the street. I'm not denying what people are saying about me."

Indeed, the chief priests and elders were fuming with anger when they perceived that Jesus did not deny the claims of the public that He was the Anointed One, the long-promised Messiah, the Son of God. They seethed with rage and thought, "That's enough for us! He just refused to deny that he is the Son of God.

We don't need to hear another word out of his mouth. Jesus must be executed!"

Jesus was not finished with putting Judaism's pompous priests in their place. He gave them another zinger that sent them through the roof with indignation. Paraphrasing Jesus, He said, "You are furious because you think I said that I will destroy the temple and rebuild it in three days, and because I am Christ, the anointed Son of God. I've got news for you! Just wait until you see Me on the final day. Your eyes will see something more shocking than the destruction of your temple!"

That sent Caiaphas over the top. He angrily ripped apart his clothing in disgust. He accused Jesus of blasphemy and asked his fellow henchmen what they wanted to do with Jesus. They promptly arrived at their predetermined conclusion: Jesus had to die.

Then the high priest rent his clothes, saying, He hath spoken blasphemy; what further need have we of witnesses? behold, now ye have heard his blasphemy. What think ye? They answered and said, He is guilty of death.

Matthew 26:65-66

What did Jesus tell Caiaphas he would witness that was more shocking than the destruction of Judaism's most sacred shrine in Jerusalem? Jesus stared directly into the eyes of Joseph ben Caiaphas, the high priest of the Sanhedrin, and said, "nevertheless I say unto you, Hereafter shall ye see the Son of man sitting on the right hand of power, and coming in the clouds of heaven."

In other words, Jesus said, "Caiaphas, I'm talking to you, big boy. Mr. Caiaphas, I will bring your old dead body out of its dusty, musty, rotten, stinking grave on the final day and make you stand and watch Me return with clouds of great glory."

Jesus' words "nevertheless I say unto you" conveyed the message to Caiaphas and the Sanhedrin that "I have something more shocking to tell you." What would be more shocking than destroying and rebuilding the temple and admitting you are the Son of God? Jesus said, "You shall see...." See whom? You shall see the Son of Man! What will Caiaphas see the Son of Man doing? "Mr. Caiaphas, you and the Sanhedrin shall see the Son of Man sitting on the right hand of the Power and coming in the clouds of heaven!"

He gave them advance notification that the innocent man they would crucify would come back someday in great power and glory. It would be more than power. He vowed to return in "the Power," meaning Almighty God. Jesus also informed them that His return would be visible. The spiritual dullness of the Jewish leaders prevented them from comprehending what Jesus told them. They did not discern that He said He would someday bring them out of their graves to witness His glorious and triumphant return personally. When He returns, Jesus will be more than King of the Jews. Every human who lived will hail Jesus as King of Kings and Lord of Lords. Caiaphas and every member of the Sanhedrin will bow their knees that day and confess that Jesus is King and Lord.

Jesus enlightened the Sanhedrin that they would see Him "sitting on the right hand of power." Why did it infuriate them? That phrase was offensive enough to make Caiaphas rip apart his expensive tailor-made robe. The Jewish rulers knew what Jesus implied. A more accurate translation of the Greek manuscripts should read that Jesus said, "the right hand of *the* Power." The power was the one and only God of the universe. Among the Hebrews, the phrase "sitting on the right hand of the Power" signified that Jesus saw Himself equal with Almighty God's divinity. "The power" speaks of the eternal Creator. The "right hand" means God's might and power. It represents the chief place of honor. "Sitting" denotes that Jesus completed His work.

Therefore, Jesus told Jerusalem's chief Jews that they would someday see Him coming in clouds representing God's divine glory and sitting with might and power in the chief place of honor as a divine prince of Almighty God the Creator and rightly chosen by God to judge humankind because He completed His work, and His enemies were under His feet. That's what made Caiaphas rip apart his robe!

Further implied in His response was the notion that He would "turn the tables" on them someday, meaning He would reverse His position with the Jews by turning His position of disadvantage at that time into an advantage later. Paraphrasing Jesus, He told the chief priests, "Presently I am a prisoner in your illegitimate court facing an unjust judgment for sins I did not commit. Boys, I've got news for you! Someday I'm going to switch positions with you. You will be a prisoner in my royal court! I will be the just and righteous Judge of the Universe on the final day. My Word will judge and convict you of sins you did commit! You will be sentenced on the final day to eternal damnation in the everlasting lake of fire. Mark my words. You will see it someday."

The universal visibility of his Second Coming is a big deal to Jesus. He guarantees that every human who ever lived will be standing on Earth in total darkness on the final day to personally see Him arrive in radiant brilliance as the triumphant king of the universe who will put all His enemies under His feet. The final day will be His day! Every eye shall be upon Jesus.

Throughout the centuries, devout Christians have longed and hoped that their generation would see the Second Coming of Jesus Christ. They went to their graves with their hope unfulfilled. Here is terrific news: They will see Jesus' return! It does not matter whether you are alive or in a grave on the final day. You will see Jesus! Every born again, baptized, Bible-believing, faith-walking, faith-talking, commandment-keeping disciple of Christ who ever lived will see Him. They will be alive when they awaken from their sleep on Resurrection Day. The whole Church of God, the Church Militant, and the Church Triumphant, will be alive and united together on the final day. Perhaps the atmosphere will reverberate with billions of voices joyfully singing, "All hail the power of Jesus' name, let angels prostrate fall."

All unrepentant sinners and wicked evildoers shall see Him too. They shall awaken from their graves to see His glorious arrival. The Jews and Romans who nailed Him to the Cross will be there too, along with every person throughout the ages who rejected Jesus, mocked Him, spat upon His holy name, and opposed His one, holy, catholic, and apostolic church. All shall see Jesus in His heavenly glory when He returns. The entire animal kingdom on Earth shall see Jesus too. Even blind bats will see Jesus.

An incomprehensible event will occur when Jesus gathers the entire human population, from Adam to the last baby born seconds before Jesus returns. Both saints and sinners, rich and poor, lowly and haughty, shall bow their knees before the triumphant King Jesus, and their mouths will audibly confess that He is Lord. Every knee means the animal kingdom too! Elephants, horses, cattle, lions, apes, rabbits, squirrels, whales, and turtles will joyfully bow before the King of Kings.

> For it is written, As I live, saith the Lord, every knee shall bow to me, and every tongue shall confess to God. So then every one of us shall give account of himself to God.
>
> Romans 14:11

They Knew Whom They Were Murdering

Caiaphas and the chief priests pretended they were shocked over Jesus' claim to be the Son of God, the Anointed One. They knew all along He was the promised Messiah. It was the real reason the Jewish rulers conspired to kill Him. Jesus told us in the Parable of the Vineyard Owner that the Jewish rulers knew that He was the Son of God. They murdered Jesus to steal His inheritance! They did not realize that God would use the crucifixion of Jesus to take away the Kingdom of God from rebellious Jews and give it to obedient Gentiles. It backfired on them. Instead of stealing Jesus' inheritance, they lost their position as God's chosen people.

After the crucifixion, resurrection, and ascension of Jesus, the unbelieving Jews were outside Israel looking in. The believing Jews, Greeks, and Romans who confessed Jesus as Lord and baptized into the Church of Christ were inside Israel as rightful citizens of the Kingdom of God. The Church did not replace Israel. Instead, God replaced the citizens of Israel. Almighty God kept the repentant Jews who believed in the name of Jesus, and He kicked out the rebellious Jews who rejected the Messiah.

Furthermore, God enlarged the population of Israel by inviting Gentiles to enter the Kingdom. Today, most Jews, including residents of the modern State of Israel, are not citizens of God's Israel. They could re-enter anytime and claim their rightful place. When the Jews crucified Jesus, God canceled all old Israeli passports. He abolished their citizenship. Yet, He cordially invited them to apply for the new Israeli passport signed by King Jesus. Heaven issues the new Israeli passport when you come up to the surface of baptism's water.

In the Parable of the Vineyard Owner, the vineyard owner (God the Father) had leased his property (the promised land) to tenants (the Jews) and went away to a far country. The vineyard owner (God) later sent servants (the prophets) to collect the harvest of fruit (praise, worship, and obedience) that the tenants rightfully owed him. The vineyard tenants (the Jews) refused to obey the vineyard owner (God) by giving him the harvest (praise, worship, and obedience) that was due to him. They killed the servants (the prophets). The owner (God) sent more servants (prophets) to them to acquire his rightful portion of the harvest. The vineyard tenants (the Jews) killed them too. Finally, the vineyard owner (God) sent his son (Jesus) to collect the fruit that rightfully belonged to him. He thought, "Surely they will respect and obey my son!" Instead, the vineyard servants said, "He sent his son. Let's kill him and steal his inheritance!"

The parable reveals that the Caiaphas Cabal was guilty of premeditated murder when its members decreed a death sentence for Jesus. What was the inheritance they lusted to possess? It was more than King David's kingdom. It was more than God's four-part promise to Abraham to give him offspring, possession of land, a blessing on him, and a blessing on all nations through Abraham's seed. God's promises to Abraham and David were not enough to

163

satisfy the Jewish rulers. The Caiaphas Cabal lusted to possess the inheritance that God promised His Son.

In Psalm 2:8, God said to His Son, "Ask of me and I shall give thee the heathen for thine inheritance, and the uttermost parts of the Earth for thy possession." God gave the entire world by covenant to His only begotten Son. The Heavenly Father bestowed to Jesus all the Gentile nations and their people as His inheritance.

God the Father gave God the Son the Kingdom of Heaven after Jesus ascended to Heaven following the Resurrection. Since the Ascension, Jesus has been the King of Heaven. Christ is ruling over His Church on Earth. In due time, Christ will extend His dominion over everybody and everything on the final day. Every knee shall bow, and every tongue shall confess that Jesus Christ is King.

The Father instructed the Son to ask for the souls of all human-kind as an inheritance. He granted Jesus' request when He went to the Cross for the sins of humanity. We are His rightful inheritance. He paid the price for our salvation and, thus, His Heavenly Father rewarded His Son for His suffering. The world's Gentile population, disrespectfully called Goyim by the Jews, were gifted to Jesus to replace the disobedient Jews cast out of His kingdom because of their unbelief.

Jesus longed to possess the souls of Gentiles, but the Jewish rulers lusted to possess the Gentiles' possessions and labor. They saw the inheritance of God's Son as their path to achieve world-wide domination.

Shortly after the Jewish-led Bolshevik Revolution in 1917 that overthrew Orthodox Christian Russia, European Ashkenazim started infiltrating Palestine. Over the next twenty-five years, Zionist paramilitary groups formed terrorist cells in Palestine and killed Palestinian Christians, Muslims, and authentic Jews who had been living together peacefully. By 1948, there were enough Zionist terrorists in Palestine to successfully overtake the Palestinian population and establish the modern State of Israel. Today, European Ashkenazim now physically occupy Palestine at the expense of Palestinian Christians, the true Semitic descendants of the early Christian saints who followed Jesus over two thousand years ago.

Today, lust for land madly drives Zionists to possess the extended borders of ancient Greater Israel. This endeavor will require perpetual warfare in the Middle East for a century to conquer all the nations currently in possession of real estate previously ruled by King David.

Zionism's goal today is to fully possess Jesus' inheritance of all Gentiles and pervert it into world domination. Perhaps they hope to achieve it through artificial intelligence, surveillance technologies, and censorship of all dissenting voices.

Our Transformation Occurs When We See Jesus

The Second Coming of Jesus Christ shall be singular, sudden, unexpected, atmospheric, and visible. Every man, woman, and child on the planet shall behold His glorious arrival with the clouds. The atmosphere will radiate with His splendor and glory when He streaks across the sky as lightning from east to west. All humans will stagger at the brightness of His coming. Saints will joyously shout in excitement, but most people will wail and mourn in terror. There will be no place for stubborn sinners to hide.

The most important thing to know about His visible appearance is that it shall transform us to be like Him. Saint Paul said we would be changed, in a moment, in the twinkling of an eye, at the last trump. Our corrupt bodies of human flesh shall put on the incorruption of the resurrected body of our Lord and Savior. We shall trade our mortality for His immortality.

When does this glorious transformation happen to us? It will happen when we see Jesus as He is! He is glorious! Our miraculous transformation from mortal beings to immortal beings is synonymous with our eyes beholding His magnificence, purity, and glory.

> ....in a moment, in the twinkling of an eye, at the last trump: for the trumpet shall sound, and the dead shall be raised incorruptible, *and we shall be changed.*
>
> **1 Corinthians 15:52**

Apostle John wrote a fascinating declaration of hope about the final day. The beloved apostle said our Heavenly Father has bestowed upon Christians the privilege of sonship. We are now the children of God. The world, however, does not recognize us as children of God because they don't acknowledge God. Indeed, the complete revelation of sonship has yet to be realized by Christians. We know that we are God's children, but we do not comprehend how awesome it shall be when this world comes to an end, and we are forever in the presence of our Heavenly Father.

Presently, it does not appear in this world that we are children of God, but we must always know that when Jesus appears, we shall be like Him! (We shall be like him, but not equal. We are made in His image, not in His essence.) What will cause this transformation to happen miraculously? John said we would become like Jesus when we see Him as he is! Yes, we are presently children, but someday we shall reach full maturity in Christ. The bud blossoms into the flower! Buds need sunlight to bloom. We are buds today, but we will fully blossom into radiant flowers when the Son's light shines upon us.

Apostle John, however, added an "and" to this beautiful promise. The "and" is a morality clause in the New Covenant. John added the caveat that qualifies who will receive this transformation. St. John the Apostle said every Christian with this hope in Jesus would keep himself pure even as Jesus is also pure.

> **Behold, what manner of love the Father hath bestowed upon us, that we should be called the sons of God: therefore the world knoweth us not, because it knew him not. Beloved, now are we the sons of God, and it doth not yet appear what we shall be:** *but we know that, when he shall appear, we shall be like him; for we shall see him as he is. And every man that hath this hope in him purifieth himself, even as he is pure.*
>
> 1 John 3:1-3

The most important thing to know about the visibility of the Second Coming is God's promise to transform us on that day to be like His Son Jesus. If you sincerely desire your physical body to be changed into a glorified body that will live forever, you better do your best in this life to live a life that is pleasing to God. It may sound old-fashioned these days, but "living right for God" will pay big dividends on the final day. You must purify yourself. How? Intimate communion with the Holy Spirit is the way to cleanse yourself.

The Second Coming of Jesus Christ on the final day shall be:

- Singular
- Sudden and Unexpected
- Atmospheric
- Visible

CHAPTER 5

HIS SECOND COMING
SHALL BE NOISY

JESUS CHRIST WILL NOT sneak into our dimension of time, space, and matter. He's going to make a scene, a huge commotion. Angels sang the first time Jesus came to Earth. Angels will shout the second time He arrives.

His Second Advent cannot be quiet. The grand kick-off event will be the mother-of-all earthquakes. St. John heard and saw it in a vision while detained as a prisoner on the island of Patmos. In Revelation 16:18, he prophesied it would be the most destructive earthquake since men were on the Earth. "Mighty" and "great" were the words he chose to describe what he saw and heard in the heavenly vision.

St. John heard lots of noises. Voices, thunders, and lightnings accompanied the mighty earthquake in the vision. The fierce tremor, "so mighty an earthquake, and so great," will rip apart the Earth's crust as its tectonic plates shift violently beneath the surface. How much noise does the ripping of the Earth's crust make when the planet splits apart? It would not be an exaggeration to say that people worldwide will hear and feel the Lord's anger.

Noises will be an integral part of the Second Coming, except for the silence that will last approximately thirty minutes after Jesus opens the seventh seal, which signifies the most severe judgment He will inflict upon the wicked. Nobody will be able to ignore the day of the Lord. Everybody will know that Jesus is back in town. He can't help it. It will be Jesus being Himself. He does not intentionally show off. Spectacular stuff happens wherever He goes. During His brief earthly ministry, Jesus ruined every funeral He attended. Dead people woke up when Jesus entered the room! Why? Because Jesus is pure life! There's nothing in Him except life. Death cannot be in His presence. When Jesus returns, Creation will tremble and shake when the Creator speaks. Dead people will sit up in their coffins to find the source of the loud commotion. It will be too noisy to continue sleeping in the dust of the Earth. Who can sleep when your casket is violently shaking?

The voice of thy thunder was in the heaven: the lightnings lightened the world: the earth trembled and shook.

Psalm 77:18

When God the Father met Moses on Mount Sinai to receive the Ten Commandments on stone tablets, the Hebrew people trembled over what they saw and heard on the holy mountain. Exodus 20:18 says, "And all the people saw the thunderings, and the lightnings, and the noise of the trumpet, and the mountain smoking: and when the people saw it, they removed and stood afar off. Like Father, like Son. Jesus looks, talks, and acts like His Papa. Therefore, we should expect similar things to happen when He returns. The people will see and hear resounding thunderings, spectacular bolts of lightning, the trumpet's blare, and mountains smoking. The righteous will reach their arms upward toward Christ, but the legs of the wicked will run to deep caves to hide from the God-Man with fiery eyes.

The Old Testament prophet Daniel saw Jesus in the second century BC. What a glorious sight he beheld! Daniel described the righteous king he saw in the vision while standing on the bank of the Hiddekel River, which some Bible scholars think is the Tigris River. In the tenth chapter of the Book of Daniel, the prophet said Jesus was clothed in linen, His loins were girded with fine gold, His body was like the beryl, His face as the appearance of lightning, His eyes were lamps of fire, His arms and feet were like polished brass, and His voice sounded like the voice of a multitude.

Centuries later, another man saw Jesus in a similar vision. It, too, was about the final day. The heavenly vision came to John the Revelator when he was a prisoner on the Isle of Patmos years after the crucifixion, resurrection, and ascension of Jesus. Apostle John, who walked with Jesus during His earthly ministry, saw the same glorious king Daniel saw in his divine vision. The Son of Man stood amid seven candlesticks. Jesus wore a garment down to His feet. His hair was like wool, as white as snow. His eyes were as a flame of fire, and His feet were like fine brass refined in a furnace. And His voice sounded like many waters. He held seven stars in His right hand, and a sharp two-edged sword came forth from His mouth. His countenance was as bright as the shining Sun. He held the keys of hell and death.

That's who is coming back to Earth on the final day of the age of humankind. The noise of His glorious and triumphant re-entry to this world will disrupt all human activity. Indeed, His arrival will disturb the entire cosmos. Every human and animal will gaze upon Him in the sky. And every ear will hear Him when He speaks like thunder, the sound of many waters, the voice of a multitude.

> **Our God shall come, and shall not keep silence: a fire shall devour before him, and it shall be very tempestuous round about him.**
>
> Psalm 50:3

The psalmist said, "it shall be very tempestuous round about him." What is a tempest? It is a violent commotion, disturbance, or tumult. In other words, Jesus will make a scene. And it will be a noisy scene. It's impossible to make a silent disturbance. The noise of His arrival will drown out all other voices and sounds on the planet. Jesus will dominate the entire cosmos on His day. Humans ignored God for ages, but nobody will ignore Him on that day. Jesus has something to say to humanity, and they will hear Him regardless of whether they want to listen or not. The final day will be His time to speak.

A Controversy with All Nations

Why does Jesus have something to say that everybody on the planet must hear? He has a long-running controversy with the nations of the world. The historical rift between Christ and the world's countries goes back to post-Great Flood days.

God made Adam. He did not create Adam but made him from Earth's elements. Contrary to popular opinions, God did not make Adam inside the Garden of Eden. God first made the Garden of Eden, formed Adam outside the garden, and placed him in the garden. When Adam sinned against God, the Lord evicted Adam from the garden and put him back where he started, the wasteland. The Garden of Eden was not Adam's birthplace; thus, he did not own it, nor did he have a claim to dwell there. It was a gift from his Maker. Adam's choice to be deceived by Satan disqualified him from living in the beautiful garden that God gifted to him.

We don't know much about the antediluvian age. That's why it is called prehistorical. It was before recorded history. There was a long gap between the post-Garden of Eden age and the pre-Great Flood age. The Book of Genesis written by Moses is our primary record of knowledge of the beginning of human civilization. From Genesis, we know that there were no nations on Earth before the Flood. The world was one. Genesis 11:1 says, "And the whole earth was of one language, and of one speech." It means people "of one lip, and one stock" of words populated the whole globe. "Lip" refers to a human organ of articulation, meaning the manner of forming and speaking words to communicate with others. People everywhere formed words in their mouths and pronounced them the same way.

Not only was the world one, but it was ruled by one too. The tyrant was Satan. How do we know that Satan ruled the world? Because humans became like him. Civilization degenerated so much that God eventually regretted the day He made Adam. Originally, God authorized Adam to have dominion over the Earth, but Adam voluntarily surrendered it to Lucifer, the serpent.

In our modern age, terms such as "one world" and "globalism," and "new world order" have become commonplace in our culture. Why has globalization become a dominant theme in government, commerce, education, and entertainment? Because presently, human civilization is subconsciously reverting to its one-world mindset when Satan ruled the world. Jesus said it would happen before He returned. He said, "But as the days of Noah *were*, so shall also the coming of the Son of man be."

Nations appeared on Earth after the Great Flood during the lifetime of Peleg, the son of Eber, who was a descendant of Noah's son Shem. Before the days of Peleg, "the whole Earth was of one language, and of one speech." A monumental event happened to humankind during Peleg's lifetime, "for in his days was the Earth divided." How was it divided? Some Creationists believe the scripture verse refers to continents drifting apart. However, the context of the biblical reference is to the division of the world according to families. Families became clans, clans became tribes, and tribes became nations, but a shared language no longer united them because something happened in the city of Babel.

These are the families of the sons of Noah, after their generations, in their nations: and by these were the nations divided in the earth after the flood.

Genesis 10:32

After the Great Flood, men and women wasted no time restarting their evil deeds. Nimrod was Noah's great-grandson. Cush was Nimrod's father, and Noah's second son Ham was Nimrod's grandfather. The Holy Bible does not state it, but we can surmise that Nimrod most likely heard his great-grandfather Noah talk about the civilization that existed before the deluge. Perhaps Nimrod resented God for destroying that world and leaving his generation with the task of rebuilding society. He had a warped scheme to make sure it did not happen again. Nimrod conspired to build a high tower to reach Heaven, enabling men to overthrow the God who destroyed the world with water.

Nimrod made headway to accomplish his goal of constructing a ziggurat to reach God's realm. Seeing their unity, the Lord said, "Behold the people is one, and they have all one language; and this they begin to do: and now nothing will be restrained from them, which they imagined to do." Following a snap inspection of the building site, the Trinitarian Godhead immediately ordered the dismantling of the tower.

Next, God scrambled the universal speech of mankind by dividing it into many languages and dialects so that no tribe could understand the words of other tribes. Is it any wonder that *Babbel* is one of today's most popular online courses to learn different languages? Humankind is subconsciously searching for its antediluvian roots; and that universal language so that nothing will be restrained from them, which they imagine doing. Man is unknowingly yearning for its pre-Great Flood universal civilization ruled by Lucifer.

And the whole earth was of one language, and of one speech. And it came to pass, as they journeyed from the east, that they found a plain in the land of Shinar; and they dwelt there. And they said one to another, Go to, let us make brick, and burn them thoroughly. And they had brick for stone, and slime had they for mortar. And they said, Go to, let us build us a city and a tower, whose top may reach unto heaven; and let us make us a name, lest we be scattered abroad upon the face of the whole earth. And the Lord came down to see the city and the tower, which

the children of men builded. And the Lord said, Behold, the people is one, and they have all one language; and this they begin to do: and now nothing will be restrained from them, which they have imagined to do. Go to, let us go down, and there confound their language, that they may not understand one another's speech. So the Lord scattered them abroad from thence upon the face of all the earth: and they left off to build the city. Therefore is the name of it called Babel; because the Lord did there confound the language of all the earth: and from thence did the Lord scatter them abroad upon the face of all the earth.

Genesis 11:1-9

Nimrod's brash attempt to overthrow God was the origin of the Creator's controversy with the world's nations. Despite our Heavenly Father's repeated attempts to reconcile fallen human-kind, the dispute never ended. When angels sang over Bethlehem, "Glory to God in the highest, and on earth peace, good will toward men," they did not envision Christmas greeting cards with those lyrics. The angels meant that God offered peace and goodwill to the world so that mankind would be reconciled to Him. God desired to end His long-running controversy with humanity. Therefore, He sent His only begotten Son to become a human embryo inside a young virgin named Mary to begin the process of reconciliation.

Over two thousand years have passed since God extended His hand of reconciliation to humanity. Throughout centuries since the Resurrection, multitudes of lost souls have accepted God's gracious offer and were reconciled to Him. Even today, reconciliation continues between God and lost souls who believe in the name of Jesus. Indeed, the Church's primary mission is to advertise Heaven's offer of reconciliation worldwide.

Sadly, millions of lost souls refused reconciliation with Christ over centuries, and the rejection continues today. Presently we are witnessing a rebirth of ancient paganism. A growing number of men and women are reverting to the spirit of Nimrod's open hostility toward Almighty God. Unwilling to be reconciled with the Creator, the age-old controversy between God and man continues today. They yearn to overthrow Him finally, but the Lord looks down on puny men and women and laughs at their ridiculous schemes for world domination.

What is a controversy? It is a dispute between two or more parties involving a matter of importance. The term denotes a legal process during which pleadings are made before a court of law. Old Testament prophet Jeremiah cried out to Israel that "the Lord hath a controversy with the nations, He will plead with all flesh...."

A noise shall come even to the ends of the earth; for the Lord hath a controversy with the nations, he will plead with all flesh; he will give them that are wicked to the sword, saith the Lord.

Jeremiah 25:31

"A noise shall come even to the ends of the Earth; for the Lord hath a controversy with the nations...." A noise shall come! What noise? It will be the tumultuous sound of a marching army advancing toward its enemy to slaughter them. Everybody will hear the thunderous movement of the Lord's angels. This mighty angelic army, with eyes glowing with flames of fire, shall gallop from Heaven to Earth to hunt down God's enemies. Their arrival will not be silent. The heavenly army shall swoop down upon sin-obsessed societies to permanently settle God's controversy. His judgment will produce much noise. The thunderous slamming of His gavel will shake the universe.

Prophet Hosea shouted, "hear the word of the Lord, ye children of Israel; for the Lord hath a controversy with the inhabitants of the land...." What was at the center of the legal dispute between Israel and God? Hosea told them the reason. "Because there is no truth, nor mercy, nor knowledge of God in the land." The prophet had a similar message for the folks in Judah. "The Lord hath also a controversy with Judah and will punish Jacob according to his ways; according to his doings will He recompense him."

Ingratitude for God's blessings has prolonged and deepened the rift between humanity and Heaven. He lovingly blessed humanity throughout the ages, but humankind's response was more wickedness, violence, bloodshed, greed, debauchery, and sexual immorality. For this reason, Jeremiah said a "noise shall come even to the ends of the Earth; for the Lord hath a controversy with the nations, He will plead with all flesh; He will give them that are wicked to the sword...." God has pleaded with humanity for over two thousand years to peacefully end the controversy by submitting to His righteous Son's lordship, but most humans rejected His plea. Therefore, God will bring swords to the wicked. The noises caused by the mass slaughter of billions of people on the final day will directly result from God's controversy with the nations. He will settle unresolved differences that day, the source of His irritation with humans. God will balance His accounting books. Angelic bailiffs will mark Heaven's court register as "case closed in plaintiff's favor."

In the days of Micah, the prophet, God brought up the touchy subject of His ongoing controversy with humanity, especially Israel, the people He chose to bless above all others on Earth. Almighty God called upon the mountains to hear His plea against Israel. Why mountains? The Creator appealed to His Creation to testify as witnesses on His behalf against the humans He richly blessed but who showed no gratitude.

If they could speak, the mountains would readily testify under oath that God abundantly blessed His people. He planted luscious fruit trees on their hillsides that abundantly fed the Israelites, broke loose rocks so that underground springs could flow down the mountains to provide sparkling clean water, and He populated the mountains with wildlife, bees, berries, herbs, and flowers.

God kept His covenant commitments, but the Israelites did not fulfill their covenant vows, nor did they appreciate all God did for them. Therefore, God filed a lawsuit against Israel. Their rebellion and ingratitude reminded Him of His long-running controversy with humanity that extended back to the days of Nimrod.

Hear ye, O mountains, the Lord's controversy, and ye strong foundations of the earth: for the Lord hath a controversy with his people, and he will plead with Israel.

Micah 6:2

A Worldwide Tumultuous Noise

Our Creator has a vast, deep memory that is beyond our mortal comprehension. He has retained remembrance of every deed done by men and women since the Garden of Eden, except sins forgiven through repentance. He could tell you what Alexander the Great ate for lunch on his thirtieth birthday or the gift that Julius Caesar gave his wife Calpurnia on their seventh wedding anniversary. Likewise, God could tell you the names and ages of the children massacred by Attila the Hun, or the color of the eyes of each Protestant saint tortured by "Bloody Mary" Tudor, the height of every Armenian Christian executed by the Turks, the birthdays of every Jew gassed in Adolf Hitler's horror chambers, or the number of hairs on the head of every Palestinian murdered by Irgun Zionists in 1948. The Great Judge will recount in stunning detail all of humankind's evil deeds on the final day when He judges the nations.

Simmering since the days of Nimrod, God's protracted controversy with the world's nations will suddenly and unexpectedly culminate in a day of worldwide judgment. St. Paul told the Athenians that Almighty God "has fixed a day in which He will judge the world in righteousness through a Man whom He has appointed, having furnished proof to all men by raising Him from the dead." When that day arrives, every dead person as far back as Adam and Eve will be awakened from their sleep and ordered to stand before the Supreme Judge. Those alive on that day will join them. God will litigate against the wicked for all to see and comprehend His righteousness, fairness, and justice.

The Almighty has meticulously documented His controversy with the world's countries. Heaven's prosecutors have collected and stored evidence against nations for as long as they existed on Earth. Some like Mexico and Canada have existed for centuries. Egypt, Syria, Greece, and other countries have lasted thousands of years. Regardless of whether each nation ruled for centuries or millennia, God has ample evidence to convict lawbreakers. Lawsuits have already been filed in Heaven's court detailing the Lord's accusations against them. The Lord will not accept any excuses on the final day. Why? Because God sent prophets and preachers to each nation. Some souls were saved, but most people had no interest in the Lord's offer of forgiveness. Jesus Christ will take His rightful place on the Great White Throne. His Word will judge the people.

A holy hush will permeate the court that houses the Great White Throne. The only sounds will be the voices of the Trinity and accompanying angels. However, everybody will hear great noises before the universal trial commences. The noises will emanate from the wicked living on Earth on the final day. God will turn them over to His angels for destruction by swords. This noisy storm of violence against them shall be like a great whirlwind that starts along the coasts and quickly encompasses all the continents and islands. The lifeless bodies of the wicked shall litter every nation like mounds of putrid, fly-covered animal dung.

A troublesome and tumultuous noise will sweep over the planet on that day. Why? Understanding why God's wrath will be so terrible on the final day requires acknowledging that God has controversies with all nations, past and present. These controversies are substantial legal disputes that demand resolution in a holy court of supreme law. Heaven's court has undisputed jurisdiction to hear these legal cases. Almighty God is the only living being in the entire universe qualified because of His absolute fairness to act as prosecutor and judge in the same court trial.

The administration of justice will be extremely noisy. Although God must mete out justice and punishment to the wicked, He dreads doing it. He instructed Amos to warn the Israelites not to wish for the day of the Lord to arrive so that their enemies would get what they rightfully deserved. Amos cried out, "Woe to you who long for the day of the Lord! Why do you long for the day of the Lord? That day will be darkness, not light." God said to them, and to us today, "You have no idea what you are wishing to happen."

Why has so many years gone by since Christ ascended to Heaven? What explains the long delay in the Lord's Second Coming? Perhaps our Heavenly Father dreads Judgment Day. Presently, the wicked are tossing and turning in agony in Hades, but they are not yet in the lake of fire. The never-ending horror of their final abode is incomprehensible to us. Our Father is deeply reluctant to send them there. He knows what awaits them there for eternity. Therefore, He has postponed the final day. However, humanity continues to delve deeper into wickedness. Eventually, God will shorten the days of tribulation for the elect's sake to end mankind's madness.

Old Testament Prophets
Heard the Noises of the Final Day

Prophet Jeremiah saw and heard that day. He prophesied, "a noise shall come even to the ends of the Earth; for the Lord hath a controversy with the nations, He will plead with all flesh; He will give them that are wicked to the sword...." Who shall make noises? God's angels will make noises, and the wicked will make noises too. Have you ever participated in an old-time country farm butchering of livestock? Hogs, cattle, goats, and sheep squeal in anguish and terror when their foreheads are shot or hammered, and their throats slit open with sharp butcher knives. No kind-hearted farmer enjoys it. The animals' screams and terrorized eyes will haunt your mind for days after the slaughter. It's enough to make you become a vegetarian.

Ezekiel warned worthless preachers that their day of slaughter was coming too. God instructed the prophet to "prophesy against the shepherds of Israel, prophesy, and say unto them, 'Thus saith the Lord God unto the shepherds: Woe be to the shepherds of Israel that do feed themselves! Should not the shepherds feed the flocks?'"

Yes, some preachers refuse to preach righteousness! Cowardly or corrupt preachers shall find no place to flee from the noisy slaughter. His fierce anger will cut them down on the Day of the Lord. They refused to tell the people to repent of their sins; therefore, the blood of unsaved souls will be upon their heads that day. They lived their best lives now, but their worst lives are ahead. Pulpit pansies will perish along with the wicked in the lake of fire. The hirelings' howls shall haunt Hell's halls.

> **So thou, O son of man, I have set thee a watchman unto the house of Israel; therefore thou shalt hear the word at my mouth, and warn them from me. When I say unto the wicked, O wicked man, thou shalt surely die; if thou dost not speak to warn the wicked from his way, that wicked man shall die in his iniquity; but his blood will I require at thine hand. Nevertheless, if thou warn the wicked of his way to turn from it; if he do not turn from his way, he shall die in his iniquity; but thou hast delivered thy soul.**
>
> **Ezekiel 33:7-9**

Prophet Jeremiah heard God's roar that will paralyze the world's wicked on the final day. What is the purpose of the Lord's war cry? Soldiers shout when they commence an invasion of a city or enemy stronghold. The commanding officer's loud shout emboldens his fellow warriors and terrorizes the inhabitants of the city that they seek to conquer. Likewise, when Yahweh roars from Heaven, it shall embolden His angelic army to lift their swords for slaughter and fill the world with sheer terror and mass confusion.

The day of the Lord shall arrive like a global tornado, executing God's vengeance upon murderers, liars, molesters, thieves, adulterers, fornicators, homosexuals, and the greedy. It will also be a day of gloom for unfaithful preachers who taught heresies or were fearful of the people and did not preach God's word or fleeced His sheep for selfish gain. Jeremiah said such preachers and religious leaders should howl and cry. The prophet said unfaithful shepherds would have nowhere to flee to escape God's fierce anger.

Warrior angels are noisy. Don't expect Heaven's air force to meet this world's governmental restrictions on airport noise levels when they burst through our atmosphere to fulfill God's military mission: rescue the righteous, slaughter the wicked. Prophet Ezekiel heard the noise made by angels. He wrote that their wings make the noise of great waters, as the voice of the Almighty, and their wings make the noise of spinning wheels and a great rushing.

Isaiah also prophesied about the final day. He heard the final day's tumultuous noise of nations when they would gather for battle with the Lord. Yahweh shall command His sanctified ones, who rejoice in God's highness, to mete out His anger upon the wicked.

I have commanded my sanctified ones, I have also called my mighty ones for mine anger, even them that rejoice in my highness. The noise of a multitude in the mountains, like

as of a great people; a tumultuous noise of the kingdoms of nations gathered together: the Lord of hosts mustereth the host of the battle.

Isaiah 13:3-4

The warriors shall travel from a "far country" carrying "weapons of His indignation" to "destroy the whole land." Their military actions will produce much howling and wailing from the world's wicked. God's warriors will crush and eliminate the fourth beast. This global monster is rising now in our present generation, and it appears that it will be a revived Pre-Flood civilization that Lucifer ruled. Humans, except the Church, will worship and conform to the image of the beast, perhaps an artificial intelligence god. How will they conform to the image of the beast? Their minds will receive and believe its propaganda. They will become like the beast when they believe its lies, and when their God-designed DNA is altered by gene therapy pseudo-vaccines produced by laboratories of pharmakeia. God's angels will destroy the beast and all who worshipped it. Isaiah said the wicked would howl.

They come from a far country, from the end of heaven, even the Lord, and the weapons of his indignation, to destroy the whole land. Howl ye; for the day of the Lord is at hand; it shall come as a destruction from the Almighty.

Isaiah 13:5-6

Isaiah said all hands would be faint. Every heart shall melt. Like a pregnant woman in great distress, pangs of sorrow shall grip them. They will be petrified. Even the bravest, most muscular men in the world will cry like sissies when they see the Lord's fiery eyes. An instantaneous awareness will grip them that humanity's long-running rebellion against God has ended abruptly.

> **Therefore shall all hands be faint, and every man's heart shall melt: and they shall be afraid: pangs and sorrows shall take hold of them; they shall be in pain as a woman that travaileth: they shall be amazed one at another; their faces shall be as flames.**
>
> Isaiah 13:7-8

God Will Not Quietly Judge the Wicked

Today's self-centered, comfort-driven, convenience-obsessed, lukewarm church members do not like to hear talk about God's wrath. Still, the Lord shall come back with fierce anger to destroy the wicked and their pride-centered civilization of rebellion against the Almighty. Righteous saints pre-marked by angels for protection have no reason to fear the final day, though terrible it shall be for everybody else. The saints, however, will safely watch it from a high altitude, humbly aware God's marvelous grace spared them.

> **Behold, the day of the Lord cometh, cruel both with wrath and fierce anger, to lay the land desolate: and he shall destroy the sinners thereof out of it.**
>
> Isaiah 13:9

In one day, Almighty God will settle His controversy with mankind. Tucked away in God's infinite mind are billions of memories He accumulated over thousands of years observing humanity's never-ending wickedness: cruelty, idolatry, wars, abortions, injustice, thievery, lying, deception, betrayal, blasphemy, molestations, adultery, fornication, homosexuality, and countless other sins that He did not forgive because the guilty never expressed remorse, nor did they repent and change their ways. He will deal with them in an instant.

He will not judge quietly. Judgment Day will be noisy. Do not expect angels to daintily tiptoe and sheepishly whisper as they bundle the wicked. The wicked will not bellow silent screams of anguish when fiery angels apprehend them. Tumultuous noises will resound worldwide. When the Sun, the Moon, and the stars go dark, the simultaneous gasping of billions of people worldwide will be noisy! King Jesus shall punish sinners for their evil deeds, the wicked for their iniquity. How can it be done quietly? Have you ever heard the pitiful screams of an animal caught in a trap? Unimaginable shall be the volume of wailing coming out of the mouths of billions of sinners caught in God's snare on the final day. It will be a day of slaughter. That is why Amos said we should not wish for the day of the Lord to punish our enemies.

For the stars of heaven and the constellations thereof shall not give their light: the sun shall be darkened in his going forth, and the moon shall not cause her light to shine. And I will punish the world for their evil, and the wicked for their iniquity; and I will cause the arrogancy of the proud to cease, and will lay low the haughtiness of the terrible.

Isaiah 13:10-11

Jerusalem Shall be Destroyed

The final day shall suddenly and unexpectedly sweep over the Earth like a global thunderstorm of righteous indignation.

Arrogant, proud inhabitants of Jerusalem shall be utterly dismayed and stunned when the thunderstorm encompasses their city too. Jerusalem's Jews rejected drinking the living water offered to them; therefore, Jesus will compel them to drink from His cup of bitter wrath.

Sadly, many good Jewish men and women in Jerusalem will perish on the final day when God brings calamity and splits the great city asunder. They listened to their rabbis and read the Talmud instead of hearing Christ's servants and believing His New Covenant. They should have emulated Abraham, who obeyed God by faith. Woe to the Christian Zionists who refused to tell modern Israel's citizens that they must repent and believe in the name of Jesus Christ whom their ancestors crucified.

Yahweh, the God of Israel, shall call for a sword upon all the inhabitants of the Earth, including the modern State of Israel. Old Jerusalem will disappear when Jesus returns because He shall entirely burn up the world in a massive ball of flames. When the smoke of the incinerated old Earth clears away, there shall only be New Jerusalem, the eternal capital of the new Earth. Jeremiah told the Jews that Jerusalem would not go unpunished:

> **Therefore thou shalt say unto them, Thus saith the Lord of hosts, the God of Israel; Drink ye, and be drunken, and spew, and fall, and rise no more, because of the sword which I will send among you. And it shall be, if they refuse to take the cup at thine hand to drink, then shalt thou say unto them, Thus saith the Lord of hosts; Ye shall certainly drink. For, lo, I begin to bring evil on the city which is called by my name, and should ye be utterly unpunished?**

Ye shall not be unpunished: for I will call for a sword upon all the inhabitants of the earth, saith the Lord of hosts.

Jeremiah 25:27-29

Judgment Day's wailing will not be confined to the streets of Jerusalem and Tel Aviv, the self-proclaimed world capital of homosexuality. Terrified cries of torment will resound from the White House, the Kremlin, Buckingham Palace, the Great Hall of the People, and the world's other palaces of power. Time will abruptly end for the occupants who governed their nations for Satan. What a noisy day it shall be when our Lord Jesus returns to Earth!

He shall shout to the angels to tread the blood out of the Earth's inhabitants like vineyard workers crushing grapes. It's no wonder that human blood will flow so deep that it will reach the height of horses' bridles. Saint John saw a lake of human blood at least five feet deep and over 200 miles wide! The angelic slaughter of the world's wicked population will be so extensive that it will produce a sea of human blood in and around Jerusalem, the harlot city. Christ the King will triumphantly overthrow and destroy the enemies of the Church so that they never rise again.

And the winepress was trodden without the city, and blood came out of the winepress, even unto the horse bridles, by the space of a thousand and six hundred furlongs.

Revelation 14:20

In the New Testament Bible, Apostle Peter said the final day should come suddenly and unexpectedly as a thief in the night. Our beloved and bold St. Peter said the heavens shall pass away with a great noise, and God's flames shall burn up the Earth.

But the day of the Lord will come as a thief in the night; in the which the heavens shall pass away with a great noise, and the elements shall melt with fervent heat, the earth also and the works that are therein shall be burned up.

2 Peter 3:10

The truth is evident: Old Testament scriptures about the day of the Lord are consistent with New Testament scriptures about the Lord's Second Advent: Jesus shall come back suddenly and unexpectedly with a thunderous shout and trumpet blast, He shall roar, an army of angels shall noisily accompany Him like a great rushing, they shall slaughter the wicked, there shall be much howling on the Earth, and if that's not enough, the angels will set the place on fire and burn up everything. Nobody and nothing, except the righteous, will survive the angels' righteous rampage.

B-Day: Operation Babylon Will be Noisy

In military terms, the Lord's return is Operation Babylon. The Commander of Heaven's Armies will wipe out prosperous and influential Babylon, Nimrod's reconstituted global empire built upon decadence, pride, debauchery, perversion, adultery, fornication, homosexuality, pornography, sorcery, witchcraft, pharmakeia, genetic manipulations, perpetual warfare, bloodshed, violence, abortions, fraud, theft, and deception. The New Nimrod's modern Babylon is held together and enforced with surveillance technology, artificial intelligence, biometrics, big data, facial recognition, and raw brute force. The fourth beast has teeth of iron to devour its prey.

How big is Operation Babylon? Its noise shall move the Earth! Every nation shall hear the cry of Babylon's great destruction when the angelic army launches its B-Day assault against the Great Harlot.

> *At the noise* of the taking of Babylon the earth is moved, and *the cry is heard* among the nations.
>
> Jeremiah 50:46

Babylon's wickedness is noisy. Why should not her destruction be noisy too? She proudly makes noises of sin, rebellion, sorcery, witchcraft, murder, lewdness, adultery, fornication, homosexuality, thievery, and war. Therefore, it should not be surprising that the harlot's incineration shall be noisier than her sin. Jesus Christ shall permanently silence her sinful noises. Waves of angelic avengers will bombard her walls, and Jerusalem shall fall. The angels' voices shall shout around the world as they carry out God's command to destroy the harlot. Her voice shall fall silent because complete silence is evidence of depopulation. No Babylonian citizens will be permitted to live. The final destruction of Babylon will be like the destruction of Sodom and Gomorrah and neighboring towns. The Lord declared: "No one will be there; no one will inhabit it." So too shall be the fate of Jerusalem on the final day.

> Because the Lord hath spoiled Babylon, *and destroyed out of her the great voice;* when her waves do roar like great waters, a noise of their voice is uttered...
>
> Jeremiah 51:55

Angelic Trumpet Blasts Are Noisy

Loud trumpet blasts from seven angels following the opening of the seventh seal in Heaven shall precede the Lord's Second

Advent. Before the seven angels sound their trumpets, there will be voices and thunderings and lightning in the heavens and an earthquake on Earth. Lots of noise and commotion! Nonstop sinning eventually begets nonstop slaying. The slaughter begins when angels burst in. The ear-splitting noise of their sudden arrival will resemble the deafening shockwave from a massive meteor explosion. Slaughtering is very noisy.

> **And when he had opened the seventh seal, there was silence in heaven about the space of half an hour. And I saw the seven angels which stood before God; and to them were given seven trumpets. And another angel came and stood at the altar, having a golden censer; and there was given unto him much incense, that he should offer it with the prayers of all saints upon the golden altar which was before the throne. And the smoke of the incense, which came with the prayers of the saints, ascended up before God out of the angel's hand. And the angel took the censer, and filled it with fire of the altar, and cast it into the earth:** *and there were voices, and thunderings, and lightnings, and an earthquake. And the seven angels which had the seven trumpets prepared themselves to sound.*
>
> **Revelation 8:1-6**

Spectacular events on earth will follow trumpet blasts from the first four angels:

- Hail and fire mingled with blood
- One-third of the planet's trees and all the grass burned up
- A mountain-sized rock burning with fire shall be cast into the sea

- One-third of the sea struck by the burning rock shall become blood; one-third of sea creatures will die, and one-third of ships destroyed
- A burning star called Wormwood shall fall from heaven, burning like a lamp. One-third of the rivers and one-third of the fountains of water shall become bitter
- The brightness of the Sun, Moon, and stars shall be dimmed by one-third.

Upon the fourth angel's trumpet blast, John heard an angel flying through the midst of heaven shouting a tremendous and ominous warning to every human: woe to the inhabitants of the Earth.

And I beheld, and heard an angel flying through the midst of heaven, *saying with a loud voice,* Woe, woe, woe, to the inhabitants of the earth *by reason of the other voices* of the trumpet of the three angels, *which are yet to sound!*

Revelation 8:13

The Roar Heard Around the World

Everybody will hear another sound on the final day. Jesus will roar mightily! Multitudes of wicked people will have heart attacks when they hear it. Jeremiah prophesied that God "shall roar from on high, and utter His voice from His holy habitation; He shall mightily roar upon His habitation; He shall give a shout, as they that tread the grapes, against all the inhabitants of the Earth." The meaning of "roar from on high, upon His habitation" means that His anger shall manifest in Heaven, but it shall be heard and felt in humanity's habitation, meaning the whole Earth.

193

Therefore prophesy thou against them all these words, and say unto them, *The Lord shall roar from on high, and utter his voice from his holy habitation; he shall mightily roar upon his habitation; he shall give a shout,* as they that *tread the grapes,* against all the inhabitants of the earth.

Jeremiah 25:30

You can compare it to a goat in a pasture, unaware that a mighty lion is crawling through the tall grass. Suddenly, the lion stands up and roars. It is too late for the goat to flee. The lion pounces upon it and devours its victim. Likewise, sudden and unexpected destruction shall come upon the wicked. They will not see it coming because their minds are dulled and defiled by sin. God's thunderings from His habitation will fill men's habitation with fear, terror, and confusion. He will trample and crush all nations. Sanctified saints, however, will be eagerly anticipating His regal roar, knowing that the dreadful war cry will be accompanied by the victorious shout and trumpet blast signifying that Christ is on His way. Christ's roar will signal the angels to commence squeezing blood out of the wicked like vineyard workers stomping juice from grapes.

The Lord shall go forth as a mighty man, he shall stir up jealousy like a man of war: he shall cry, yea, roar; he shall prevail against his enemies.

Isaiah 42:13

The Lord also shall roar out of Zion, and utter his voice from Jerusalem; and the heavens and the earth shall shake: but the Lord will be the hope of his people, and the strength of the children of Israel.

Joel 3:16

And he said, The Lord will roar from Zion, and utter his voice from Jerusalem; and the habitations of the shepherds shall mourn, and the top of Carmel shall wither.

Amos 1:2

Who is this roaring King of glory? He is Yahweh, the Lord strong and mighty, the Lord mighty in battle. His Son shall come to save His people Israel, the one, holy, catholic, and apostolic Church, the holy Christian nation of people who love Him and keep His commandments. His people, true Israel, are waiting for the noisy sound of the great trumpet blast and glorious shout! The heavenly noises shall blend into a symphony of salvation on that glorious day.

For the Lord himself shall descend from heaven with a shout, with the voice of the archangel, and with the trump of God: **and the dead in Christ shall rise first: then we which are alive and remain shall be caught up together with them in the clouds, to meet the Lord in the air: and so shall we ever be with the Lord.**

I Thessalonians 4:16-17

Everybody Will Hear
the Shout to Open All Graves

When Jesus returns, He will shout with joyous delight. Why? Because "that day" will have finally arrived. That day is the final day. The controversy with the nations shall finally be over. On that day, Jesus shall "send His angels, and gather together His elect from the four winds, from the uttermost part of the Earth to the uttermost part of Heaven."

His shout will thoroughly and permanently disrupt the entire cosmos. It will signify that the Creator has returned to His Creation. The repercussions of His cry shall be innumerable and immeasurable, but the first to respond to it shall be the bodies of the departed saints. They are the virgins in Jesus' parable who slumbered and slept. All ten bridesmaids shall awaken from their sleeping places, but not all ten shall go up in the air to meet the Lord in the clouds. Only the five wise virgins who acquired sufficient supplies of the oil of grace shall participate in that atmospheric journey. They shall fly when they hear the midnight cry, "Behold, the bridegroom is coming; go out to meet him." Wedding ceremonies are joyfully noisy too. The happier the participants, the more noise they make.

The arrival of the wedding day necessitates Jesus dispatching legions of angelic reapers to bundle the wicked for perpetual burning and to gather His elect from every nation to dwell in New Jerusalem on the new Earth. A mighty trumpet blast shall signify the time for Heaven's angels to gather all righteous souls on Earth.

And he shall send his angels *with a great sound of a trumpet,* and they shall gather together his elect from the four winds, from one end of heaven to the other.

Matthew 24:31

Old Graves Creak When Cracked Open

Meanwhile, all humankind in their graves since the Garden of Eden shall also suddenly awaken. The heavenly noise will notify them that Jesus is back in town. His command to come out of their graves will be heard by those who sleep. All dead bodies shall listen to His voice and come out of their graves. Adam and Eve, Cain and Abel, Enoch, Methuselah, Noah, Abraham, Moses, Jeremiah, Genghis Khan, George Washington, Adolf Hitler, Mother Teresa, Billy Graham, Winston Churchill, Elvis Presley, John Wayne, Mohammed, Confucius, Buddha, indeed, everybody who ever lived. All the people buried one minute before the trumpet blast will pop out too. They will set the world record for the shortest time in a grave.

When will the dead come out of their graves? When they hear the divine shout! It will be the shout heard round the world. All the dead, righteous and wicked, shall be resurrected. The righteous shall receive glorified bodies that know no pain, disease, weariness, or death. For the righteous, it shall be a resurrection of life. For evildoers, it will be a resurrection of damnation. They too shall be given new bodies, but not bodies to live forever, but bodies to perpetually die in continuous punishment and anguish, forever separated from God.

> **Marvel not at this: for the hour is coming, *in the which all that are in the graves shall hear his voice, and shall come forth*; they that have done good, unto the resurrection of life; and they that have done evil, unto the resurrection of damnation.**
>
> **John 5:28-29**

The bodies of all departed saints in Christ who are blissfully resting in Paradise shall come out of their graves. God will give them incorruptible bodies designed for eternal living in His presence. Christians who are alive when Jesus returns must undergo a radical change because flesh and blood cannot inherit the Kingdom of God and dwell eternally in New Jerusalem. They shall be changed in a moment, in the twinkling of an eye, and given incorruptible bodies too. When do these things happen? Sight and sound will trigger this glorious transformation of our bodies. When our eyes see Jesus after our ears hear the trumpet, our mortal bodies will experience an instantaneous metamorphosis to become immortal bodies.

> **Now this I say, brethren, that flesh and blood cannot inherit the kingdom of God; neither doth corruption inherit incorruption. Behold, I shew you a mystery;** *We shall not all sleep, but we shall all be changed, in a moment, in the twinkling of an eye, at the last trump: for the trumpet shall sound,* **and the dead shall be raised incorruptible, and we shall be changed.**
>
> **I Corinthians 15:50-52**

Seven Noisy Bowls

Sound is measured in units called decibels. The louder the noise, the higher the decibel level. A whisper has a decibel level of 30. A clap of thunder, however, registers a decibel level of 120. What about hundreds of millions of people singing praises to God in appreciation of receiving glorified bodies? What decibel level will their combined voices reach on the final day? The experience will be so glorious that high church Anglicans will joyfully shout, and Pentecostals will be speechless.

Although wails and screams of anguish and horror will cover the surface of the Earth, joyful shouts and songs of praise will fill the sky. God will fulfill Isaiah's prophecy when He swallows up death, wipes away tears from all faces, and takes away the rebuke of His people heaped upon the saints by mockers and scoffers who arrogantly asked, "Where is the promise of your messiah's return?"

He will swallow up death in victory; and the Lord God will wipe away tears from off all faces; and the rebuke of his people shall he take away from off all the earth: for the Lord hath spoken it.

Isaiah 25:8

In his vision on the island of Patmos, Apostle John saw another great sign in Heaven. He saw seven angels who each held a bowl containing a plague that they would pour upon the world's rebellious population. The release of the seven plagues would end God's wrath. John saw what looked like a sea of glass mingled with fire: and those who had gotten the victory over the beast, and over his image, and over his mark and the number of his name. They stood on the sea of glass, holding harps of God. John heard the saints sing the Song of Moses, the servant of God, and the song of the Lamb.

Great and marvelous are thy works, Lord God Almighty; just and true are thy ways, thou King of saints. Who shall not fear thee, O Lord, and glorify thy name? for thou only art holy: for all nations shall come and worship before thee; for thy judgments are made manifest.

Revelation 15:3-4

St. John heard the Church Militant singing the Song of Moses. Viciously attacked by one of the horns upon the head of the fourth beast, the worldwide Holy Christian Church shall sing and shout when King Jesus triumphantly arrives to rescue them from the beast. Suddenly, the blood-soaked, sin-saturated, and tumultuous age of humankind will end. Thousands of years of wars, violence, bloodshed, disease, hatred, suffering, pain, tears, and death will abruptly halt, never to restart.

Our blessed hope shall come for His beloved Church, faithful Israel. The Church Militant shall become one with the Church Triumphant. Together, they shall ascend into the air to meet their king. They are the flying humans that Isaiah prophetically described when he wrote about the end of the age when darkness covers the earth, and gross darkness covers the people. Full of hope, Isaiah proclaimed to all saints that the time would come that they should rise and shine for their light is come, and the glory of the Lord has risen upon them. Isaiah saw the saints of God lifted into the atmosphere to join the resurrected saints who came forth from their graves. The Old Testament prophet paused in his prophecy to ask a question: "Who are these that fly as a cloud, and as the doves to their windows?"

The noisy arrival of the Messiah is throughout the writings of the Old Testament prophets. At the First Advent of Jesus Christ, the daughter of Zion greatly rejoiced and shouted. Zechariah prophesied that Israel's king would come riding humbly on a donkey bringing salvation to the world. The Old Testament prophet encouraged them to cry out far and wide by rejoicing greatly over the good news that "thy king cometh to thee." He did not say a king, but thy king, the One who is worthy of our praises and adoration. This king is the promised Messiah, the Son of David. Loudly shout and rejoice because thy king, who is just and righteous, "cometh to thee" to save your soul.

Rejoice greatly, O daughter of Zion; shout, O daughter of Jerusalem: behold, thy King cometh unto thee: he is just, and having salvation; lowly, and riding upon an ass, and upon a colt the foal of an ass.

Zechariah 9:9

Jesus publicly entered Jerusalem only one time. He deliberately chose to ride a colt as an example of meekness and humility. The multitude of Jerusalem's citizens responded with loud, joyful shouts of praise and adoration. With the streets adorned with palm branches and garments, the elated people shouted, "Hosannah, blessed is the king who cometh in the name of the Lord." Will not His people shout His praises even louder at His second appearance? He will not ride a donkey on the final day. The One who is called Faithful and True shall enter Earth's atmosphere regally sitting upon a majestic white horse. He shall come to judge and make war.

Rejoice greatly, O daughter of Zion; shout, O daughter of Jerusalem: behold, thy King cometh unto thee: he is just, and having salvation; lowly, and riding upon an ass, and upon a colt the foal of an ass.

Zechariah 9:9

And I saw heaven opened, and behold a white horse; and he that sat upon him *was* called Faithful and True, and in righteousness he doth judge and make war.

Revelation 19:11

In the eleventh and twelfth chapters of the Book of Isaiah, the prophet spoke to the daughter of Zion, meaning the Church. Both chapters foretell the coming of the Messiah, Jesus Christ. Isaiah said, "there shall come forth a rod out of the stem of Jesse, and a Branch shall grow out of his roots: and the spirit of the Lord shall rest upon him, the spirit of wisdom and understanding, the spirit of counsel and might, the spirit of knowledge and of the fear of the Lord; and shall make him of quick understanding in the fear of the Lord." Isaiah said that "in that day" the people shall say, "O Lord, I will praise you...." The daughter of Zion, the Church, shall praise the Lord because He is the God of our salvation, strength, and song. "In that day" shall the daughter of Zion call upon His name, declare His doings among the people, make mention that His name is exalted, sing unto the Lord because He has done remarkable things, and cry and shout for great is the Holy One of Israel amid thee.

Why will the Second Coming of Jesus be noisy? The sudden and glorious appearance of the Holy One will cause an instantaneous eruption of indescribable joy from two groups of Christians. The formerly dead saints whose bodies are released from their graves and reunited with their souls will be the first group to burst into loud shouting and singing. The second group of singing saints will be Christians alive on Earth on the final day, viciously and ruthlessly pressed on all sides by the Antichrist, who will patiently endure to the end as their Master instructed them.

The daughter of New Zion shall gleefully sing joyous songs of praise and adoration. Their voices shall fill the atmosphere above the whole Earth. Faithful Israel shall burst out into thunderous rejoicing, shouting, and singing because the Lord has taken away her judgments, cast out her enemy, and removed evil from her sight forever. The King of Israel shall be home with His people. The righteous shall be glad in the Lord and rejoice. All who are upright in heart shall shout for joy.

The Restoration of All Things Shall be Noisy Too

More than saints will sing when Jesus returns in all his splendor and glory. God's big plan is to bring Heaven and Earth together into a perfect union through Christ." Theologically, this plan is called the consummation of all things. St. Paul said God has "made known to us the mystery of His will, according to His good pleasure which He had purposed in Himself: that in the dispensation of the fulness of times *He might gather together in one all things in Christ*, both which are in Heaven, and which are on Earth, even in Him."

God's grand plan began before the foundation of the world and is scheduled to conclude on the final day. Adam's sin disrupted and separated God's beautiful and perfect Creation. He never meant immorality, lying, thievery, lust, murder, war, poverty, hatred, strife, division, sickness, disease, and death would be behavior in human societies. Such things are an aberration of God's original intent for humanity's dominion of the Earth.

Whenever God decrees that the time has come to wind up the age of humankind, He will gather all things made by Him and bring them together in Christ. The grand union started with the incarnation of the Son of God as a human embryo inside the womb of a virgin, Mary, whose womb was the ark of the New Covenant. Therefore, the Church rightfully called her the Christotokos, meaning Christbearer, or the mother of Christ.

Apostle Paul told the Galatian saints that the fullness of time arrived when "God sent forth His Son, made of a woman, made under the law, to redeem them that were under the law, that we might receive the adoption of sons." The word dispensation means administration or management. God not only had a grand goal to unite all things in Christ, but He also had a grand plan to manage the achievement of His goal.

For thousands of years, the Creator's unwavering goal has been to undo the damages caused by Adam's sin and restore Creation to its original state of purity. The death, burial, resurrection, and ascension of the Creator's only begotten Son was necessary to restore Creation. The sinless Last Adam had to die for the sinful First Adam. A God-Man's blood was the currency needed to ransom humanity from Satan's deadly captivity.

Adam's sin not only introduced disorder into the spirits, minds, and bodies of men and women but also into Creation's matter. Sin desecrated the Earth. God did not create carnivores to devour the flesh of animals and humans. He also did not establish weather patterns that produced hurricanes, cyclones, typhoons, earthquakes, volcanoes, and hailstones. He created a peaceful planet to bless humanity. Continuous disorder, however, has been Earth's fate since Adam's fall.

The good news is that the Creator has a perfect plan to restore a harmonious order to Creation. Presently, Heaven and Earth are separated. The plan is to bring Earth and Heaven into harmony. The Ancient of Days will renew His original intent for Creation by making a new planet for faithful humans who repented of their sins and believed in the name of Jesus Christ. After the last day, the first day will usher in one glorious kingdom that unites all Christians with all spiritual beings in Heaven. The first day shall have no end. Our Heavenly Father has "a plan for the fullness of time, to unite all things in Christ, which are in Heaven and on Earth."

The culmination of the plan is the restitution of all things. Standing atop Solomon's Porch in Jerusalem, Apostle Peter told his fellow Jews that God spoke about the restoration of all things through the mouths of all His holy prophets since the world began. That means since the fall of Adam, Methuselah, Noah, and all Heaven-inspired prophets preached about the restoration of all things. Preachers of righteousness promised that someday God would restore life to its original state and proper order in a new Garden of Eden.

Old Testament prophet Ezekiel prophetically saw "that day" in the far future. He said the people shall say, "This land that was desolate is become like the garden of Eden...." Our Heavenly Father's heart yearns to gather the children who love Him and place them in a new Garden of Eden where He will dwell with them forever. He will reimage Creation and make all things new.

The new Creation will sing and shout. O, what a happy day it shall be for the righteous! The heavens and the Earth shall sing! Isaiah prophesied that the mountains shall break forth in singing. St. John the Revelator prophesied that the animals shall also sing praises to King Jesus.

Yes, the new Earth's animals shall talk! If they can sing, they must also know how to talk. Do you think they will bark, meow, moo, and chirp the lyrics of *Amazing Grace*? No, my friend. Instead, animals shall make wonderful sounds praising their Creator. Animals did not sin against God, but they suffered death because of Adam's sin. We must consider the possibility that God will fully restore them on the New Earth. If so, the entire animal kingdom shall worship God! What an incredible sound the animals shall make when they sing to Jesus Chris for being delivered from death caused by Adam. Going to church will never be the same after hearing Handel's *Messiah* sung by an all-frog choir.

And every creature which is in heaven, and on the earth, and under the earth, and such as are in the sea, and all that are in them, heard I saying, Blessing, and honor, and glory, and power, be unto him that sitteth upon the throne, and unto the Lamb for ever and ever.

Revelation 5:13

God made everything in six days for His glory. The universe, planets, stars, humans, animals, mountains, trees, oceans, indeed everything exists for God's glory. It is the duty and privilege of everybody, and everything, made by God to praise Him.

Life in New Jerusalem will be noisy too. Eternal singing and praising will fill the city's homes, streets, parks, and theaters. Saints, angels, and animals will continuously praise King Jesus forever. Why not? Death will die, sadness banished, and tears wiped away forever.

And after these things *I heard a great voice* of much people in heaven, saying, Alleluia; Salvation, and glory, and honor, and power, unto the Lord our God: for true and righteous are his judgments: for he hath judged the great whore, which did corrupt the earth with her fornication, and hath avenged the blood of his servants at her hand. And again they said, Alleluia. And her smoke rose up for ever and ever. And the four and twenty elders and the four beasts fell down and worshipped God that sat on the throne, saying, Amen; Alleluia.

And a voice came out of the throne, saying, Praise our God, all ye his servants, and ye that fear him, both small and great. And I heard as it were the voice of a great multitude, and as the voice of many waters, and as the

206

voice of mighty thunderings, saying, Alleluia: for the Lord God omnipotent reigneth. Let us be glad and rejoice, and give honor to him: for the marriage of the Lamb is come, and his wife hath made herself ready. And to her was granted that she should be arrayed in fine linen, clean and white: for the fine linen is the righteousness of saints. And he saith unto me, Write, Blessed are they which are called unto the marriage supper of the Lamb. And he saith unto me, These are the true sayings of God.

Revelation 19:1-9

The Second Coming of Jesus Christ on the final day shall be:

- Singular
- Sudden and unexpected
- Atmospheric
- Visible
- Noisy

CHAPTER 6

HIS SECOND COMING SHALL BE DISRUPTIVE

I F ELVIS PRESLEY WROTE a song about the final day he would sing that there would be a "whole lotta shaking going on."

The moment Jesus Christ enters our physical dimension, there will be brilliant lightning, deafening thunder, violent earthquakes, unusual noises, blustering storms, tumultuous tempests, and raging red-hot fires.

> **And the angel took the censer, and filled it with fire of the altar, and cast it into the earth: and there were voices, and thunderings, and lightnings, and an earthquake.**
>
> **Revelation 8:5**

The grand arrival of Jesus Christ on the final day is known as the Parousia. It announces the arrival of a significant person, along with their regal presence. When a king or queen enters a building, so too does his or her royal power and prestige. Everything associated with the monarch's throne travels with the king or queen: the divine right to rule, absolute power, absolute authority, and regal majesty. Imagine a typical scene when King Jesus leaves His throne room and strolls down Heaven's Main Street. Tens of thousands of angels bow down and cry, "Holy, holy, holy!" It's just another day in Heaven. The presence of Jesus disrupts the ordinary.

Should we not expect similar things to happen when the Parousia occurs? Heaven's King Jesus and His kingly presence shall arrive in humankind's world. Traveling with Him will be everything associated with His throne in Heaven: the divine right to rule, absolute power and authority, and regal majesty. Jesus cannot tiptoe through the backdoor of our natural dimension of reality and not be seen nor heard. His glory and greatness are too much for our physical world. Our ordinary world will tremble in His extraordinary presence. His reentry into our realm will violently disrupt the universe. The cosmos will rupture, and His presence will rip apart the fabric of the universe. Jesus will not have to make it happen. Stuff just happens when He arrives on the scene. His kingdom travels with Him.

The supreme King of Zion suddenly and unexpectedly disrupted Jerusalem's idolatry and debauchery on a day many centuries ago. Her people did not see it coming. Isaiah, however, forewarned the inhabitants of Jerusalem that God would visit them in their state of sinful rebellion. In Isaiah 29:1, God called the city Ariel. The meaning of Ariel is obscure. It possibly refers to lion-like men or the lion of God. The prophet cried out, "Woe to Ariel, to Ariel, the city where David dwelt...."

Isaiah warned that God would disrupt Jerusalem. There would be heaviness and sorrow. The Lord's army would encamp about the city and lay siege to it. The proud city would be incredibly humbled. Brave men would whisper in fear of what was happening to Jerusalem. Their faint and shrill voices would come from the Earth as the voices of spirit-charmers and necromancers.

And then Isaiah gave Jerusalem's arrogant inhabitants the awful news. God would visit them in their state of prideful sin. In Isaiah 29:6, the prophet declared, "Thou shalt be visited of the Lord of hosts with thunder, and with earthquake, and great noise, with storm and tempest, and the flame of devouring fire." Such shall be the day of the Lord, but on a grander scale beyond human comprehension.

Several centuries later, God instructed another prophet to warn the descendants of the Jews who Isaiah had warned. Divine judgment was rapidly approaching Judah. Prophet Joel cried out to Judah's elderly men to listen to him: "Hear this, ye old men, and give ear, all ye inhabitants of the land." The people were astonished by the sight of farmlands, pastures, and vineyards stripped bare by hungry hordes of locusts. The prophet asked Judah's aged men, "Has anything like this happened in your lifetime or in the days of your fathers?" Joel instructed the older men to educate Judah's children that divine chastisement so severe had never happened in Judah's history. The prophet desired that the people fully understand that the destruction of their food supply was only the beginning of their troubles. The army of insects was merely a fore-runner of far greater calamities on their way. Joel wanted Judah's future generations to know what happened and, more importantly, why it happened. Perhaps they would learn from their ancestors' mistakes and avoid a similar fate.

It was God's sovereign right to remove His blessings from Judah. Almighty God knew it was necessary to humble the people.

They had to be motivated to repent of their wicked ways. Humans can slide so deep into evil behavior that prophetic warnings no longer get their attention, whether individuals or national populations. If not confronted, individuals or nations will eventually become reprobates. When they reach that saturated state of sinfulness, there is no way to bring them back. The people of Judah were prime candidates to become reprobates. Only a sudden and extreme disruption to their daily lifestyles could halt their downward slide. Therefore, the aerial invasion of locusts was the opening act to a land invasion of enemy soldiers who would slaughter the inhabitants, plunder their possessions, and occupy their homes, farms, and vineyards. Judah's jolt was speedily on its way.

The prophet shouted a dire command to the country's lazy priests, "Blow ye the trumpet in Zion, and sound an alarm in my holy mountain." Joel said, "let all the inhabitants of the land tremble." Tremble means to shake involuntarily from fear, be troubled with fear or apprehension, and quake or quiver. Why did Joel tell Judah's people to shake and tremble in great fear? There was one reason: "for the day of the Lord cometh, for it is nigh at hand." The prophet prepared the people to stand with contrite hearts in awe of God's majesty and with their consciences stricken with fearful trembling at the thought of their Maker's disgust of their sinful ways.

Locust Creatures from the Abyss

Prophet Joel saw the dark clouds of locusts as precursors of the real invaders marching toward Jerusalem. He warned that "a nation powerful and innumerable has invaded my land; its teeth are like the teeth of a lion, like the fangs of a lioness." In other words, Joel informed Judah's sinful citizens that God had inspired a foreign army to conquer them. The locusts ate only the vegetation. The invading soldiers would devour everything in sight with teeth of iron, meaning swords.

Judah's priests were spiritually slothful. The people would never have sunk so deep into wickedness if the priests had been faithful to God. Therefore, it was the duty of priests to blow their trumpets. The sin-stupefied population had to be startled to face a stark reality: a day of judgment was quickly approaching Judah. Their refusal to repent and turn from their wicked ways would produce severe consequences for everybody. The rain falls on the just and the unjust.

The principle remains the same today. All Christian pastors, evangelists, and teachers must warn their flocks of the consequences of sin. Joel warned Judah, "for the day of the Lord cometh." Judah's judgment did arrive. There have been many more "day of the Lord" visitations over thousands of years to cities and nations. The day of the Lord is any day God avenges sin. There is coming, however, a final visitation. God will avenge the evil of the whole world. The final day of the Lord shall come suddenly and unexpectedly upon humankind like the Great Flood. Therefore, it is the solemn duty of every Christian pastor, evangelist, and teacher to blow their spiritual trumpets and sound the alarm. They must wake up their congregation and proclaim that Christ is coming.

St. James admonished early Christians to establish their hearts "for the coming of the Lord draweth nigh." James told them not to hold grudges against others because "the judge standeth before the door." Old Testament prophet Joel prophesied, "The earth shall quake before them; the heavens shall tremble: the sun and the

moon shall be dark, and the stars shall withdraw their shining...."
Jesus echoed Joel's prophecy by using similar language when He
prophesied about the final day. Jesus said, "there will be signs in the
sun, in the moon, and in the stars; and on earth distress of nations,
with perplexity, the sea and the wave roaring."

The darkening of the Sun, Moon, and stars will only be the
commencement of the complete disruption of the cosmos, harbin-
gers of even more significant judgments to befall humanity. As
God sent massive swarms of locusts to Judah as forerunners of
worse things to come, so too will the Lord send locusts to warn
the modern world that far worse judgments will swiftly arrive. In
his vision on the Isle of Patmos, St. John wrote in Revelation 9 that
he saw "a star fall from heaven unto the earth." God gave the star
the key to the bottomless pit, the abode of evil spirits.

John saw the abyss open and smoke like from a great furnace
ascended from it. When the smoke reached the surface of the
Earth, it darkened the atmosphere and dimmed the Sun's light.
From the smoke came fierce-looking locusts shaped like horses
prepared for battle. They wore headgear that looked like golden
crowns. They had faces like human men, hair like mortal women,
and teeth like lions. The locust creatures from the pit wore breastplates of iron. Their wings sounded like chariots pulled by many
horses running to battle. Most frightening, the locust creatures had
tails like scorpions with venomous stingers.

St. John the Revelator said God commanded the locust creatures
not to harm trees, grass, and other green vegetation. Their victims
were men and women who did not have the seal of God on their
foreheads. The locust creatures were not permitted to kill their
victims but only torment them for five months. Their stings were as

painful as scorpion stings. Those who were stung begged to die, but death did not come. The king of the bottomless pit ruled the locust creatures. The ruler is an angel whose name in Hebrew is Abaddon, and in Greek, his name is Apollyon, which means "destroyer."

Who is Apollyon? Most Christian Zionists prophecy teachers say he is Satan or another mighty fallen angel. Is he the devil or a powerful fallen angel? The Bible says, "and they had a king…." The locust creatures did not elect Apollyon as their king because, ordinarily, those ruled did not choose their ruler. A more accurate translation would read, "They have over them as king an angel of the abyss…."

Who appointed and empowered the angel of the abyss? Was it Satan or Almighty God? Who rightfully owned the key given to the angel to unlock the abyss? That question leads us to the following question: who locked the abyss in the first place? Logic would deduce that the person who rightfully owned the key was the same person who authorized the bottomless pit to be locked. It would also be reasonable to assume that the person who commanded the pit to be sealed would also be the same being who would authorize it to be opened at a specific time in the future. Furthermore, one would have to ask, "Who is locked up in the abyss and who jailed them?" Would not the judge who sent them to the abyss be the same judge who owns the prison key?

Is Satan a king? Does Satan own the key to the bottomless pit? Did Satan lock up his devoted devils? And why would the locust creatures torment Satan's followers on Earth? Why would they not sting Christians? The claim that Satan is the angel with the key implies that the Dragon can act as he wishes. Once again, Christian Zionist eschatology is woefully wrong. It doesn't matter.

Christian Zionists have a story, and they are sticking to it. For them, everything must fit inside their Darby-Scofield-Moody prophecy box. The Christian Zionist enchilada comes fully loaded. You must eat the whole thing or reject all of it.

Is it possible that the angel with the key who rules over the locust creatures imprisoned inside the abyss is a prison warden sent and deputized by God? Where are the fallen angels? Apostle Peter wrote in his second epistle, "For if God spared not the angels that sinned, but cast them down to hell, and delivered them into chains of darkness, to be reserved unto judgment...." The New Testament Bible's Greek manuscripts do not say "hell." St. Peter used the Greek word *tartarosas*, derived from the place called Tartarus. The fallen angels are locked up in Tartarus. The King James Bible translators called it hell. Who imprisoned the fallen angels in caves of deep darkness? Who has the key to this subterranean cavern of divine punishment? Could it be the same divine being who owns the key to the bottomless pit? Who owns the abyss? Satan or God?

In the twentieth chapter of the Revelation of Jesus Christ, St. John "saw an angel come down from heaven, having the key of the bottomless pit and a great chain in his hand." Who came down? An angel. From whence did he come? From Heaven. What did the angel from Heaven carry in his hand? The key to the bottomless pit and a great chain. What did the angel do with the key and chain? St. John wrote, "And he laid hold on the dragon, that old serpent, which is the Devil, and Satan, and bound him a thousand years, and cast him into the bottomless pit, and shut him up...."

Christian Zionists want us to believe that the angel with the key in Revelation 9 is Satan, but the angel in Revelation 20 is from

Heaven and sent by God. Theologically, it makes sense to conclude that both biblical references to an angel with a key to the abyss are talking about the same angel, the same key, and the same abyss.

Jehovah rules over the bottomless pit. The One who locked the abyss is the only One authorized to unlock it. God alone decrees the time His angel will open it. He will unlock the bottomless pit at the end of the age. God will restrict the movements of the locust creatures who ascend from the pit in the smoke, perhaps volcanic eruptions. The locust creatures will not torment the disciples of Christ, but instead, they will persecute Satan's disciples.

The locust creatures will be very disruptive. Will they be physically visible on Earth? They are spirit creatures from another realm. Most likely, they will be invisible to human eyes. Apostle John said, "in those days shall men seek death, and shall not find it; and shall desire to die, and death shall flee from them." What is their stinger? Is it a vaccination needle? Is the venom that drives men mad a gene therapy vaccine from Hell's biological warfare research laboratory? Will saints escape the painful madness because they will refuse to be vaccinated? The Holy Bible does not reveal the nature and manner of their venomous stings. Only the saints alive at that time will know the answers to such questions. Regardless, the locust creatures will be very disruptive to human civilization.

St. John wrote that the locusts "were like unto horses prepared unto battle." They had the teeth of lions, wore breastplates of iron, and their wings made a loud noise that sounded like many horses running to battle. Approximately eight hundred years earlier, Old Testament prophet Joel warned the Jews that the palmerworms, locusts, cankerworms, and caterpillars that devoured Judah's farmlands and vineyards were forerunners of a greater army of invading soldiers who would finish them with swords. In his spirit, the prophet saw an innumerable army of invading soldiers from another nation. They were strong and without numbers. The invaders were marching toward Judah. Joel described them as having the "teeth of a lion."

The prophet cried out to the people of Judah that the invaders were a strong people. Their soldiers would "leap on the mountaintops" as with "the sound of chariots." In the Revelation of Jesus Christ, St. John saw the locust creatures as having "the teeth of lions." Their wings made the sound of "chariots of many horses running to battle." The Old Testament prophet said the invaders would "run to and fro in the city; they shall run upon the wall, they shall climb upon the houses; they shall enter in at the windows like a thief." Apostle Paul said, "the day of the Lord so cometh as a thief in the night."

Prophet Joel knew when the invaders would "climb upon the houses" and shall "enter in at the windows like a thief." He said it should occur when the Sun and the Moon go dark, and the stars shall withdraw their shining. Jesus said, "immediately after the tribulation of those days shall the sun be darkened, and the moon shall not give her light, and the stars shall fall from heaven, and the powers of the heavens shall be shaken...." The mighty Old Testament prophet said the "Lord shall utter his voice before his army." New Testament Apostle Paul said that the "Lord himself shall descend from heaven with a shout, with the voice of the archangel, and with the trump of God..." Joel prophesied that "his camp is very great: for he is strong that executeth his word." Jesus said He "shall send his angels with a great sound of a trumpet, and they shall gather together his elect from the four winds, from one end of heaven to the other."

Joel revealed to Judah's stunned inhabitants that the incoming invaders would have the appearance of horses. In the vision on Patmos, St. John saw locust creatures in the bottomless pit that were "like unto horses prepared unto battle...and their faces were as the faces of men." Joel prophesied that "the people shall be much pained: all faces shall gather blackness." St. John saw locust creatures that stung the wicked and gave them much pain for five months. Their victims begged to die, but death would not come to them.

Speaking through the fiery prophet Joel, God told the people of Judah what would happen before the day of the Lord. God will show humankind wonders in the heavens, and in the Earth, blood, and fire, and pillars of smoke. "The day of the Lord" and "that day" refer to various visitations of God to cities and nations over thousands of years. Nineveh experienced a "day of the Lord" forty years after Jonah warned them to repent. The city's population repented after Jonah preached, but it did not last a generation. They lapsed back into their wicked ways, and God rescinded Heaven's reprieve. When Joel prophesied, he spoke of an immediate "day of the Lord" for Judah. Yet, his prophetic utterances also foretold the future of humanity. Joel saw the last days. He prophesied about the final "day of the Lord."

Confirming that Joel's prophecy referred to the last days, Apostle Peter quoted Joel in his first public sermon immediately after receiving the indwelling of the Holy Spirit on Pentecost. Like Joel, St. Peter spoke to the "men of Judea and all you who dwell in Jerusalem." Thus, he addressed the descendants of the men and women who heard Joel prophesy about the last days. Apostle Peter said, "But this is that...." This is what? This is that which was prophesied by Joel eight centuries earlier.

> **And it shall come to pass in the last days, saith God, I will pour out of my Spirit upon all flesh: and your sons and your daughters shall prophesy, and your young men shall see visions, and your old men shall dream dreams: and on my servants and on my handmaidens I will pour out in those days of my Spirit; and they shall prophesy: and I will shew wonders in heaven above, and signs in the earth beneath; blood, and fire, and vapor of smoke: the sun shall be turned into darkness, and the moon into blood, before that great and notable day of the Lord come: and it shall come to pass, that whosoever shall call on the name of the Lord shall be saved.**
>
> Acts 2:17-21

The prophet Joel saw "that day," the final visitation of God to Earth when God would do more than disrupt time. He will abolish time as we presently know it. When the Creator disposes of the Sun, Moon, and stars as necessary items, there cannot be 24-hour days and 365-day years in God's new world order. The Sun, Moon, and stars darkening shall announce that the King of Glory will soon step out on the center stage for the main act. As it was in Joel's day, so too will it be as we gallop toward the final day. The end-time locust invasion from the abyss is a sure sign that the worst judgments are on their way for the wicked, scoffers, mockers, and unbelievers.

The Gospel is Disruptive

The First Advent of Jesus Christ was very disruptive. Although the Lord confined the disruptions to a small geographical area, they produced cosmic happenings. An angelic choir in the nighttime sky over Bethlehem proclaimed to shepherds the birth of the Savior. Later, a delegation of wise men came from the East to Jerusalem to worship the Christ child. A mysterious star brightly "went before them" and led them to the house in Bethlehem where the infant Messiah lived with Mary and Joseph. (The Magi did not go to the manger where Jesus was born.) Angels led Joseph in dreams to flee Bethlehem and later to depart Egypt.

Likewise, the introduction of the Gospel was disruptive too. This disruption was worldwide, not local. Old Testament prophet Haggai prophesied the coming of the Messiah. Haggai said God would shake the heavens, and the Earth, and the sea, and the dry land, and all nations when the Messiah would appear. He prophesied that the glorious incarnation of the Son of God was Heaven's response to "the desire of all nations." The miraculous virgin birth of Jesus and the preaching of the Gospel of the Kingdom would agitate the world and "shake all nations."

God's introduction of the Gospel of the Kingdom was more significant and meaningful than Him giving the Law to Moses on Mount Sinai, thus making the rejection of the Gospel more dangerous than breaking the Law. The giving of the Law on Mount Sinai shook the mountain and nearby vicinities. The introduction of the Gospel, however, would shake the nations of the world. The shaking has continued for over two thousand years. Foretelling of the resurrection of Jesus and the destruction of the Jewish temple, Haggai said the Messiah's unsurpassed glory would be superior to the glory and splendor of the gold and silver in the Jewish temple in Jerusalem.

For thus saith the Lord of hosts; Yet once, it is a little while, *and I will shake the heavens, and the earth, and the sea, and the dry land; and I will shake all nations, and the desire of all nations shall come:* and I will fill this house with glory, saith the Lord of hosts. The silver is mine, and the gold is mine, saith the Lord of hosts. The glory of this latter house shall be greater than of the former, saith the Lord of hosts: and in this place will I give peace, saith the Lord of hosts.

Haggai 2:6-9

Jesus's earthly ministry was disruptive. He performed supernatural miracles that suspended the laws of physics. He turned water into wine. He made eyeballs with mud. He fed thousands of men, women, and children with a handful of loaves and fish. He cured the incurable, cast out demons, and raised the dead.

Staying true to His ways, Jesus' departure from this world also disrupted the planet. Darkness fell over the land when the Romans crucified Jesus to satisfy the delirious bloodlust of the Jewish rulers to murder the Son of God.

Now from the sixth hour there was darkness over all the land unto the ninth hour.

Matthew 27:45

Many strange occurrences shocked the people of Jerusalem on the day Jewish religious leaders and Roman government officials, religion and state united, physically killed the Messiah. A mighty earthquake shook Jerusalem when Jesus' divine soul separated from His human body. Rocks split apart. Angels ripped from top to bottom the massive, thick curtain in the temple. God also opened graves in Jerusalem. Dead saints came out and walked Jerusalem's streets and were seen by many.

> Jesus, when he had cried again with a loud voice, yielded up the ghost. And, behold, the veil of the temple was rent in twain from the top to the bottom; *and the earth did quake, and the rocks rent; and the graves were opened; and many bodies of the saints which slept arose, and came out of the graves after his resurrection, and went into the holy city, and appeared unto many.* Now when the centurion, and they that were with him, watching Jesus, saw the earthquake, and those things that were done, they feared greatly, saying, Truly this was the Son of God.
>
> Matthew 27:50-54

There was an earthquake when Jesus' body died at Golgotha. Although it did not cause widespread structural damage to Jerusalem's buildings, the rumble was felt and heard far and wide. The tearing asunder of the rocks signified God's wrath against the Jewish people for rejecting and killing His Son. Days later, an angel of the Lord triggered another earthquake in Jerusalem when he rolled back the stone from Jesus' burial tomb opening.

> *And, behold, there was a great earthquake:* for the angel of the Lord descended from heaven, and came and rolled back the stone from the door, and sat upon it.
>
> Matthew 28:2

If His crucifixion and resurrection triggered earthquakes, atmospheric darkness, and supernatural phenomena, should we not expect even more spectacular disruptions when He returns?

His Second Advent Will Disrupt the Cosmos

The birth of Jesus disrupted Bethlehem and the surrounding villages. The introduction of the Gospel disrupted the world. His Second Coming shall disrupt the universe.

Let's start with the warm-up to the Big Event. Jesus called it "the beginning of sorrows." After walking out of the temple in Jerusalem, Jesus was asked three questions by His disciples.

- When will the temple be destroyed?
- What shall be the sign of your coming?
- What shall be the sign of the end of the age?

He responded by giving them a very detailed description of what will happen regarding all three questions. Today, many people mistakenly omit the first question about the temple's destruction. They wrongly interpret his comments about the future destruction of the temple as a prophecy about the Second Advent. Whenever you read Matthew 24, keep in mind that Jesus answered all three questions asked by the disciples. When asked, all three questions were about future events. God destroyed the Jewish temple in 70AD. Therefore, the answer to the first question already happened, but the temple's destruction was a future event when the disciples questioned Him. The coming destruction of the temple was the reason Jesus mentioned the abomination of desolation standing in the temple and His warning to flee the city.

We are discussing in this chapter the two remaining questions: What shall be the sign of His coming, and what shall be the sign of the end of the age? Jesus said we should expect to see people coming in His name claiming to speak for Him but deceiving many. We will hear of wars and rumors of wars. Nations shall rise against nations and kingdoms against kingdoms. There will also be great earthquakes here, there, everywhere; plus, famines and pestilences. Such things are only the beginning of sorrows. Calamities much more horrible shall come.

Jesus-haters shall despise Jesus-lovers throughout the world for the sake of the name of Jesus Christ and shall gather up the saints to be afflicted and killed. When Christians are hated and killed worldwide, the resolve of many spiritually weak Christians will buckle and collapse. Their faith shall melt in the furnace of adversity. Such are they who shall be offended by strong Christians who refuse to draw back from the true apostolic faith despite severe persecution and cruel executions. Thus, Babylonian Churchianity members will betray true Christians who stand for righteousness while living in a vile, disgusting, sin-obsessed world that is on a collision course with Almighty God.

In these Last Days, we should expect to see apostate Christian religious rulers conspiring with government authorities, religion and state united again to persecute authentic Christians, faithful Israel. Courageous disciples of Christ should be on guard now for signs that a spirit of Judas is operating among religious zealots posing as Christians. Identification with Jesus Christ will become increasingly dangerous and risky as the world races toward the final day.

Only a portion of Christendom will still be in the game in the last inning. Intense social, economic, and political pressure will be too much for many weak church members to endure. Many people who foolishly believe that Jesus will remove them from Earth before the start of tribulation will succumb to the temptation to deny His name. Cowardly, timid, fearful, and faithless church members will have their part in the lake that burns with fire and brimstone.

> **Then shall they deliver you up to be afflicted, and shall kill you: and ye shall be hated of all nations for my name's sake. And then shall many be offended, and shall betray one another, and shall hate one another. And many false prophets shall rise, and shall deceive many. And because iniquity shall abound, the love of many shall wax cold. But he that shall endure unto the end, the same shall be saved. And this gospel of the kingdom shall be preached in all the world for a witness unto all nations; and then shall the end come.**
>
> **Matthew 24:9-14**

In addition to disruptions caused by earthquakes, famines, and pestilences, Jesus also said there would be fearful sights and great signs from heaven. The Greek word for fearful sights means "things of terror." Most likely, things of terror and great signs from heaven refer to comets, asteroids, meteors, and other things in outer space sent by God to warn humanity that their end is near. There shall be signs in the Sun and the Moon, and in the stars too.

On Earth, nations will be distressed and bewildered about the things coming upon the world. Sea waves shall roar. Politicians, scientists, environmental activists, and journalists will likely tell frightened citizens that the Earth's ecosystem is collapsing because of extreme climate change. Many people will believe anything but the Holy Bible. Terrifying sights in the sky will not be enough to move them to repentance.

God sent many supernatural signs to warn the Jews before the destruction of Jerusalem and the temple in 70 AD. Still, they grossly misinterpreted the signs as messages of divine favor and protection. They thought God was telling them they would defeat their military enemies. Instead, God was warning them that their destruction was on its way to Jerusalem. Misunderstood omens can be fatal.

Planet Earth's Popeye Moment

What explains such bizarre cosmic disruptions in the natural order of the universe? Creation's groaning will eventually become a scream of anguish, pleading with the Creator to deliver it from the crushing burden of accommodating humankind's sins for thousands of years. In Matthew 24:8, Jesus said the things coming upon the Earth, meaning earthquakes, famines, pestilences, wars, and tribulation, are the beginning of sorrows. The "beginning of sorrows" represents the beginning of birth pangs.

Who or what will be in labor? Who or what will suffer birth pangs? God's beautiful Creation presently seeks deliverance from mankind's awful sins. The Creator never intended for His masterpiece to coexist with evil. Sin is a foreign substance, a deadly virus that entered Creation at the fall of Adam and Eve and made it sick. Apostle Paul said the whole Creation, the entire universe, is groaning in travail caused by the proliferation of sin. Christ will deliver Creation from the bondage of sin.

....because the creature itself also shall be delivered from the bondage of corruption into the glorious liberty of the children of God. For we know that the whole creation groaneth and travaileth in pain together until now.

Romans 8:21-22

Animated Popeye cartoons were popular among American children in the 1950s and 60s. Popeye was cool. He was a happy, easy-going, skinny sailor who tried to get along with everybody.

Popeye's good-natured personality, however, was frequently challenged by mean, nasty bullies such as Brutus. In each cartoon, Popeye would reach his tipping point. He would shout, "That's all I can stands. I can't stands no more!" Now that's when the cartoon hero would whip out a big can of spinach, squeeze it until the lid popped off, gulp down the spinach, flex his muscles, and go after Brutus with a vengeance. For Brutus, it was "lights out." The big, bearded goon would find himself knocked out on the floor, seeing twinkling stars and hearing chirping birds. And Popeye would go on his way in each cartoon episode whistling a happy tune and often holding hands with his girlfriend, Olive Oyl. The end of the story.

Planet Earth is rapidly approaching Popeye's tipping point. The planet will shout to God, "That's all I can stands. I can't stands it no more!" It will be "lights out" for sinful humanity—the end of the story. God will speak into existence a new planet that will whistle a happy tune for eternity. A perpetual happy ending!

Strange things are already happening, yet few people connect the dots to Matthew 24. Earthquakes have occurred since Noah's Flood, but our planet is now experiencing "great earthquakes" as prophesied by Jesus. The Great Sumatra-Andaman Earthquake of December 26, 2004, struck the Indian Ocean with a whopping 9.1 magnitude. It generated a terrifying tsunami that suddenly and unexpectedly swept hundreds of thousands of people into the sea. The powerful quake moved the Earth off its axis and shortened the day. Likewise, the monstrous magnitude 8.9 super-quake that struck Japan in April 2011 carried the Earth off its axis by four inches and shifted Japan's main island by eight feet. Another mega-quake that shifted the planet off its axis and shortened the day struck Chile in March 2010 with a whopping 8.8 magnitude.

Yes, our planet is speaking to God now. It is groaning in travail like a pregnant woman suffering painful birth pangs. Someday, however, it will beg for immediate relief from the unbearable burden of sin. Did you know that our planet can speak? The Earth has a mouth, and blood has a voice. Innocent blood speaks to God through the Earth's mouth. The Holy Bible says so in its account of Cain's murder of his brother Abel over their offerings to God.

And the Lord said unto Cain, Where is Abel thy brother? And he said, I know not: Am I my brother's keeper? And he said, What hast thou done? *the voice of thy brother's blood crieth unto me from the ground. And now art thou cursed from the earth, which hath opened her mouth to receive thy brother's blood from thy hand...*

(Genesis 4:9-11)

Almighty God placed explosive charges deep in the bowels of the Earth. Foolish men and women on the planet's surface are unaware of what God hid beneath their feet. He will detonate those explosive charges at His appointed time. God has scheduled a mega seismic convulsion deep inside the Earth at the end of the age, the mother of all earthquakes. In 1 Samuel 2:8, Prophet Samuel said, "for the pillars of the earth are the Lord's, and he hath set the world upon them."

Humanity has a date with destiny when God will suddenly and unexpectedly knock the Earth off its pillars. Isaiah prophesied that God would move the Earth off its axis and rock it back and forth like a drunkard. It will be ripped up and removed like a flimsy hut in a violent windstorm. Isaiah saw the day when the Earth totters under the weight of humanity's unceasing, accelerating, and worsening decadence. The Creator will remove the planet He created by His spoken words. Why? Because the transgressions of mankind shall be heavy upon it. Disruptive is too mild of a word to describe what will happen to the planet. The Earth shall split wide open, be thoroughly shaken, tremble, fall, and not rise again.

The earth is utterly broken down, the earth is clean dissolved, the earth is moved exceedingly. The earth shall reel to and fro like a drunkard, and shall be removed like a cottage; and the transgression thereof shall be heavy upon it; and it shall fall, and not rise again.

Isaiah 24:19-20

That day will spring upon the unsaved human population suddenly and unexpectedly, like a thief in the night bursting into a home after midnight while its drunken inhabitants are sleeping. Three things shall pounce upon them: fear, a pit, and a snare. The snare is God's trapping net. Escaping the cosmic disruption will be impossible. Judgment will be unavoidable. Only the saints marked by angelic seals upon their foreheads will be spared and rescued when the foundations of the Earth violently shake. Angels will transport everybody else to the eternal barbeque pit.

> **Fear, and the pit, and the snare, are upon thee, O inhabitant of the earth. And it shall come to pass, that he who fleeth from the noise of the fear shall fall into the pit; and he that cometh up out of the midst of the pit shall be taken in the snare: for the windows from on high are open, and the foundations of the earth do shake.**
>
> Isaiah 24:17-18

The Creator is the World's First Environmentalist

One reason God will be wroth with furious indignation is humanity's ongoing destruction of His beautiful planet made for their enjoyment and benefit. Beginning in the Twentieth Century with the invention of the atomic bomb, humans ventured onto a path they had never traversed since the Garden of Eden. Powerful nations now possess military weapons beyond the comprehension of most people. Nuclear warheads that can destroy our planetary home multiple times arm intercontinental ballistic missiles, submarines, and bomber aircraft. Presently, the world has entered the age of hypersonic missiles that can rapidly encircle the globe and deliver a nuclear payload on a target city and nuclear-armed drone torpedos capable of generating massive tsunami waves to wipe out a coastline.

Such nuclear weapons pale in destructive power compared to new top-secret weapons. Gene-specific biologically engineered viruses could decimate an entire race of humans. Space-based scalar and directed energy weapons will unleash horrifying acts of war never seen on Earth. Weather warfare could starve a population with drought or drown them in floods. Imagine the horrors of future wars fought with armies of self-energizing human flesh-eating robotic warriors, genetically modified cyborg soldiers, and genetically engineered hybrid creatures that have never existed in human history. The Nephilim have returned as they were in the days of Noah.

This is madness! We permit defense contractors, university research laboratories, pharmaceutical companies, international corporations, scientists, and politicians to destroy God's planet. There is coming a day when the Creator will stop the people who are destroying His Earth. In the eleventh chapter of the Revelation of Jesus Christ, St. John wrote, "And the nations were angry, and thy wrath is come, and the time of the dead, that they should be judged, and that thou shouldest give reward unto thy servants the prophets, and to the saints, and them that fear thy name, small and great; and shouldest destroy them which destroy the earth."

Rebellious, sin-obsessed humankind will make such a mess of our planet that there will be no way to save it. Jesus said His Father would shorten the days of tribulation because it shall be so great that no flesh could be saved. Blood soaks Earth's soil. Blood has a voice, and the earth has a mouth. The blood speaks to God every hour through the Earth's mouth, pleading for justice. God has no choice but to start over. He will make a new planet. The Holy Bible calls it "the restitution of all things." It will be the restoration of His glorious Creation.

Repent ye therefore, and be converted, that your sins may be blotted out, when the times of refreshing shall come from the presence of the Lord; and he shall send Jesus

Christ, which before was preached unto you: *whom the heaven must receive until the times of restitution of all things, which God hath spoken by the mouth of all his holy prophets since the world began.*

Acts 3:19-21

Satan, his demons, which are the disembodied spirits of the Nephilim, and his human progeny disrupted the Creator's beautiful, excellent plan for humankind. There's coming a day when God will permanently disrupt their disruptions. He will end the old Creation and start over. You can easily understand many troubling things in society by recognizing that Satan's minions, spiritual and human, are madly driven to mar, defile, and destroy all good things: religion, the environment, culture, art, music, values, theater, sports, entertainment, families, and education. Almighty God is very aware of the destruction of His planet. He is coming someday to destroy those who have destroyed His beautiful Earth.

Mankind's damage to the planet, along with its blood-saturated soil, will necessitate its obliteration and replacement. Supernatural fire from Heaven shall dissolve the Earth. God will create a new Earth that is not deformed by humanity's endeavors nor soaked with blood. How will God create a new Earth, and how long will it take Him to do it? It is reasonable to assume that God will create the new Earth the same way He created the old Earth: He will speak it into existence. It won't take a lot of time to do it. From His mouth may come the words, "Let there be a new Earth!" He may be ancient, but He is still the one and only Creator. He is as much God today as He was when he spoke this present world into existence. His power has not diminished.

Almighty God will be finished with His old Creation when He dispatches Jesus Christ to wind up His affairs with humankind and dissolve the cosmos. He will even discard His present Heaven and make a new Heaven. Why? Because Lucifer's rebellion marred the old Heaven. The first sin occurred in Heaven. God cast out Lucifer and many rebellious angels. The old Heaven reminds God of Lucifer's rebellion, and the old Earth reminds Him of Adam's fall.

Behold, He will make all things new: a New Heaven, a New Earth, and New Jerusalem. All three are closely related. Our Heavenly Father will relocate His home from Heaven and move in with His children in New Jerusalem on the New Earth. What will God do with the old Heaven? Place a "for sale by owner" sign on it? Will He board it up like a vacant building? No, He will make it disappear. His heart's desire has always been to dwell with His children in the Garden of Eden. The glorious arrival of the King to the New Earth will bring along His kingdom and regal presence. His presence shall unite the New Heaven, the New Earth, and the New Jerusalem for eternity.

But the day of the Lord will come as a thief in the night; in the which the heavens shall pass away with a great noise, *and the elements shall melt with fervent heat, the earth also and the works that are therein shall be burned up.* Seeing then that all these things shall be dissolved, what manner of persons ought ye to be in all holy conversation and godliness, looking for and hasting unto the coming of the day of God, wherein the heavens being on fire shall be dissolved, and the elements shall melt with fervent heat?

Nevertheless we, according to his promise, look for new heavens and a new earth, wherein dwelleth righteousness.

2 Peter 3:10-13

Mother of All Earthquakes Reserved for Jerusalem

Disruption will disturb Jerusalem for centuries of sinful behavior, rebellion, stubbornness, and Kabbalah sorcery. Although there will be great earthquakes in many places of the world as we approach the end, God has one extraordinary earthquake scheduled for that most wicked city, Jerusalem, which God calls Sodom and Egypt. It's going to be a doozy. You do not want to be riding in a religious tour bus in Jerusalem on that day. There will be no refunds.

God still remembers the day they crucified His only begotten Son. At the appointed hour, His fury shall explode on Jerusalem and the city's wicked Kabbalah wizards, rabbis, Freemasons, proud politicians, bloodthirsty military commanders, treacherous intelligence agents, homosexuals, and greedy business people. Almighty God will trigger an extreme earthquake that will strike Jerusalem with a vengeance, splitting the "great city" into three parts. Simultaneously, there shall be a collapse of cities worldwide. God will remember Babylon, meaning Jerusalem, and make her lick every drop from His cup of wrath. The disruptive earthquake is part of the grand finale of the age of humankind.

And *the great city was divided into three parts, and the cities of the nations fell:* and great Babylon came in remembrance before God, to give unto her the cup of the wine of the fierceness of his wrath.

Revelation 16:19

235

The Jerusalem quake will be preceded by the seventh angel pouring out his vial and a great voice. The voice originates from the temple of heaven, from the throne. Therefore, Almighty God, not an angel or prophet, makes a powerful proclamation just before the earthquake that will devastate Jerusalem. He shall say, "It is done." God the Father will echo the words of God the Son when Jesus cried, "It is finished!" Our Heavenly Father will shout, "It is done!" to signify the final destruction of Babylon the Great and the harlot's entire Satanic empire on Earth. It also represents the end of the age of humankind and this present world.

> **And the seventh angel poured out his vial into the air; and there came a great voice out of the temple of heaven, from the throne, saying, It is done.**
>
> **Revelation 16:17**

Jerusalem, along with her tabernacle-of-Moloch star god Remphan, the so-called Star of David, shall be destroyed by God in His final judgment on Satan's Babylonian civilization. Jerusalem is Babylon the Great, "the great city," the harlot, the city that killed God's prophets, the city that crucified our Lord, the seat of the synagogue of Satan. In the Old Testament, God often called rebellious and idolatrous Jerusalem a harlot and promised that divine judgment would cut her down.

> **....but if ye refuse and rebel, ye shall be devoured with the sword: for the mouth of the Lord hath spoken it. *How is the faithful city become an harlot! it was full of judgment; righteousness lodged in it; but now murderers.***
>
> **Isaiah 1:20-21**

God accused Jerusalem of being worse than a harlot by speaking through Old Testament prophet Ezekiel. He said the city is vile like a prostitute that pays men for sex.

> **How weak is thine heart, saith the Lord God, seeing thou doest all these things, the work of an imperious whorish woman; in that thou buildest thine eminent place in the head of every way, and makest thine high place in every street; and hast not been as an harlot, in that thou scornest hire; but as a wife that committeth adultery, which taketh strangers instead of her husband!** *They give gifts to all whores: but thou givest thy gifts to all thy lovers, and hirest them,* **that they may come unto thee on every side for thy whoredom.**
>
> Ezekiel 16:30-33

The seventeenth chapter of the Apocalypse describes Mystery Babylon as a great whore with whom the kings of the Earth have committed fornication, and the inhabitants of the Earth have been made drunk with the wine of her fornication. John is shown a woman sitting upon a beast, full of names of blasphemy. Furthermore, John said the great city has a name written upon her forehead: MYSTERY, BABYLON THE GREAT, THE MOTHER OF HARLOTS AND ABOMINATIONS OF THE EARTH.

The Apocalypse mentions the "great city" ten times. Each reference is to Mystery Babylon, the place that God shall destroy. Does the Holy Bible identify Mystery Babylon? Yes, it does. It is Jerusalem, the great city that crucified Jesus Christ! God called Jerusalem "Sodom and Egypt." It is called great because of the pride of its inhabitants. It is called Sodom because of its wickedness. It is called Egypt because it represents bondage and oppression. It is called Jerusalem because it is the world capital of idolatrous apostasy, the global seat of hostility against Jesus Christ and His Church. Jerusalem represents worldwide Zionism. The kings of the Earth have committed fornication with Zionism. The Earth's inhabitants have been made drunk with the wine of Zionism's fornication.

> **And their dead bodies shall lie in the street of the great city, which spiritually is called Sodom and Egypt, where also our Lord was crucified.**
>
> **Revelation 11:8**

Crucifying the Son of God was expected of the people of Jerusalem. They have a long history of murdering God's holy prophets. Old Testament prophet Isaiah cried out to God that "the children of Israel have forsaken Thy covenants, thrown down Thy altars, and slain Thy prophets with the sword." Many Bible scholars believe Isaiah was later sawn into two pieces by his Jewish enemies.

Centuries later, Jesus accused them to their faces of being murderers. The Lord called them vipers and whitewashed tombs in a fiery tirade against Judaism's scribes and Pharisees. He then tore into them by accusing them of being "the children of them which killed the prophets." In the Book of Acts of the Apostles, Stephen confronted the Jews who crucified Jesus by asking, "Which of the prophets did your fathers not persecute?" The bold deacon also accused Jerusalem's Jewish rulers of collectively sharing the bloodguilt with their forefathers who killed those who prophesied the coming of the Righteous One. That was all the Sanhedrin judges could bear hearing from Stephen's mouth. Stephen's words "cut to the heart." The Jewish judges gnashed their teeth at him. They murdered Stephen the moment he accused them of killing the prophets.

It Won't be the First Time God Splits Apart Jerusalem

It will not be the first time God divides Jerusalem into three parts. He did it in the days of Ezekiel. God instructed Ezekiel to shave his head and beard with a sharp knife. The sharp knife represented the sword of war that was coming to Jerusalem. God's judgment would be a time of calamity and ruin. Even in modern times, most Arab societies consider shaving off a man's hair and beard an act of utter humiliation.

God told the prophet to weigh the cut hair and beard on scales and accurately divide the hair into three parts. Symbolically, Ezekiel's head represented the chief Jewish rulers of the city. His hair represented the citizens. The cutting of his hair represented God removing His grace and glory from Jerusalem. Each pile of hair cut by the sword represented a third of Jerusalem. One-third of the city was burned in a fire. The second third of Jerusalem was cut to pieces with swords. The remaining third of the city was scattered to other nations like chaff in the wind.

And thou, son of man, take thee a sharp knife, take thee a barber's razor, and cause it to pass upon thine head and upon thy beard: then take thee balances to weigh, and divide the hair. Thou shalt burn with fire *a third part* in the midst of the city, when the days of the siege are fulfilled: and thou shalt take *a third part*, and smite about it with a knife: and *a third part* thou shalt scatter in the wind; and

I will draw out a sword after them. Thou shalt also take thereof a few in number, and bind them in thy skirts. Then take of them again, and cast them into the midst of the fire, and burn them in the fire; for thereof shall a fire come forth into all the house of Israel. Thus saith the Lord God; *This is Jerusalem: I have set it in the midst of the nations and countries that are round about her.*

Ezekiel 5:1-5

God's roar shall trigger the cataclysmic worldwide earthquake that shall rip apart Jerusalem someday. He shall roar in righteous indignation because He is wroth with sinful humans who repeatedly rejected His generous offer of mercy, forgiveness, adoption, and eternal life made possible by repentance, faith in the name of the crucified and resurrected Jesus Christ, and baptism into His holy Church. It is Jerusalem that represents the world's hatred of Jesus Christ. It was in Jerusalem that the Christ-haters crucified the Son of God on a wooden cross.

The Lord shall go forth as a mighty man, he shall stir up jealousy like a man of war: *he shall cry, yea, roar;* he shall prevail against his enemies.

Isaiah 42:13

The wrath expressed by the King of the Universe shall be like the roaring of a mighty lion that strikes its prey suddenly and unexpectedly. Yahweh's anger will manifest as a roar from Heaven because He has a legal dispute with all the nations that He must settle forever. Jeremiah prophesied that the Lord would roar from on high and utter His voice from His holy habitation.

The Lord shall roar from on high, and utter his voice from his holy habitation; he shall mightily roar upon his habitation; he shall give a shout, as they that tread the grapes, against all the inhabitants of the earth. A noise shall come even to the ends of the earth; for the Lord hath a controversy with the nations, he will plead with all flesh; he will give them that are wicked to the sword, saith the Lord.

Jeremiah 25:30-31

God's sudden, unexpected, and swift intervention into humanity's affairs will astonish the people of the Earth. His victorious utterance will announce that judgment is unstoppable. God's roar from Heaven will physically shake the Earth. The shaking will greatly agitate and stir up the dead spirits in Hades, including the "chief ones of the earth," meaning the he-goats who ruled nations as monarchs. The great goats still sit upon their thrones in Hades, ruling over the spirits of dead men and women. Isaiah prophesied that "Hell from beneath is moved for thee to meet thee at thy coming: it stirreth up the dead for thee, even all the chief ones of the earth; it hath raised up from their thrones all the kings of the nations."

The Lord also shall roar out of Zion, and utter his voice from Jerusalem; and the heavens and the earth shall shake: but the Lord will be the hope of his people, and the strength of the children of Israel.

Joel 3:16

Old Testament prophet Habakkuk said that when God stands up to judge, He measures the Earth, drives asunder the nations, the mountains are scattered, and the hills bow. Habakkuk said when the mountains see God, they tremble; and the Sun and Moon stand still as the light of His arrows go by and the shining of His glittering spear. God shall furiously march through the world, threshing the wicked and going forth for the salvation of His people.

> He stood, and measured the earth: he beheld, and drove asunder the nations; and the everlasting mountains were scattered, the perpetual hills did bow: his ways are everlasting.
>
> Habakkuk 3:6

> The mountains saw thee, and they trembled: the overflowing of the water passed by: the deep uttered his voice, and lifted up his hands on high. The sun and moon stood still in their habitation: at the light of thine arrows they went, and at the shining of thy glittering spear. Thou didst march through the land in indignation, thou didst thresh the heathen in anger. Thou wentest forth for the salvation of thy people, even for salvation with thine anointed; thou woundedst the head out of the house of the wicked, by discovering the foundation unto the neck.
>
> Habakkuk 3:10-13

Accompanying the splitting asunder of Jerusalem by a mega-earthquake before the second coming of Jesus Christ, every island and mountain on Planet Earth shall disappear! If that's not disruptive enough, massive hailstones, estimated to be over 100 pounds each, will rain down on nations signifying God's heavy judgments upon unrepentant sinners. People too stubborn and proud to repent will curse God for the hailstorm and die in their rebellion.

And every island fled away, and the mountains were not found. And there fell upon men a great hail out of heaven, every stone about the weight of a talent: and men blasphemed God because of the plague of the hail; for the plague thereof was exceeding great.

Revelation 16:20-21

Jeremiah Saw God Rewind Time to Genesis

A tremendous disruption will be the reversal of Creation. God will rewind His time machine to His first words in the Book of Genesis. Jeremiah saw the final day. The Old Testament prophet saw the Earth as it was in its primitive state in Genesis 1:2, described by Moses as "without form, and void; and darkness was upon the face of the deep."

What caused it to happen? Disruptive judgment! In the Old Testament days, Jeremiah focused his ministry on preaching a warning of divine judgment if the people of Israel did not repent of their evil ways. God, however, revealed something to Jeremiah infinitely more shocking than the impending judgment of Israel. It is a pattern seen throughout Old Testament scriptures.

Jeremiah saw God rewind His time machine! God gave Jeremiah a fleeting glimpse of the final day when the Creator would rewind time to its primordial starting point. The prophet gazed into the distant future at the end of time. He saw the final judgment that God will wreak upon humanity's wicked world. All was gone. The Earth returned to its primitive state at the beginning of time. Using the exact Hebrew words in Genesis 1:2, Jeremiah saw the planet's formlessness, emptiness, nothingness, and confusion. Earth was without beauty and surrounded by stark darkness. Jeremiah saw no light in the universe.

In Jeremiah 4:23-25, the Old Testament prophet declared, "I beheld the earth, and, lo, it was without form, and void; and the heavens, and they had no light. I beheld the mountains, and, lo, they trembled, and all the hills moved lightly. I beheld, and, lo, there was no man, and all the birds of the heavens were fled."

The Spirit revealed to Jeremiah that the world would be tossed back to its primitive state of formless chaos before God spoke the words, "Let there be light." He was allowed to peek into the future when the Sun goes dark, the Moon has no light to reflect, and the stars fall from the heavens. In the vision, everything was out of order. Jeremiah said the heavens, the abode of the stars, "had no light." The primeval Earth was in a state of formlessness, confusion, and chaos. The mountains and hills quivered and swayed from the power of God's fury released through the worldwide earthquake at the end of the age. The prophet saw a lifeless, empty planet. No humans were alive, and all birds had disappeared.

Jeremiah saw the ultimate judgment of sin and rebellion: the complete abolition of the existing cosmos. The Creator will abolish it to make way for a new universe, a new creation. God will not slap a fresh coat of paint on our old planet marred by massive earthquakes, volcanic eruptions, meteor strikes, massive hail-stones, pestilences, famines, and wars involving nuclear, biological, chemical, and scalar weapons. Even worse, violent men and women soaked the planet's soil with innocent blood, especially the blood of hundreds of millions of aborted babies. The Earth has a mouth, and blood has a voice. The blood of all innocent humans killed since the murder of Abel is continually crying out to God for justice. Our old Earth is already beyond repair. No refurbishment will suffice. It is only fit for a fire—flames so hot that even the cinders and ash vanish. A fire from Heaven that consumes the element of fire itself.

Judgment is Disruptive

You can't ignore the fact that the Second Coming of Jesus Christ will disrupt the cosmos. Jesus will initiate a universal blackout immediately after the days of Satan's tribulation against the saints come to an end. Tribulation and wrath are two separate and different things. The time of great tribulation is Satan's wrath against God's holy Church. The day of the Lord is God's wrath against Satan and his wicked synagogue. God's saints will suffer tribulation. They will not suffer God's wrath. Before it's over, however, the wicked shall experience great tribulation. They shall suffer God's wrath.

When God interrupts Satan's persecution of Christians, it will be His turn to persecute Satan's disciples. The Almighty will pull the plug and cut off the universe's electricity. Why waste electricity when you're ready to implode the entire building? Demolition experts know that they must first cut off the electrical power before imploding buildings. In this case, the demolition contractor is Almighty God. He will power down the stars before imploding the universe. He will recall and rescind His words spoken in Genesis.

Jesus said the Sun shall be darkened, the Moon shall not give her light, the stars shall fall from heaven, and the powers of the heavens shall be shaken. When shall these things happen? Jesus told us in easy-to-understand words. He said the universe shall go dark "immediately after the tribulation of those days." How can there be a one-thousand-year Jewish kingdom in Jerusalem if the Sun,

Moon, and stars have disappeared? Will the Millennial Kingdom's inhabitants use flashlights?

When Jesus prophesied about the end of the age, it was not the first time His Jewish disciples heard that Yahweh would someday turn out the lights in the universe. They knew that Jesus was referring to Isaiah's prophecies about the Medes' destruction of Babylon, a type of the final "day of the Lord" at the end of the age. In the Last Days, Jerusalem is identified in the Apocalypse as "the great city," the harlot, Sodom and Egypt, Mystery Babylon. Isaiah prophesied that her people would howl, their hearts shall melt, they shall be afraid: pangs and sorrows shall grip them, their faces shall be inflamed, because the day of the Lord had arrived, and it shall come as a destruction from the Almighty.

> Howl ye; for the day of the Lord is at hand; it shall come as a destruction from the Almighty. Therefore shall all hands be faint, and every man's heart shall melt: and they shall be afraid: pangs and sorrows shall take hold of them; they shall be in pain as a woman that travaileth: they shall be amazed one at another; their faces shall be as flames. Behold, the day of the Lord cometh, cruel both with wrath and fierce anger, to lay the land desolate: and he shall destroy the sinners thereof out of it. *For the stars of heaven and the constellations thereof shall not give their light: the sun shall be darkened in his going forth, and the moon shall not cause her light to shine.* And I will punish the world for their evil, and the wicked for their iniquity; and I will cause the arrogance of the proud to cease, and will lay low the haughtiness of the terrible.
>
> **Isaiah 13:6-11**

Isaiah uttered numerous prophecies about significant cosmic disruptions that will accompany the final day of the Lord. In Isaiah 24:23, the prophet said, "the moon shall be confounded, and the sun ashamed." In Isaiah 60:19, he prophesied that the "sun shall be no more thy light by day, neither for brightness shall the moon give light unto thee." Isaiah told the Israelites why they would no longer need the sun and moon in the same verse. He said, "the Lord shall be unto thee an everlasting light, and thy God thy glory." The Old Testament prophet did not prophesy about a future Jewish empire. He spoke about New Jerusalem, the authentic, eternal capital city of faithful Israel, the glorious Church of God.

How dreadful shall the wrath of God be for unrepentant sinners and the wicked when the final day catches them by surprise? The magnitude of the cosmic disruption is unimaginable. Mountains will be removed. Islands will disappear. The seas will roar. The Sun, the Moon, and stars will turn to darkness. The planet will be ripped apart by a worldwide earthquake. God will remove the pillars holding the Earth in space, thus making the planet tossed to and fro like a drunkard. Massive hailstones shall pummel the wicked as they hide in caves seeking to escape the Lord's indignation as the blood of hundreds of millions of aborted babies cries out from the soil for revenge and justice. His angels shall crush the wicked as grapes.

Both Old and New Testament scriptures speak about the physically disruptive nature of God's presence when He enters our dimension. Job said God would overturn and remove mountains in His anger, shake the Earth out of its place and its pillars, command the Sun not to rise, and seal up the stars (Job 9:5:8). Ezekiel said there shall be a great shaking in the land, all creatures shall shake at God's presence, and mountains shall be thrown down (Ezekiel 38:19-20).

Joel prophesied that the Earth would quake, the heavens shall tremble, the Sun and Moon shall be dark, and the stars withdraw their shining when the Lord utters His voice before His army (Joel 2:10-11). Joel also prophesied that there shall be wonders in the heavens and in the Earth: blood, fire, and pillars of smoke, the Sun shall be turned into darkness and the Moon into blood (Joel 2: 30-32), and the Sun and the Moon shall be darkened, and the stars shall withdraw their shining (Joel 3:15). The Old Testament prophet said an unstoppable army would invade, a fire would devour everything before them, and a flame behind them would set everything on fire. Joel lamented that humankind lost the Garden of Eden, the paradise that God lovingly prepared for them. (Joel 2:3)

Isaiah prophesied that the stars of heaven and the constellations would cease giving light, the Sun shall be darkened, and the Moon will cease to shine (Isaiah 13:10), and the Moon shall be confounded, and the Sun ashamed (Isaiah 24:23).

King David prophesied that God would rain upon the wicked snares, fire, brimstone, and a horrible tempest (Psalms 11:6). Asaph wrote that God shall not keep silent when He comes on the scene. A fire will devour His enemies as he goes forth. There shall be a storm around Him (Psalm 50:3). Asaph also wrote that God's thunderous voice is heard in Heaven, lightnings will lighten the world, and the Earth will tremble and shake (Psalm 77:18).

The sons of Korah wrote that God shall remove kingdoms and nation-states on Earth when heathen nations rage. The Earth shall melt when He utters His voice (Psalm 46:6). King David wrote that God's stare at the Earth would trigger earthquakes. His will touch hills and set off volcanic eruptions (Psalm 104:32). The psalmist who wrote Psalm 114 said that the Earth trembles at the presence of the God of Jacob.

In the New Testament, Jesus Christ said the day of the Lord would be like Lot departing Sodom. Immediately, fire and brimstone fell from heaven and destroyed everybody (Luke 17:29-30). Apostle Paul wrote to the saints in Thessalonica that when the Lord Jesus is revealed from Heaven with His mighty angels, His flaming fire will take vengeance on everybody who does not know God nor obeyed the Gospel of the Lord (2 Thessalonians 1:7-8). Apostle Peter wrote that "the day of the Lord will come as a thief in the night, the heavens shall pass away with a great noise, and the elements shall melt with fervent heat, and the earth shall be burned up (2 Peter 3:10).

However, Jesus revealed to St. John the most detailed vision about the day of the Lord. In his vision on Patmos, Apostle John saw angels pour out vials containing judgments like the plagues of Egypt. The first vial shall release noisome and grievous sores upon everyone who received the beast's mark and worshiped his image. The second vial shall turn the sea to blood and kill everything in it. The third vial will turn rivers and fountains of water into blood (Revelation 16:2-4). The fourth angel's bowl shall be poured out upon the Sun: power shall be given to him to scorch men with fire (Revelation 16:8-9). The fifth angel will pour out his vial upon the seat of the beast, and his kingdom will be full of darkness, and they will gnaw their tongues for pain (Revelation 16:10-11). The sixth angel will pour out his vial upon the Euphrates River, and it shall dry up (Revelation 16:12). The seventh angel will pour his vial into the air. God will shout from Heaven, "It is done." There shall be voices, thunder, lightning, and hail. A mega-earthquake will strike Jerusalem and split the city into three parts, the cities of nations shall fall, islands and mountains shall disappear (Revelation 16:17-20).

The Second Coming of Jesus Christ on the final day shall be:

- Singular
- Sudden and unexpected
- Atmospheric
- Visible
- Noisy
- Disruptive

CHAPTER 7

HIS SECOND COMING SHALL BE FIERY

JESUS WILL COME WITH flaming fire!

When the Lord and his angelic special forces commandos suddenly and unexpectedly kick open sinful humanity's front door, they will burst into Babylon and all her daughters with flamethrowers the size unlike anything seen by men.

He will set everything ablaze! People, houses, skyscrapers, parliaments, palaces, military bases, shopping malls, universities, schools, museums, vehicles, aircraft, ships, bridges, nuclear power facilities, film studios, farms, ranches, forests, mountains, theaters, cafes, restaurants, hair salons, clothing boutiques, candy stores, nightclubs, stock exchanges, banks, shrines, temples, mosques, churches, cities, nations—everything!

He's coming to burn abortionists. He's coming to burn child molesters. He's coming to burn pornographers. He's coming to burn rapists. He's coming to burn homosexuals, adulterers, fornicators, and sexually immoral men and women. He's coming to burn liars and deceivers. He's coming to burn the wicked. He's coming to burn warmongers. He's coming to burn swindlers and thieves. He's coming to burn those who oppress the poor and weak. He's coming to burn murderers and those who shed innocent blood. He's coming to burn people who cheat widows out of their houses and savings.

He's coming to burn drunkards, drug addicts, and gluttons. He's coming to burn perverted preachers and deviant deacons. He's coming to burn Judaizers. He's coming to burn all antichrists. He's coming to burn revilers. He's coming to burn those who cause strife and division in His Church. He's coming to burn idolaters, witches, warlocks, sorcerers, gurus, mystics, astrologers, necromancers, numerologists, diviners, soothsayers, occultists, New Agers, Freemasons, and members of all secret societies. He's coming to burn the greedy, the jealous, the envious, and those who covet. He's coming to burn those who destroy His Earth. He's coming to burn all humans who rejected His gracious offer of forgiveness and salvation.

Will anybody be safe? Yes, every abortionist, child molester, pornographer, rapist, homosexual, adulterer, fornicator, immoral man or woman, liar, deceiver, wicked person, warmonger, swindler, thief, murderer, drunkard, drug addict, glutton, perverted preacher, deviant deacon, Judaizer, antichrist, reviler, agitator, idolator, witch, warlock, sorcerer, guru, mystic, astrologer, necromancer, numerologist, diviner, soothsayer, occultist, New Ager, and Freemason who remorsefully repented of their sins, confessed faith in Jesus Christ and were baptized into the Church, before they died or before Jesus Christ appears on the final day.

Born again men and women have no reason to fear God's wrath. His fiery wrath is for the wicked and unbelievers. Angels will douse this planet with a flammable liquid that men cannot extinguish, and Jesus will light the match. God's sin amnesty is still in effect. Time is running out to accept His gracious offer of forgiveness and eternal life.

A spectacular five-stage separation of souls will precede God's consuming fire:

1. Jesus Christ will open all graves. Every human who ever lived will come out of their graves and tombs.
2. Angelic reapers shall seize the wicked, bundle them, and take them away to be burned later in the lake of fire.
3. The resurrected bodies of saints that come out of their graves will be taken into the atmosphere to meet Jesus Christ.
4. Immediately after that, Christ will also transport all living saints into the atmosphere to join their resurrected brethren.
5. King Jesus will separate all humans who ever lived into two camps: goats and sheep. Angels will lead the goats to the lake of fire. The angels will guide the sheep to the gates of New Jerusalem.

....and before him shall be gathered all nations: and he shall separate them one from another, as a shepherd divideth his sheep from the goats: and he shall set the sheep on his right hand, but the goats on the left.

Matthew 25:32-33

What is the final day? It is the day of the Lord, the last visitation of God to humanity. It is a day without increments of time. No hours, no minutes, and no seconds. Time will cease to exist when the time maker appears on the scene. The Ancient of Days does not need humans' clocks and calendars. He will accomplish His objectives according to His schedule, not ours. Who are theologians to tell the Almighty that He must spread out His to-do list over a thousand years? Is not God able to do everything instantaneously? He is the ultimate multitasker. The final day is the consummation of all things. It encompasses:

1. The darkening of the cosmos
2. The appearance of the sign of the Son of Man
3. The Parousia
4. The opening of all graves
5. The bundling of the wicked
6. The resurrection of the dead bodies of departed saints
7. The transformation of the bodies of living saints
8. The catching up of resurrected and living saints into the atmosphere to meet Jesus
9. The separation of all humans who ever lived since the beginning of the world into two categories: saved and unsaved
10. The Great White Throne of Judgment
11. The casting of Satan and the wicked into the lake of fire
12. The testing of the earthly works of all saints in God's crucible of fire
13. The fiery destruction of the Earth
14. The rolling up of the cosmos like a scroll
15. The creation of a new Earth and heavens
16. The descent of New Jerusalem to the new Earth
17. The relocation of God from Heaven to New Jerusalem.

Operation Bundle and Burn

Jesus' arrival will swiftly usher in judgment upon the world as a mighty flood. It will come suddenly and unexpectedly as in the days of Noah. People were sinning like there was no tomorrow. And they were right! There was no tomorrow for them. The sky turned black, brilliant streaks of lightning flashed across the sky, ominous claps of thunder reverberated above, and a deluge of heavy rain fell nonstop for 40 days and nights. The Earth's crust was ripped asunder by mighty earthquakes. Fountains deep inside the planet were released through massive fissures in the planet's crust and flowed like mighty rivers onto the Earth's surface. All drowned except Noah and his family and the creatures that dwelt in water.

God has scheduled another global flood for wicked humanity. The next time it will be a flood of fire. The commander of Heaven's armies will signal to the angels that it is time to commence Operation Bundle and Burn. Before the incineration of the planet, a tremendous aerial armada of angelic reapers shall descend with the Lord. Tens of millions of them will fill the sky. The reapers will fan out across continents in search of men and women who have the mark of the beast, or the name of the beast, or the number of his name. Heaven's law enforcement officers will apprehend all rebels and lawbreakers who rejected or ignored the merciful King's sin amnesty.

First, however, they will snatch up unrepentant sinners and vile, wicked people who pop out of their graves when Jesus shouts. Sleepytime for the wicked will suddenly end. The unsaved dead will be startled out of their sleep in their dusty burial places. There will be no time to yawn for those who awaken from death. As

255

quickly as dead people shoot out of their graves, angelic reapers will snatch them faster than lizards eating crickets. It will be "off to the fire pit" to be flame-broiled for eternity! The Holy Bible says they will be bundled and burned. It will be no different than a gardener who pulls weeds, bundles them in piles, and tosses them into a fire pit to ensure that the seeds never reproduce.

> **If a man abide not in me, he is cast forth as a branch, and is withered; and men gather them, and cast them into the fire, and they are burned.**
>
> **John 15:6**

After lassoing and bundling startled, dazed, and freaked out dead sinners awakened from their graves, the angelic reapers will quickly turn their attention to the terrified living sinners. They will run, scream, and wildly curse as they try to hide from the fury of the Lord, but they will not go far. Not even deep caves will provide cover from God's wrath. Indeed, the wicked will beg cave rocks to fall and crush them. Better to be smashed by boulders than captured by angels with fiery eyes and glistening swords.

> **And the kings of the earth, and the great men, and the rich men, and the chief captains, and the mighty men, and every bondman, and every free man, hid themselves in the dens and in the rocks of the mountains; and said to the mountains and rocks, Fall on us, and hide us from the face of him that sitteth on the throne, and from the wrath of the Lamb....**
>
> **Revelation 6:15-16**

It will not matter whether they are crushed or captured. The wicked will be hauled away to Beelzebub's Barbeque Pit located at 666 Beast Street, Hell. They'll be turning forever on skewers over roaring flames and hot coals. They'll have plenty of time to remember their sins, their rejection of God's forgiveness through faith in Jesus Christ. Even worse, they'll have eternity to contemplate their complete separation from God, who will no longer remember they ever existed! They will forever fry in black fire. The flames in the lake of fire are invisible because the darkness is so great that not even roaring fires can produce light in a lightless world totally separated from God.

Let them be blotted out of the book of the living, and not be written with the righteous.

Psalm 69:28

The good news is that the Church shall escape God's wrath upon the wicked. The fire shall not burn righteous men, women, and children who were saved by faith in Jesus Christ. Glorified bodies will not burn. The saints, however, shall feel the heat on their feet as they are caught up into the atmosphere to meet our glorious King Jesus. They will know that the triumphant Church was rescued by Jesus a split second before the fireball engulfed the planet. As saints gaze at the burning world below them, each man and woman will say, "There but for the grace of God, go I."

Our present age is a repeat of the pre-flood age. Humankind's wickedness and evil are increasing at an alarming rate of speed in the twenty-first century. Violence, bloodshed, and sexual immorality are vexing the whole world, and it's getting worse each year. Creation is groaning to be released from humanity's wickedness.

Just as Creation is moaning for release from humanity's sins, God too will once again regret ever making humankind. However, the second time will be different from the first global judgment. In the first worldwide judgment, God destroyed the wicked with water. God spared the Earth the first time, but He will destroy the planet with fire and start over the second time.

In his second epistle to the Church in Thessalonica, Saint Paul wrote that Jesus and his angels shall come back to Earth in flaming fire to take vengeance on humans who do not know God nor obey the Gospel of our Lord Jesus. They shall be punished by fire and separated from God forever. Could there be a worse punishment?

> ....*when the Lord Jesus shall be revealed from heaven with his mighty angels, in flaming fire taking vengeance on them that know not God, and that obey not the gospel of our Lord Jesus Christ: who shall be punished with everlasting destruction from the presence of the Lord, and from the glory of his power;* when he shall come to be glorified in his saints, and to be admired in all them that believe (because our testimony among you was believed) in that day.
>
> 2 Thessalonians 1:7-10

John the Baptist bravely warned the Jewish religious leaders about the day when God would separate all humans into two groups: wheat and chaff. The chaff shall burn up with unquenchable fire.

> And now also the axe is laid unto the root of the trees: *therefore every tree which bringeth not forth good fruit is hewn down, and cast into the fire.* I indeed baptize you with water unto repentance: but he that cometh after me is mightier than I, whose shoes I am not worthy to bear: he

shall baptize you with the Holy Ghost, and with fire: whose fan is in his hand, *and he will thoroughly purge his floor, and gather his wheat into the garner; but he will burn up the chaff with unquenchable fire.*

Matthew 3:10-12

Prophecy in Parables

One of the best places in the Holy Bible to find scriptures about the end of the world are the parables of Jesus. His parables contain valuable insights into what will happen on the final day of humankind. For some unknown reason, many modern Bible prophecy teachers ignore the parables of Jesus when teaching about His Second Coming and the punishment of the wicked. Could the reason be that their doctrines contradict the parables?

The thirteenth chapter of the Gospel According to St. Matthew contains seven parables and two explanations. Jesus came out of a house and sat beside the sea. A great crowd assembled around Him to hear His wisdom. He entered a boat and made it His platform to teach many things to the people standing on the shore. His first lesson was the Parable of the Sower. According to St. Mark, Jesus said the Parable of the Sower is the master key to understanding all other parables.

And he said unto them, Know ye not this parable? and how then will ye know all parables?

Mark 4:13

The sower is Jesus, who proclaims the Gospel of the Kingdom of Heaven. Contrary to popular Evangelical beliefs, the seed is not the Word of God. The seeds are people who hear the Gospel. The

259

field is the world. Jesus sows in the world people who hear the Gospel. Therefore, He expects a harvest from the people He plants in the world. Where did He plant you in His field? Is your life producing the crop desired by Him? The condition of your soul's soil determines your willingness and ability to receive, believe, and act on the Word of God.

After teaching His disciples the Parable of the Sower, without skipping a beat, Jesus immediately taught them the following parable. The Parable of the Tares, however, has noticeable differences from the Parable of the Sower. In the Parable of the Tares, two people sow two different seed types. The first sower is Jesus. The second sower is Satan. The first group of the seed represents the saints of God. The second group of the seed represents Christian lookalikes. Jesus identified the first group as wheat, and the second group as tares, a noxious weed that mimics wheat.

Another parable put he forth unto them, saying, The kingdom of heaven is likened unto a man which sowed good seed in his field: but while men slept, his enemy came and sowed tares among the wheat, and went his way. But when the blade was sprung up, and brought forth fruit, then appeared the tares also. So the servants of the householder came and said unto him, Sir, didst not thou sow good seed in thy field? from whence then hath it tares? He said unto them, An enemy hath done this. The servants said unto him, Wilt thou then that we go and gather them up? But he said, Nay; lest while ye gather up the tares, ye root up also the wheat with them. Let both grow together until the harvest: and in the time of harvest I will say to the

reapers, Gather ye together first the tares, and bind them in bundles to burn them: but gather the wheat into my barn.

Matthew 13:24-30

After the crowd departed, Jesus and His disciples entered the nearby house. The puzzled disciples asked Jesus to explain the Parable of the Tares. Jesus gave them the explanation. There are no mysteries about the parable's meaning. There can be no differences of opinion in interpreting it without contradicting the Lord's words. Jesus gave us the key to unlocking the code. Using His key, we know that:

- The sower of the good seed is Jesus Christ
- The field is the world
- The good seed are the children of the Kingdom of Heaven
- The tares are the children of the wicked one, Satan.
- The enemy who sowed the tares is Satan
- The harvest is the end of the world
- The reapers are the angels
- Jesus shall dispatch His reapers
- The reapers shall gather out of His kingdom all things that offend Him and those who do iniquity; the list includes the wicked, rebellious, disobedient, enemies of the Christian faith and people who place stumbling blocks in the path of souls desiring salvation
- The reapers shall toss the tares into a furnace of fire
- There shall be wailing and gnashing of teeth among the tares in the furnace of fire
- Then shall the righteous shine forth as the sun in the kingdom of their Father.

He answered and said unto them, He that soweth the good seed is the Son of man; the field is the world; the good seed are the children of the kingdom; but the tares are the children of the wicked one; the enemy that sowed them is the devil; the harvest is the end of the world; and the reapers are the angels. As therefore the tares are gathered and burned in the fire; so shall it be in the end of this world. *The Son of man shall send forth his angels, and they shall gather out of his kingdom all things that offend, and them which do iniquity; and shall cast them into a furnace of fire: there shall be wailing and gnashing of teeth.* Then shall the righteous shine forth as the sun in the kingdom of their Father. Who hath ears to hear, let him hear.

Matthew 13:37-43

Beware the Tares, but Don't Uproot Them

Using the interpretation provided by Jesus, the Parable of the Tares teaches us that there are two classes inside the worldwide Church: wheat and tares. They are in every local church, ministry, Bible college, seminary, Christian radio station, Christian television station, religious publishing house, and every other entity that claims it represents the Kingdom of God. The sower, of course, is Jesus Christ, the Son of Man, the seed of the woman, the son of David, who goes throughout the world sowing people who heard the Gospel. The field is the world which Jesus, the seed sower, claims full ownership. The enemy is Satan, the fallen angel who is the enemy of Christ. In the parable, the enemy deliberately committed a malicious act of revenge by sowing tares among the wheat.

262

The wheat represents the saints for whom the Savior died, the fruit of His work on the Cross, and resurrection. The tares are the offspring of Satan. They are worthless weeds that resemble wheat, spiritual impostors that mimic wheat but are false. The reapers are angels, the harvest is the end of the world, and the furnace is the lake of fire.

Why did Jesus classify humanity into two groups: wheat and tares? Grain is the substance used worldwide to produce life-sustaining bread. Jesus called Himself the bread of life. He said that man does not live by bread alone but by every word that proceeds out of the mouth of God. Jesus said whoever comes to Him shall never hunger because He is the true bread from Heaven that gives life unto the world. He is the Bread of Life. Thus, Jesus referred to His disciples like wheat. Each fruitful stalk of wheat produces grain which supplies bread to spiritually hungry souls. Therefore, Christ identifies His disciples by their fruitfulness for the growth and expansion of the Kingdom of Heaven.

Jesus also used wheat to teach a lesson about His death and resurrection. He said that unless a grain of wheat falls into the ground and dies, it will remain alone on the surface of the land. However, when it dies in the soil, it will germinate and produce a rich grain harvest. Therefore, God had to permit the death and burial of Jesus so that Christ could be resurrected and bring forth much fruit for God's kingdom, meaning the Church. Thus, wheat represents life and resurrection. That is why many traditional churches use works of art that feature wheat and grapes to represent the Eucharist, the Lord's Supper.

What about tares? The Biblical Greek word is *zizanion*. Most likely, Jesus was referring to darnel, ryegrass that grows in Palestine and has a life cycle like wheat. Darnel is a worthless noxious weed that so closely resembles wheat during the growth cycle that farmers can only distinguish the difference between it and wheat as harvest time draws near. It is a lookalike plant that has no useful purpose. Darnel, however, is poisonous and can contaminate wheat grain. A fungus that often infects the darnel can produce dizziness and nausea when consumed by humans and livestock. The Latin word for darnel is the root of the English word "drunk."

Spiritually, tares are fruitless persons who mimic wheat in the Church of God. The Word of God does not dwell in tares. Often, they possess an intellectual knowledge of the Holy Bible, but it does not reside in their hearts. Tares waste valuable resources by entangling the wheat and usurping needed soil nutrients and moisture.

Churches and ministries that cater to the whimsical, superficial needs of tares who have no interest in knowing the Word of God and expanding the Kingdom of Heaven on Earth waste vast amounts of financial resources donated each year worldwide for the Gospel. Tares are toxic too. They infect wheat grains with funguses that cause dizziness. Doctrines and rituals contrary to the Word of God interspersed by tares in churches globally have produced much confusion in the Body of Christ.

A similar metaphor for wheat and tares is wheat and chaff. Technically, the chaff is the husk, the shell that encases the wheat grain. The farmer must remove the worthless husks before using the gain to make food. Threshing and winnowing are the methods used in ancient times and still today in third-world countries to separate the husks and dispose of them. Threshing involves pounding the wheat sheaves against wooden bars to separate the grains from the stalks. Winnowing separates the chaff from the grains by pouring the wheat on a windy day from a height and allowing the wind to blow away the useless husks.

John the Baptist told his disciples that he baptized sinners with water unto repentance, but there was One coming who would baptize them with the Holy Spirit and fire. He said the Messiah would have a fan in His hand to thoroughly purge His floor, to gather His wheat into the garner, and to burn up the chaff with unquenchable fire.

In the Parable of the Tares, Satan deceitfully planted tares to grow next to the wheat while the farmers slept. Sleep represents spiritual laziness, apathy, indifference, and neglect. In Psalm 1:4, the Holy Bible says that the ungodly "are like the chaff which the wind drives away." King David prayed that his enemies would be "as chaff before the wind, and may the angel of the Lord cast them down."

Isaiah said God would destroy evildoers "as the fire devours the stubble and the flame consumes the chaff." The Old Testament prophet also said that God's enemies "shall become like fine dust, and the multitude of the ruthless ones as chaff which blows away; and it shall happen in an instant, suddenly."

Yes, the tares shall be blown away to Hell's furnace in an instant. Jesus Christ shall come suddenly and unexpectedly, visibly and noisily, to sweep useless husks into a fiery furnace encased in spiritual darkness so deep that the flames will be invisible. Nobody will be able to rescue them no matter how loud they scream because their shouts of agony will not penetrate Hell's walls to reach the saints living on the New Earth.

In the parable, Jesus said the man, meaning Himself, planted good seed in his field. The field represents the world. Thus, Jesus declared His ownership of the world. While men slept, the evil one maliciously planted the tares in the farm field that did not belong to him. He got away with the dastardly crime because good men and women were too drowsy to stay awake to guard the field against the devilish intruder. Satan most heavily scatters his darnel seed in the places where the Word of God is flourishing the most. The Dragon weakens the harvest by sowing confusion and compromise in local church congregations zealous for God.

During the growing season, tares are often indistinguishable from wheat. Only God and His angels know who are the wheat and who are the tares within His Church. In every organization that claims to represent Jesus Christ, there are tares mingled among the wheat. Physical appearances can be deceiving. A heavily tattooed Bible college janitor may be walking closely with Christ while the polished, well-dressed college dean is inwardly working against Christ by slyly introducing doctrines of devils into his students' minds. Meanwhile, a young man or woman delivered from homosexuality could be living a chaste life before the Lord in deep brokenness and humility. At the same time, that person's self-righteous pastor may be secretly living a decadent private life filled with pornography, adultery, and drunkenness.

Only God's eyes see the true hearts of people. Only He knows who is genuine and who is fake. Born again, baptized, command-ment-keeping Christians are the wheat, and they are in every Christian church in the world. Hypocrites, heretics, apostates, liars, homosexuals, fornicators, adulterers, liars, and thieves are in every church in the world. God prohibits His saints from pulling up tares. Satan planted darnel seeds in thousands of churches. Some of them are growing tall behind pulpits! Some are esteemed professors in

Christian colleges and seminaries. Others are famous authors and hosts of television and radio shows and podcasts.

Faithful Christians may identify and expose the imposters, but they are not authorized to rip them out of the ground. Likewise, the Lord does not expect His saints to allow tares to flourish in churches unchallenged. Vigorous defense of the Apostles' Doctrine will expose the tares and drive them away from faithful saints.

So shall it be at the end of the world: the angels shall come forth, and sever the wicked from among the just, and shall cast them into the furnace of fire: there shall be wailing and gnashing of teeth.

Matthew 13:49-50

God does not punish the wicked now because He is waiting until the end of the age. Until Christ returns, wheat and tares will grow and flourish together. If God sends judgment upon the wicked, the wheat will suffer too. The identity of tares will become more evident the closer we get to harvest time. Meanwhile, the Lord allows His wheat to grow alongside Satan's tares. It's always been that way. It will remain that way until the final day. When harvest time comes, God will commission His reapers to separate the wheat and tares into two groups: the righteous saved and the wicked lost. Angels will pursue the tares, bundle them, and cast them into the lake of fire's eternal flames of torment. Let the professionals pull up the tares.

Jesus could not be more straightforward and direct in His message to humanity. Useless tares shall spend eternity in Hell's flames. Judgment Day will not be a court trial where defendants can present their case and call witnesses in their defense. Instead, it will be a very short sentencing hearing. They will arrive in God's courtroom already convicted as guilty. Why? Because during their lifetime on Earth, they rejected salvation through Jesus Christ or mocked the Lord by pretending to be His disciple while secretly offending Him. The Supreme Judge of the Universe shall sentence the guilty: eternity in the everlasting lake of fire, complete separation from God, and the blotting out of their names from God's memory forever. Their resurrected bodies will burn forever in extreme agony.

The Parable of the Tares is a prophecy parable about the end of the age of humanity. Many modern Bible prophecy teachers overlook it because it refutes the Christian Zionists' adamant assertion that Jesus will first secretly gather His saints in an invisible Rapture event before the start of great tribulation and return seven years later. That doctrine is utter nonsense.

In the Parable of the Tares, Jesus gave us easy-to-understand teaching about what will happen when He returns. Who gets plucked up first by the angels on the final day? The righteous or the wicked? Clearly, Jesus said His angels would first gather the wicked. Jesus will say to the angels, "Gather together first the tares…." When will Christian saints be caught up in the air to meet Jesus? The Lord said, "then shall the righteous shine forth as the sun in the kingdom of their Father." It follows the gathering, binding, bundling, and burning of the tares. The righteous shall shine after angels bundle the wicked.

The message is clear. Tares shall be bundled for the firepit immediately upon Jesus' arrival on the final day. Gehenna's roaring flames are unextinguishable. The excruciating, unbearable, agonizing pain of perpetual burning in roaring flames forever is too much for mortals to comprehend. God will not send anybody into the fire. The tares will plunge themselves into Hell's fiery pit by their refusal to submit in this life to the lordship of Jesus Christ, the King of Glory.

The World's Biggest Fish Fry

Friday night fish-fry dinners attract lots of hungry diners in many American communities each week. Battered or breaded fish fillets are deep-fried and served with potato pancakes, coleslaw, hushpuppies, and other side dishes.

Jesus, too, attended many fish-fry dinners during His days on Earth. His last meal with the disciples was a fish-fry breakfast on the shore of the Sea of Tiberias. The resurrected Messiah fried fish on charcoal and served the fish to seven of His disciples, including fresh bread. His last meal on Earth was a fish fry. One of His first actions on Earth, when He returns, will be a fish fry too.

Jesus cast His net into the Sea of Mankind a long time ago, the day Adam and Eve were evicted from the Garden of Eden. His fishnet has been subtly present in humanity's oceans of life for thousands of years. Generations of men and women have come and gone, but few were mindful of the net's presence.

The Parable of the Net teaches us that the world is a vast sea populated by diverse races, ethnicities, cultures, languages, and customs. All dwell inside the great drag net deliberately placed in the world by the Creator. The net calmly floats in the world's Sea of Mankind. Throughout centuries, men and women lived their lives unaware or denied that they existed inside a massive divine drag net. The Master Fisherman gave them plenty of room to move inside His global net and exercise their free will to make choices.

Some made the right choices. Most made bad decisions while living inside His net.

The drag net is still floating in the world's seas of humanity today. The current population of humans is making choices as individuals swim to and fro inside the great drag net. Some people know the net is there, others inwardly know but outwardly deny its existence, and many simply don't care that an end-of-the-world drag net surrounds them.

What is God's drag net? It is the Gospel of the Kingdom. The world is a vast sea of humanity, and the preaching of the pure Gospel of the Kingdom is the casting of a net into that sea to catch men and women. God called men to become fishermen of human souls and charged them to oversee His net in each generation. The preaching of the Gospel of the Kingdom is how the Holy Spirit draws lost souls in the net to salvation through faith in Jesus Christ.

The net is colorblind. It makes no distinctions between skin colors. All varieties of human beings are within the net. The net does not prefer one social class over another, nor one type of education, one level of wealth, or nationality. The Great Gospel Net seeks human fish of every kind. There is no discrimination regarding which fish are allowed in the net. The Great Gospel Net surrounds all humanity. No humans are swimming outside of it.

The discrimination, however, will occur on the final day. In this life, good people and evil people dwell side by side. Neither side cares much for the company of the other. Good people and bad people will continue to mingle in this life until the final day. On that day, the Master Fisherman will instruct His angelic assistants to yank the Great Gospel Net and close it forever suddenly. The angels will haul it to shore and begin the process of separating the fish within its meshes into two piles: Saved and unsaved. The putrid evil fish caught in the net will be separated and burned in a fiery furnace. It will be the biggest fish fry ever.

> **Again, the kingdom of heaven is like unto a net, that was cast into the sea, and gathered of every kind: which, when it was full, they drew to shore, and sat down, and gathered the good into vessels, but cast the bad away. So shall it be at the end of the world: the angels shall come forth, and sever the wicked from among the just, and shall cast them into the furnace of fire: there shall be wailing and gnashing of teeth.**
>
> **Matthew 13:47-50**

In the Parable of the Net, Jesus said not a single word about a secret, pre-tribulation Rapture event. Christian Zionists would have us believe that the Gospel Net will be closed twice and pulled to shore. According to them, the first angelic drawing of the net will occur at their infamous Rapture event seven years before the Second Coming. If you accept this theology, you must believe that Jesus meant to say that the angels will gather out the good fish on the Rapture day and leave the bad fish in the net and cast it back into the sea where it will remain for another seven years. Furthermore, you must convince yourself that during those seven years, some bad fish will decide to become good to avoid the big fish fry dinner they suddenly know is awaiting them if they don't get away from all the bad fish.

According to Christian Zionists, the angels will haul in the net a second time when Jesus returns seven years after the Rapture. That's not the end of the Rapture fable. God will delay Judgment

Day for a thousand years, according to their narrative. Where do the bad fish reside during the thousand years? Do they stay in the net awaiting their eternal fate? Will they be placed in holding ponds on Earth? Christian Zionists have no logical answers that do not contradict the clear words of Jesus Christ.

Jesus said when the net is fully populated, meaning when God decrees that humanity's time is over, the angels will draw it to shore. The angels will separate good fish from bad fish. Angels will cast away the rotten fish. When will the great separation happen? Jesus, not Darby nor Scofield, said, "so shall it be at the end of the world." Angelic reapers will sever the wicked from the righteous. God's angels will throw the evil fish in the furnace of fire where there will be eternal wailing and gnashing of teeth.

The Great Separation of Souls

The Parable of the Tares is like the Parable of the Net. Both parables teach that there will be a great separation of souls on the final day. Jesus said the Kingdom of Heaven is like a net cast into the sea and gathered every kind of fish.

When the net was full, the fishermen pulled it to shore, sat down, and separated the fish into two piles: good and bad. The fisherman kept the good fish but threw away the bad. Likewise, in the Parable of Tares, Jesus said it would be the same at the end of the world when the angels come to Earth and separate the tares from the wheat, meaning the wicked from the righteous. The reapers will cast the tares into the fiery furnace where there shall be wailing and gnashing of teeth.

Both parables are about the great separation of souls. This frightening warning that all human souls, dead and alive, will be separated into two piles on the final day was prevalent in Jesus' teachings. When Jesus departed the temple, his disciples asked him about the temple's future destruction and the sign of his coming, and the end of the age. Jesus gave a long answer that spans across the pages of the twenty-fourth and twenty-fifth chapters of the Gospel According to St. Matthew. His lengthy reply included the Lesson of the Fig Tree, the Parable of the Unfaithful Servant, the Parable of the Ten Virgins, and the Parable of the Talents. These prophecy parables are about the final day.

The New Testament Bible clearly states that there will be a great separation of souls that will happen suddenly, without warning, at the end of the age when Jesus returns. Only baptized, commandment-keeping saints walking in grace and love will be ready for it. In Matthew 25, Jesus said the entire human population would be separated into two groups, beginning with Adam and Eve.

When the Son of Man comes in His glory, and all the holy angels with Him, then He will sit on the throne of His glory. Before Him will be gathered all nations, and He will separate them one from another as a shepherd separates his sheep from the goats. He will set the sheep at His right hand, but the goats at the left.

Matthew 25:31-33

First, Almighty God shall convene the entire human race according to their respective nations. All Asian, South Pacific, and African tribes will congregate. Likewise, all the tribes that ever lived on the European and American continents will assemble too. From the beginning of time, every member of every tribe will take their place for the special meeting. Europe's Saami, Franks, Gothi,

273

Longobardi, and Saxons tribes will be there, along with Africa's San, Nama, Hadza, Hamar, Zulu, and Maasai tribes. King Jesus will convene and preside over the greatest ever United Nations general assembly.

Next, Jesus will instruct His angels to divide each tribe into two groups: sheep and goats. Angels will guide the sheep to stand next to Jesus' right side. They shall lead the goats to His left side. What will happen to the goats on the left? They will be tied and fried!

> **Then He will say to those at the left hand, 'Depart from Me, you cursed, *into the eternal fire*, prepared for the devil and his angels.'**
>
> **Matthew 25:41**

The sheep and goats will go in two different directions and stay in their respective dwelling places for eternity. Undoubtedly, the goats will wail and scream as they are led away by angelic bailiffs, but the Great Judge will not acknowledge their pleas just as they did not acknowledge Christ while they lived on Earth.

Meanwhile, another group of angels will lead the sheep to the gates of New Jerusalem, where they shall enter to find eternal rest. Both goats and sheep made their choices for eternity while living on Earth. Life is fair, after all.

> **And these shall go away into everlasting punishment: but the righteous into life eternal.**
>
> **Matthew 25:46**

Jesus conveys the same truth in multiple parables and sermons. All graves shall open when Jesus shouts. Every dead person since Adam and Eve shall come out of their graves, both righteous and wicked. Angelic reapers shall separate the awakened dead and those living when Jesus returns into two groups: righteous and wicked. The soul reapers will usher the righteous into eternal bliss in the presence of Almighty God, Father, Son, and Holy Spirit, but they shall shove the wicked into Gehenna's blazing furnace of flames where the worms never die. Both groups of humans made choices in this life.

The Parable of the Wedding Banquet

The final day's great separation of souls is present in the Parable of the Wedding Banquet. The parable's message is that religious imposters will be bundled and burned first when the day of the Lord suddenly and unexpectedly arrives and stuns all the mockers and scoffers who laughed at preachers' warnings that the Day of Judgment is coming. The parable in Matthew 25 is about an imposter who sneaked into a wedding banquet improperly dressed.

And Jesus answered and spake unto them again by parables, and said, The kingdom of heaven is like unto a certain king, which made a marriage for his son, and sent forth his servants to call them that were bidden to the wedding: and they would not come. Again, he sent forth other servants, saying, Tell them which are bidden, Behold, I have prepared my dinner: my oxen and my fatlings are killed, and all things are ready: come unto the marriage. But they made light of it, and went their ways, one to his farm, another to his merchandise: and the remnant took his servants, and entreated them spitefully, and slew them. But when the king heard thereof, he was wroth: and he

sent forth his armies, and destroyed those murderers, and burned up their city.

Matthew 22:1-7

In this parable, the certain king, meaning Almighty God, lovingly made way for His wayward, rebellious children's reconciliation to Him through His abundant grace and mercy. The bridegroom is Jesus Christ, the Son of God, the mediator and reconciler between God and man. The servants sent forth to announce the invitation to attend the banquet were the Old Testament prophets, from Methuselah to John the Baptist. The other servants were the Christian apostles and disciples who continued Jesus' ministry after His crucifixion, resurrection, and ascension to Heaven.

The Jews scoffed at God's invitation and stubbornly declared they would not come to the banquet for His Son. They went about their daily affairs while mocking their Jewish brethren in Palestine who believed in the name of Jesus. The rapid growth of the Christian faith throughout Palestine and the surrounding areas provoked Jewish religious rulers to viciously persecute both Jews and Gentiles who believed in the name of Jesus as the promised Messiah. Finally, God sent the Roman army to Jerusalem to destroy the city and its temple and execute the Jews who corporately were guilty of crucifying Jesus and torturing, imprisoning, and killing Christian saints.

Eventually, our Heavenly Father commissioned other servants to go into the highways to find people who would be delighted to be guests at His Son's wedding banquet on the final day. God took this action when it was apparent the Jews would continue to stubbornly refuse His gracious offer of forgiveness and reconciliation because of their wickedness and pride. Therefore, God gleefully opened the doors of Israel to invite everybody to become a citizen. No longer was citizenship in Israel confined to one race of people.

The other servants sent later represent Christian pastors, evangelists, preachers, and teachers who were, and still, today, sent into all the world to preach the Good News. Indeed, other servants include every baptized believer who cheerfully spreads the glory of His name to people near and far.

The Gospel, with all its privileges meant for the Jewish people, was rejected by most Jews. Therefore, the jilted King opened His kingdom to Gentiles and offered them all the blessings intended for the Jews and more! His servants, meaning the Christian saints, have been authorized for over two thousand years to provide anybody and everybody the opportunity to attend the grand wedding banquet on the final day.

Jesus instructed His disciples to gather as many as they found, both bad and good. In the Parable of the Tares and the Parable of the Wedding Banquet, the servants are neither equipped nor authorized to decide who is worthy of being saved nor deciding who is a genuine Christian or an imposter. The Church's assignment is to invite all to come to the wedding party. Church membership rolls contain both wheat and tares. The angelic reapers will do the sorting at harvest time.

Christianity does not discriminate among sinners. Everybody is welcome to come to the fountain and freely drink Christ's living water. There are no prohibitions based on race, skin color, gender, ethnicity, nationality, social status, or financial assets. Likewise, the grossness of a person's sins does not disqualify them from accepting the invitation. The ground is level at the Cross, and the Blood of

Christ can cleanse all stained souls. All people are equal in the eyes of their Maker. Any discrimination or segregation today in local congregations is offensive to God.

> **Then saith he to his servants, The wedding is ready, but they which were bidden were not worthy. Go ye therefore into the highways, and as many as ye shall find, bid to the marriage. So those servants went out into the highways, and gathered together all as many as they found, both bad and good: and the wedding was furnished with guests.**
>
> **Matthew 22:8-10**

The introduction of good and bad people into the story sets up the next scene in the Parable of the Wedding Banquet. Firstly, we must note that none of us are good apart from Jesus Christ. Many people in the world are said to be "good people." However, good people can still be lost if they were never born again through faith in Jesus Christ and water baptism. Christians must invite everybody to attend the banquet. Let each invitee make their own decision about what to do with the invitation. You are not responsible for their decision. Your responsibility is to deliver the invitation.

In the parable, the keen eyes of the King inspected the wedding party's guests. One man caught the attention of the observant host. He was not wearing attire suitable for a wedding party of such royal splendor and nobility. It was not uncommon in ancient times for a king to own a vast wardrobe of elegant garments for classy women and luxurious clothes for dignified men invited to attend royal social events. Thus, the king made sure his guests were properly attired.

In the parable, one man came to the palace inappropriately dressed for the majestic wedding ceremony of the king's son. It was an act of great disrespect. This man brazenly crashed the stately party wearing his dirty work clothes. He casually mingled with guests dressed in spotless wedding garments while wearing filthy rags. His attitude and behavior insulted the imperial host. The gate crasher was disqualified from attending the wedding party because he never bothered to be cleansed before entering the event. He foolishly believed his own merits and worthiness entitled him to participate in the palace party.

The insolent intruder's arrogant act of disrespect was the second offense suffered by the benevolent king. The original list of invitees snubbed the king by declining his invitation. He responded to their rude insult by dispatching the palace servants to the highways to invite anybody who desired to participate in his son's marriage ceremony. Many of the people who eagerly accepted his invitation had no means to acquire royal robes to attend a palace party of such grandeur. The warm-hearted nobleman went out of his way to provide spotless royal garments for everybody so that they could enter and participate while appropriately dressed.

In the sixty-first chapter of the Book of Isaiah, the man of God prophetically spoke in the voice of the Christian Church, thanking God for His kindness in providing to sinners the garments of salvation. Through Isaiah's mouth, the Church said, "I will greatly rejoice in the Lord, my soul shall be joyful in my God; for He hath clothed me with the garments of salvation, He hath covered me with the robe of righteousness, as a bridegroom decketh himself with ornaments, and as a bride adorneth herself with her jewels."

Despite the king's gracious and generous provision of wedding garments for all, the parable's boorish brute butted into the priestly son's wedding party. His rude behavior was an expression of utter contempt for the king. The king had no option other than to confront and remove the intruder from his kingdom's palace.

> **And when the king came in to see the guests, he saw there a man which had not on a wedding garment: and he saith unto him, Friend, how camest thou in hither not having a wedding garment? And he was speechless.** *Then said the king to the servants, Bind him hand and foot, and take him away, and cast him into outer darkness; there shall be weeping and gnashing of teeth. For many are called, but few are chosen.*
>
> **Matthew 22:8-14**

What gave away the imposter when the king's eyes surveyed the festive crowd? The trespasser was outed by his clothing. He dressed inappropriately for a grand ceremony for the king's beloved son at the palace. Would you wear faded blue jeans with holes in both knees, a tattered old sweater, muddy boots, and a baseball cap to attend a state dinner at the White House or a royal garden party at Buckingham Palace? Even if you succeeded in getting past the guards, you would still be the odd duck in the banquet if all the other guests dressed in tuxedos and gowns. You would stand out in the crowd and be quickly spotted.

The king's question, "Friend, how camest thou in hither not having a wedding garment," can be translated as, "My friend, how did you get in here? You are not wearing proper attire. What door did you use to enter this party?" On the final day, Jesus will say to the tares, "How did you get inside my wedding? You are not clothed with robes of righteousness. I am the door. If any man or woman enters in through me, he or she shall be saved. If you had entered the only correct door, you would have been given a proper wedding garment."

When confronted by the king, the imposter was speechless. He had no excuse or defense to justify his behavior. The indignant king summoned the palace security guards and ordered them to evict the imposter. They escorted him through the crowd of merrymakers, festive lights, tables of food, and musicians and tossed him into the pitch darkness of the night where he was vulnerable to wild beasts and violent thieves. He could have stayed inside had he only dressed for the occasion.

Will something make you conspicuous to the reaper angels on the final day? Will something cause you to stand out from the masses of humankind as someone unfit to attend the grand and glorious wedding of Jesus Christ and His bride? When the final day suddenly arrives, each of us must be clothed with garments of salvation, covered with the robe of righteousness, and adorned with jewels. If you are not wearing them, the reaper angels will bind your feet and hands and toss you into outer darkness where you will wail and gnash your teeth forever.

Be silent before the Lord God! For the day of the Lord is at hand; the Lord has prepared the sacrifice; He has consecrated His guests. On the day of the Lord's sacrifice, I will punish the officials and the king's sons, and all who clothe themselves with foreign attire.

Zephaniah 1:7-8

Zephaniah admonished the people to "hush your mouth" in the terrifying presence of Almighty God. There was nothing for them to say. The day of judgment had arrived. Habakkuk, another prophet, cried out, "Let all the earth be silent before Him." Zephaniah said God had prepared a sacrifice. The grossness of Israel's sin became disgusting to the Lord. When men and women refuse to humble themselves and repent of their sins and offer themselves as a living sacrifice, holy and acceptable to God, at that point, the Lord will make those stubborn men and women the sacrifice and victim of their sins.

The king ordered his servants to "bind him hand and foot, take him away, and cast him into out darkness...." Men and women commit sins with their hands and feet. What sinful acts have you ever done with your hands? Where did your feet take you to sin? Therefore, angels shall bind sinners' hands and feet on the final day. They will have no way to escape from Hell's flames.

Once again, we see the same pattern: The wicked, the unrepentant, the hypocrites, the tares, and the imposters shall be bundled and burned first before the grand wedding ceremony commences. The moral of the story is clear: You must be clothed with a robe of righteousness in this life if you expect to wear a garment of salvation in the next life. At a significant expense, the king has provided pure wedding garments for all who desire to attend His Son's glorious wedding on the final day. Only fools would dare attempt to enter the festive event wearing filthy rags of their self-righteousness, not the spotless clean robe of Christ's righteousness. On that day, the angelic reaper angels will gather all unclean people attired in filthy rags, place them on a fiery altar, and present them to God as the sacrifice and victims of their sins.

Reserved Unto Fire Against That Day

As sure as the sun shall rise in the morning, there will be a generation that shall live to see the final day. Perhaps it is your generation. Maybe it will be your grandchildren's generation. It doesn't matter because time does not exist in Heaven. God does not wear a Rolex, nor does He look at a calendar to make plans. The One who created time does not need to measure time for His purposes. Apostle Peter wrote to the churches in Asia Minor that "with the Lord one day is as a thousand years, and a thousand years as one day."

In his second epistle to the churches, St. Peter said he desired to stir up the minds of the saints to remember the predictions of the holy prophets and the commandment of Jesus delivered to them through himself and the other apostles.

> **This is now the second letter that I am writing to you, beloved. In both of them I am stirring up your sincere mind by way of reminder, that you should remember the predictions of the holy prophets and the commandment of the Lord and Savior through your apostles, knowing this first of all, that scoffers will come in the last days with scoffing, following their own sinful desires. They will say, "Where is the promise of his coming? For ever since the fathers fell asleep, all things are continuing as they were from the beginning of creation."**
>
> **2 Peter 3:1-4**

Apostle Peter underlined for emphasis the critical message in his epistle. "Knowing this first of all..." Knowing what first? He reminded them of Old Testament prophecies and New Testament apostolic teachings. What did Apostle Peter proclaim as paramount to remember? The sign that the final day was near would be the prevalence of scoffers in societies worldwide. Such scoffers will pursue their lustful desires and laugh at warnings about the final day.

The rise of cocky, proud mockers of God is a sure sign to Christian saints that the end of the world is rapidly approaching. Mockers and scoffers will exhibit no fear of God. Instead, they will laugh at the mere mention of an all-seeing, all-knowing God who will suddenly and unexpectedly declare a day of judgment for the entire human population, both living and dead. To them, divine judgment is a joke. They laugh at preachers who warn that the day of the Lord is drawing near for humanity. They don't believe there is a supreme being in the universe, let alone a day of judgment.

They see religious people as relics of the past, not members of an enlightened society ruled by an educated class of people who worship technology and science. Today's ruling classes in most Western nations tout their allegiance to values of inclusiveness, tolerance of sexual preferences, diversity, and multi-genderism.

Apostle Peter taught Christians to remember the prophets' prophecies, Jesus and the apostles. Know this first: in the last days, scoffers will appear in societies who will brazenly laugh at and mock righteous men and women who speak about repentance before a day of judgment. Such people will openly flout their lustful sins, brag about them, and encourage others to join them in their lewd and rebellious behavior to display to the world their independence from archaic religious thoughts and values.

A chorus of derisive, contemptuous disdain for God will achieve ascendancy in all levels of society. Atheism will become chic. Faith in God will become an impediment to career advancement. The more insolent atheists become in their hatred of God, the more intimidated will weak Christians become in their fear of social, financial, political, or even physical persecution. The good news is that there will be a remnant of God's people who will not cower before the God-haters. Indeed, they will double-down in their open worship of Jesus Christ and obedience to His commandments. The louder the atheists shout at them to stop saying the name of Jesus, the louder the faithful saints will proclaim the glory of His name.

What will be the familiar cry of the atheistic mockers of God? Their universal question will be, "Where is the promise of his coming?" Characterized by their contempt of God and wicked disdain for righteousness, these scoffers will arrogantly ask the saints, "Where is your god? Where is the evidence he exists? Where is proof your god will manifest himself in our dimension and judge us?"

Mockers and scoffers will say to Christians, "You religious zealots have existed since the beginning of mankind, always threatening the rest of us with divine judgement if we do not obey your invisible god's old book of religious rules. Where is this god? Where is his mighty rod of judgment?"

The Christian faith says Jesus Christ will return on the final day to open the graves, raise the dead, gather His saints in the air, judge the wicked, destroy the world, and usher in New Jerusalem. Today's incredulous mockers and scoffers exclaim in disbelief, "We have heard this stuff since the beginning of time!" Apostle Peter admonished saints to be ready for the arrival of mockers and scoffers laughingly asking the Church, "Where is the evidence of your god's promise to come back to Earth?" Such mocking will be a primary sign that the end of the age is approaching rapidly.

Mockers voluntarily choose to be ignorant; thus, they will automatically believe Satan's lies because they willfully do not desire to know the truth. Heaven's response to such people is to send them a delusion that will spiritually seal their eyes forever, thus preventing them from ever seeing the truth. The Lord will give them over to reprobate minds because they possess no desire to acquire knowledge of God and the Kingdom. Consequently, God will prevent them from entering His kingdom.

As humanity marches toward its final day, many will deliberately ignore crucial information: Noah's Great Flood! St. Peter the Apostle prophesied that in the last days, people would be willingly ignorant that God flooded the world with water ages ago and that He would burn the planet in the subsequent global judgment. Peter said God had reserved the Earth and cosmos in storage as they await the grandest inferno in world history. Our planet, atmosphere, and universe will be engulfed and consumed in flames.

The only souls who will survive the fire flood will be people sealed in the ark of baptism. In the third chapter of his first epistle to the churches, St. Peter compared water baptism with entering Noah's Ark. The saving of eight souls by water, said Peter, is a figure whereunto baptism does now save us by the resurrection of Jesus Christ.

Apostle Peter warned that people should not foolishly think that God is forgetful or slow to fulfill His promises. He is holding back the final day to give sinful men and women more time to repent and be saved through faith in the name of Jesus Christ and baptism into His Church. God does not desire to punish the wicked. His heart longs for them to know Jesus Christ as the Savior of the world. God's sin amnesty commenced at the Cross on Calvary's hill. The unconditional pardon of all sins is readily available to all who will come to Jesus, seeking forgiveness and salvation. The sin amnesty ends when the final day begins.

The Final Day Shall Come as a Thief in the Night

Every passing day brings us one day closer to the expiration date of God's merciful sin amnesty. Saint Peter said the final day would come suddenly and unexpectedly like a thief who barges into your house after midnight and sets your home on fire, engulfing you in consuming flames as you sleep. The thief in the night is the day of the Lord.

The Lord is not slack concerning his promise, as some men count slackness; but is longsuffering to us-ward, not willing that any should perish, but that all should come to repentance. *But the day of the Lord will come as a thief in the night; in which the heavens shall pass away with a great noise, and the elements shall melt with fervent heat, the earth also and the works that are therein shall be burned up.*

2 Peter 3:9-10

Therefore, how shall we live knowing that a consuming fire from Heaven shall dissolve our planet? In what spiritual state should Jesus Christ find us upon His glorious return? Before both men and God, Peter said our conversations and behavior must be holy and godly. Our thoughts, words, prayers, and actions must attest to an earnest, heartfelt yearning for Jesus Christ to return. All humans will see the fiery destruction of the cosmos on the final day. The awakened dead and those alive when Christ return shall see it. The righteous and the wicked shall see it too. Thus, Apostle Peter encourages all men and women by asking, "Since you will see everything dissolved by fire, what kind of person ought you be now while you are still living?"

Seeing then that all these things shall be dissolved, what manner of persons ought ye to be in all holy conversation and godliness, looking for and hasting unto the coming of the day of God, *wherein the heavens being on fire shall be dissolved, and the elements shall melt with fervent heat?* Nevertheless we, according to his promise, look for new heavens and a new earth, wherein dwelleth righteousness.

2 Peter 3:11-13

Payday is coming. The Creator will bestow upon every man and woman who ever lived in the history of the world their just rewards for the way they lived. Persecutors of the righteous should take heed! God will punish those who caused trouble for Christians who sought to live holy lives for God. As the antichrist forces greatly persecute the saints of God, the Lord will spring a reversal upon them. He will transfer to themselves the affliction and pain they impose upon the Church but in more significant measure. Simultaneously, Christ will bestow rest to the afflicted righteous saints. It will happen suddenly and unexpectedly when Jesus and His angels are revealed in flaming fire to repay the wicked who persecuted His disciples with persecution.

...seeing it is a righteous thing with God to recompense tribulation to them that trouble you; and to you who are troubled rest with us, when the Lord Jesus shall be revealed

from heaven with his mighty angel in flaming fire taking vengeance on them that know not God, and that obey not the gospel of our Lord Jesus Christ: who shall be punished with everlasting destruction from the presence of the Lord, and from the glory of his power; when he shall come to be glorified in his saints, and to be admired in all them that believe (because our testimony among you was believed) in that day.

2 Thessalonians 1:6-10

Psalms 104:4 says God makes angels His ministers of flaming fire. In his second epistle to the church in Thessalonica, Apostle Paul said God's mighty angels would arrive to take "vengeance" on all who did not know God and did not obey the Gospel of Jesus. They shall be sentenced to everlasting destruction, separated from the presence of the Lord and His glory and power.

Psalms 21:9 says God shall make His enemies "as a fiery oven in the time of thine anger...swallow them up...and the fire shall devour them." Psalms 97:3 says a fire goes before God "and burneth up his enemies." Psalms 106:18 declares that "a fire was kindled" amidst the Hebrews who worshipped the golden calf, and "the flame burned up the wicked."

New World Order Religion

Presently, human societies are decoupling from their religious past and embracing atheism. Western nations are increasingly becoming godless. Many prophecy teachers have taught that the future Antichrist will establish a worldwide religion. Reformation-era theologians and preachers wrongly predicted it would be

Roman Catholicism. More recent teachers have taught that a future universal religion will synthesize many religions.

Presently, it appears that the universal religious mindset of the world will someday be global atheism. The New Nimrods are currently promoting and using atheism to decouple the world's population from Christianity. However, the denial of God's existence is merely the path the New Nimrods must take humankind to prepare them to accept their ultimate world religion: Luciferianism. The nations' ruling classes will someday openly embrace and worship their true god, Lucifer, the devil. Luciferianism will eventually become the only religion permitted to exist in the world. Daniel's fourth beast will be a revived Luciferian empire, the government of Satan that ruled the world before the Great Flood.

Therefore, do not be dismayed by the God-haters' loud voices in the last days. Understand that they hate Jesus because they love Satan. Mockers' loud voices of scorn are the key sign that Jesus' return is imminent. St. Peter said they would scornfully ridicule anybody who brings up Noah's name and points to the Great Flood as evidence that God destroyed all humans except for eight people.

Noah preached righteousness and repentance for many years as he constructed the ark. People foolishly ignored Noah's warnings of impending judgment. People heard Noah's preaching, but they scoffed at his sermons. Noah was smeared as a conspiracy theory-believing lunatic until the downpour began and the underground rivers burst onto the Earth's surface.

The worldwide flood came suddenly and unexpectedly. Nobody, except Noah and his family, was prepared to live through the deluge. Why? Because Noah was moved by faith and fear. Fear is not always a bad thing. Sometimes faith and fear work together to accomplish God's will on Earth. In the Book of Hebrews, Apostle Paul wrote, "By faith Noah, being warned of God of things not seen as yet, moved with fear, prepared an ark to the saving of his house; by the which he condemned the world, and became heir of the righteousness which is by faith."

Noah's fear was in response to the divine warning of impending judgment. He heard God, and he believed. Therefore, Noah was very afraid. He got busy building an ark to escape the judgment. Without fear, Noah most likely would have never finished building the ark. The normalcy bias would have replaced his motivation to complete the assignment on time. Noah's obedience was evidence of his fear of God and his faith in his Maker. He had faith in God, but he was "moved with fear" to get busy with his hands building an ark. Faith without works is dead. His obedience in response to the divine warning also made visible the unbelief of the world that mocked the divine warning. Thus, God declared Noah to be righteous.

Everybody who hears divinely inspired messages that the final day is coming must, by faith, be moved with fear to prepare for that day. They must ignore scoffers and mockers. The Creator promised Noah He would never flood the world again with water. Rain will not fall from the sky, nor will rivers spring up from beneath the planet's surface. Instead, fire will rain down from above and erupt from below. The deluge came quickly in Noah's day. So too will the fire in our day.

Isaiah said Hell had enlarged itself and opened its mouth without measure, and multitudes shall descend into it. Who will descend into Hell's wide mouth? Every life that does not bring forth good fruit for God's kingdom, all names that not in the

Book of Life, whoever does not know God, and whoever offends children. Hell's mouth shall swallow such people, and they shall descend to the lake of unquenchable fire.

The Second Coming of Jesus Christ on the final day shall be:

- Singular
- Sudden and unexpected
- Atmospheric
- Visible
- Noisy
- Disruptive
- Fiery

CHAPTER 8

HIS SECOND COMING SHALL BE GLORIOUS

H IS FIRST ARRIVAL ON Earth attracted little attention. Yes, a small number of shepherds watching sheep on the hillsides outside Bethlehem saw and heard angels singing in the nighttime sky. At first, those eyewitness accounts stirred excitement among the town's inhabitants. However, as the years passed, the fantastic stories faded into folklore told by older adults and women to children. Besides, the family moved away from Bethlehem to Nazareth. The singing angels, the bright star, and the mysterious wise men were old news.

His second arrival will be a global showstopper. The first time, few people on Earth were aware of His arrival. The second time, everybody will know He's back. The first time, Jesus brought grace. The second time, He will bring glory.

For the grace of God that bringeth salvation hath appeared *to all men,* teaching us that, denying ungodliness and worldly lusts, we should live soberly, righteously, and godly, in this present world; *looking for that blessed hope, and the glorious appearing of the great God and our Savior Jesus Christ;* who gave himself for us, that he might redeem us from all iniquity, and purify unto himself a peculiar people, zealous of good works.

Titus 2:11-14

The humble Savior who came with grace for the forgiveness of sin is the same Savior who will come again with great glory for the final judgment of sin and the consummation of all things. The saving work of Jesus Christ began at the Cross: He willingly bore our sins, died to pay the ransom for our souls, descended to the place of the dead, rose from the grave, and ascended to Heaven to intercede for us. We now wait for Jesus to return in great glory to deliver us from God's wrath that will pour out upon the wicked and to usher in the full manifestation of the Kingdom of God.

We look back to the First Advent of Jesus Christ to remind ourselves of God's grace bestowed upon sinners by purchasing our redemption. We look forward to the Second Advent of Jesus Christ with anticipation of Him completing our redemption. Jesus will complete your salvation when He transforms your physical body to a glorified body to house your spirit permanently. The Second Coming of Jesus Christ will change your mortal physical body like His glorious, resurrected body. Thus, your salvation needs both advents of Jesus Christ to be complete because your physical body is still subject to death, which is the curse that came upon all life because of sin. The glorious metamorphosis will happen when your eyes see Jesus in His glorified body.

For our conversation is in heaven; *from whence also we look for the Savior, the Lord Jesus Christ: who shall change our vile body, that it may be fashioned like unto His glorious body,* according to the working whereby he is able even to subdue all things unto himself.

Philippians 3:20-21

The last days began with the First Advent of Jesus Christ and will conclude with His Second Advent. St. John the Apostle wonderfully saw both manifestations of Jesus Christ. The apostle traveled and lived daily with Jesus during our Lord's ministry on Earth. John's eyes saw Jesus as a man who knew hunger, thirst, weariness, and pain in a physical human body. However, in a vision on the Isle of Patmos, Apostle John saw King Jesus reigning in Heaven. His hair was white as snow. His eyes were like flames of fire, and His feet were like polished brass. His voice sounded like many rivers.

And I turned to see the voice that spake with me. And being turned, I saw seven golden candlesticks; and in the midst of the seven candlesticks one like unto the Son of man, clothed with a garment down to the foot, and girt about the paps with a golden girdle. His head and His hairs were white like wool, as white as snow; and His eyes were as a flame of fire; and His feet like unto fine brass, as if they burned in a furnace; and His voice as the sound of many waters. And he had in His right hand seven stars: and out of His mouth went a sharp two-edged sword: and His countenance was as the sun shineth in His strength. And when I saw him, I fell at His feet as dead. And he laid His right hand upon me, saying unto me, Fear not; I am the first and the last: I am he that liveth, and was dead; and, behold, I am alive for evermore, Amen; and have the keys of hell and of death.

Revelation 1:12-18

Three of Jesus' disciples saw the glory of the Lord. Jesus took Peter, James, and John, His brother, to a high mountain. Their eyes beheld the transfiguration of Jesus. His face was as bright as the Sun, and His clothing was white as light. Moses and Elijah appeared and talked with Jesus.

Jesus is no longer the suffering servant. He is now the King of Glory! Every human will see Jesus coming in the clouds with power and great glory. It will not be ordinary glory. He shall come with great glory! His glorious appearance in the sky above the Earth will occur immediately after the tribulation and the darkening of the Sun, the Moon, and stars. Angels will dim the cosmic theater lights so that the show's star can make His grand entrance onto the center stage. There will be no cheap seats in the house with an obstructed view. Every view will be center orchestra seats, and every eye shall see Him! The King Jesus Show will have only one star performing on stage that day.

> Immediately after the tribulation of those days shall the sun be darkened, and the moon shall not give her light, and the stars shall fall from heaven, and the powers of the heavens shall be shaken: and then shall appear the sign of the Son of man in heaven: and then shall all the tribes of the earth mourn, *and they shall see the Son of man coming in the clouds of heaven with power and great glory.* And he shall send His angels with a great sound of a trumpet, and they

shall gather together His elect from the four winds, from one end of heaven to the other.

Matthew 24:29-31

Behold, he cometh with clouds; and every eye shall see him, and they also which pierced him: and all kindreds of the earth shall wail because of him. Even so, Amen.

Revelation 1:7

Why will the Second Advent of Jesus Christ be glorious? His triumphant return will be glorious for only one reason: Jesus is glorious! Therefore, everything He does is glorious. How can we imagine a future event that is unimaginable? How can we comprehend the arrival of a king who is incomprehensible? There is no historical event in humankind's past to reference as an example of what will happen on the final day. No human in history ever saw anything comparable to the grand and glorious arrival of the King of Glory. Waves of eternal praise and thunderous ovations shall resound as the saints of God worship the King of Kings and Lord of Lords.

There will be nobody left to stop you from worshipping Jesus with all your heart, mind, and soul. How long will the first standing ovation last? None of us know. Besides, there will be no more time when Jesus arrives. Unrestrained and joyous cheering, shouting, singing, and worshiping our triumphant King Jesus will fill the sky above the New Earth forever.

Old Testament Prophet Isaiah Saw Jesus

The Holy Bible gives us glimpses of Almighty God's magnificent glory. Old Testament prophet Isaiah saw the Lord's glory. Isaiah saw Jesus. It happened in a vision in the year that King

Uzziah died. The scripture does not indicate whether the vision occurred before or after Uzziah died. We only know it happened in the same year. We also don't know if Isaiah meant the king's physical death or the civil death of his kingship due to leprosy that ravished His body. We simply know that the prophet used the year of the king's civil or physical death to mark the time of the vision. However, one thing we know, is that the Old Testament prophet saw Jesus Christ. How do we know it? We know it because Apostle John said the deity was Jesus Christ.

These things said Isaiah, when he saw His glory, and spake of him.

John 12:41

The sixth chapter of the Book of Isaiah describes the prophet's vision. Isaiah saw Jesus Christ sitting upon a throne, high and lifted up, and His majestic robe filled the ornate temple in Heaven. Above the throne were six-winged seraphim that shouted, "Holy, holy, holy, is the Lord of hosts: the whole earth is full of His glory."

In the year that king Uzziah died I saw also the Lord sitting upon a throne, high and lifted up, and His train filled the temple. Above it stood the seraphim: each one had six wings; with twain he covered His face, and with twain he covered His feet, and with twain he did fly. And one cried unto another, and said, Holy, holy, holy, is the Lord of hosts: the whole earth is full of His glory.

Isaiah 6:1-3

Isaiah did not describe the divine essence of the trinitarian Godhead. No man has seen the face of Almighty God and lived.

In the New Covenant age, the physical manifestation of God given to humanity to behold with their eyes is Jesus Christ, the last Adam. Likewise, the Old Covenant prophet Isaiah was given the manifestation of Yahweh in the personhood of the Messiah, our Lord Jesus Christ.

Interestingly, Isaiah also did not describe the form and appearance of Jesus. Instead, he told the physical setting around Jesus. He beheld the Lord's stately and majestic throne. It was "high and lifted up." He said a spectacular royal robe clothed the Lord. Isaiah was particularly amazed by the grandeur and size of the majestic garment's flowing skirt that filled the holy temple. Isaiah was awestruck by the seraphim that flew above the throne, crying, "Holy, holy, holy is the Lord of hosts: the whole earth is full of His glory." Isaiah said not a word about Jesus' features. He only spoke about His glorious attire, throne, and adoring seraphim.

Moses Saw God's Goodness

The Israelites knew that nobody had ever seen the face of God and lived. Moses encountered Almighty God shortly after the Hebrews greatly sinned by dancing naked around a golden calf idol. Moses took the tabernacle of the congregation and pitched it far from the camp of the rebellious Hebrews. The Hebrews who sincerely sought God went out unto the tabernacle. Moses went too. When the people saw Moses enter the tabernacle, a cloud-like pillar descended and stood at the door of the tabernacle while Moses talked to God. Seeing the pillar, the Hebrews rose and worshipped God. The Book of Exodus says God spoke to Moses as a man speaks to a friend. For a moment, Moses had regained the tremendous privilege and lofty position enjoyed by Adam and Eve, who talked to God daily in the Garden of Eden as friends.

> And Moses took the tabernacle, and pitched it without the camp, afar off from the camp, and called it the Tabernacle of the congregation. And it came to pass, that everyone which sought the Lord went out unto the tabernacle of the congregation, which was without the camp. And it came to pass, when Moses went out unto the tabernacle, that all the people rose up, and stood every man at His tent door, and looked after Moses, until he was gone into the tabernacle. And it came to pass, as Moses entered into the tabernacle, the cloudy pillar descended, and stood at the door of the tabernacle, and the Lord talked with Moses. And all the people saw the cloudy pillar stand at the tabernacle door: and all the people rose up and worshipped, every man in His tent door. And the Lord spake unto Moses face to face, as a man speaketh unto His friend. And he turned again into the camp: but His servant Joshua, the son of Nun, a young man, departed not out of the tabernacle.
>
> **Exodus 33:7-11**

What did Moses say to his friend, Almighty God? After securing God's restoration of the Hebrew people, Moses boldly made one personal request: He asked to see God's glory! His soul hungered to see God's face. He craved the immediate knowledge of Almighty God, which the Lord reserved for angelic spirits and the souls of saints who have departed this world. Moses previously encountered God on the mountain, yet it did not satisfy his soul's hunger for

God. Moses craved a more profound experience with his Maker, the Almighty Creator of the Universe.

In Exodus 33:18, Moses cried to God, "I beseech Thee! Show me thy glory." Yahweh could not fully grant the heartfelt request of His servant and friend Moses. God did, however, allow Moses to see and experience all the divine presence that a mortal human can handle and remain alive on Earth. He gave Moses a fleeting glimpse of a portion of His glory. What Moses saw was God's goodness. Moses' eyes beheld only the afterglow of the glory of God's backside as He walked past him. Had Moses seen anything more, he would have instantly dropped dead because his mortal body's neurons would have been overwhelmed and short-circuited from an electrical overload.

> **And the Lord said unto Moses, I will do this thing also that thou hast spoken: for thou hast found grace in my sight, and I know thee by name. *And he said, I beseech thee, show me thy glory. And he said, I will make all my goodness pass before thee,* and I will proclaim the name of the Lord before thee; and will be gracious to whom I will be gracious, and will shew mercy on whom I will shew mercy. And he said, Thou canst not see my face: for there shall no man see me, and live.**
>
> Exodus 33:17-20

God's goodness and glory are inseparable. Wherever God's goodness is made known, so too is His glory. Likewise, God's goodness is also present whenever His glory is revealed.

As Moses met God at the rock in Horeb, we first met and continue to meet God through Christ the Rock daily. Through the incarnation of Jesus Christ in Mary's womb and His birth in Bethlehem, God revealed Himself to humanity. Blessed Mary's undefiled womb was the holy Ark of the New Covenant.

When the Virgin Mary, whose name and memory is blessed by all generations, gave birth to the Christ child, a heavenly choir of angels sang in the nighttime sky above Bethlehem, "Glory to God in the highest, and on earth peace, good will toward men." God's glory returned to Earth to announce that humankind could have peace and reconciliation with their Maker through faith in the only begotten Son of God. If we hunger to see God the Father, we must first see God the Son.

> **No man hath seen God at any time; the only begotten Son, which is in the bosom of the Father, he hath declared him.**
>
> **John 1:18**

> **Ye have neither heard His voice at any time, nor seen His shape.**
>
> **John 5:37**

> **Not that any man hath seen the Father, save he which is of God, he hath seen the Father.**
>
> **John 6:46**

> **And Jesus cried out and said, "He who believes in Me, does not believe in Me but in Him who sent Me. "He who sees Me sees the One who sent Me.**
>
> **John 12:44-45**

When the day of His crucifixion drew near, Jesus prepared His disciples that He would return to His Father in Heaven. In reassuring them, Jesus admonished them not to allow their hearts to be troubled. He promised that He was going home to prepare a place for them. Jesus said, "and if I go and prepare a place for you, I will come again...." Thomas asked how they would know the way there. Jesus replied by declaring that He *is* the way! Jesus said no human could come to the Father except by him. Philip demanded, "Show us the Father." In John 14:9, Jesus replied, "Have I been with you such a long time, and yet you have not known Me, Philip? He who has seen Me has seen the Father. So how can you say, ‹Show us the Father?"

Philip's heart's cry "show us the Father" was identical to Moses asking God to "show me Thy glory." Yahweh spoke with Moses as a friend. Jesus talked to Philip as a friend. If you see God, you will first see His glory. If you see the Son, you will see His glory. The complete revelation of Almighty God to humanity in this present age is found only in Jesus Christ, the Son of God. Jesus is the Bread of Life and Living Water which abundantly satisfies our hungry, thirsty souls that long to be reconnected with the divine Creator who walked with Adam and Eve in the Garden of Eden and spoke with them as friends.

> **Ye are my friends,** if ye do whatsoever I command you. **Henceforth I call you not servants; for the servant knoweth not what His lord doeth:** *but I have called you friends;* **for all things that I have heard of my Father I have made known unto you.**
>
> John 15:14-15

During the Old Testament times, it was upon the rock in Horeb that Yahweh granted Moses' desire to see His goodness and glory. In New Testament times, it is only upon Christ the Rock that we

303

see God's goodness and glory. When Jesus returns on the final day, all humans will see the fullest and brightest display of His glory. We will not look at His backside as He passes by. Everybody will see His radiant face as He arrives on clouds of great glory.

> ....and then shall appear the sign of the Son of man in heaven: and then shall all the tribes of the earth mourn, *and they shall see the Son of man coming in the clouds of heaven with power and great glory.*
>
> Matthew 24:30

Blow the Trumpet in Zion

God's glory is associated with clouds in the Holy Bible. Scripture references to clouds describe the presence of God on Earth. In the magnificent exodus of the Hebrews out of Egypt, God told Moses that He would come to him in a thick cloud that the people may hear when God spoke to Moses.

> And the Lord said unto Moses, *Lo, I come unto thee in a thick cloud,* that the people may hear when I speak with thee, and believe thee forever. And Moses told the words of the people unto the Lord.
>
> Exodus 19:9

God descended from Heaven to Mount Sinai for a divine visitation with the Hebrew people. Lightning and thunder, a thick cloud, the voice of the trumpet, fire, smoke, and an earthquake heralded His arrival.

> And it came to pass on the third day in the morning, *that there were thunders and lightnings, and a thick cloud upon*

the mount, and the voice of the trumpet exceeding loud; so that all the people that was in the camp trembled. And Moses brought forth the people out of the camp to meet with God; and they stood at the nether part of the mount. *And mount Sinai was altogether on a smoke, because the Lord descended upon it in fire: and the smoke thereof ascended as the smoke of a furnace, and the whole mount quaked greatly.*

Exodus 19:16-18

The same things will happen when Jesus Christ returns on the final day. In the Apocalypse vision seen by Apostle John on the island of Patmos, the apostle saw and heard lightning, thundering, voices, great hail, and a mighty earthquake. As the ancient Hebrews heard "the voice of the trumpet exceeding loud," all inhabitants of the Earth would hear the last trumpet blast when Jesus descends from Heaven to Earth with a mighty shout. He will come with clouds. All who rejected Christ and persecuted His Church shall wail.

Behold, he cometh with clouds; and every eye shall see him, and they also which pierced him: and all kindreds of the earth shall wail because of him. Even so, Amen.

Revelation 1:7

Old Testament prophet Joel foretold of the extraordinary event. He said the saints should blow the trumpet in Zion, sound an alarm in God's holy mountain, and let all the inhabitants tremble for the day of the Lord is coming. The saints are to shout, "Repent! The day of the Lord is coming!"

In the second chapter of the Book of Joel, the prophet said the day of the Lord "is nigh at hand." It will be a day of darkness and gloominess, a day of clouds and thick darkness. He saw an army coming that humanity had never seen in history, nor would ever see again. They will torch everything as they march across the Earth. A great fire will devour everything before them, and a mighty flame will burn after they march through the land. Nothing shall escape their military march through all nations. The Earth will quake before God's army. The heavens above shall tremble as the Sun, Moon, and stars go dark. Joel said the Lord shall utter His voice before His army because His camp is more extensive and mightier than humans can comprehend. He said the day of the Lord is great and very terrible, and nobody can live through it.

Joel prophesied that "it shall come to pass afterward" that God shall pour out His spirit upon all flesh. Sons and daughters shall prophesy, old men shall dream dreams, and young men shall see visions. Joel said God would show wonders in the heavens and the Earth. There shall be blood, fire, and pillars of smoke. The Sun shall be turned into darkness and the Moon into blood. All of it shall happen before the great and terrible day the Lord comes. The good news is Joel's assurance that "whosoever shall call on the name of the Lord shall be delivered: for in mount Zion and in Jerusalem shall be deliverance."

Apostle Peter quoted prophet Joel on the Day of Pentecost when Jesus gave the Holy Spirit to His Church. When the men and women of Jerusalem marveled at the sight and sound of Spirit-filled saints speaking in other languages as they came out of the upper room, Peter told them, "But *this is that* which was spoken by the prophet Joel...." The Jews immediately knew that "this" (the disciples speaking in other languages known by others hearing them) was "that" (the Lord pouring out His spirit on all flesh).

Speaking about the coming day of the Lord, Old Testament prophet Joel said the priests of God must "blow the trumpet in Zion, sanctify a fast, call a solemn assembly, gather the people, sanctify the congregation, assemble the elders, gather the children...." He said the ministers of the Lord should weep and pray that God would spare the people.

"Sanctify the congregation" means the people who claim to be Christians must clean up their lives before the Lord returns. Christians must repent of their sins, turn from their wicked ways, and abstain from unlawful sensual pleasures outside marriage. In short, they must embrace holiness if they desire to see Jesus' glory forever.

Almighty God Desires to Live with the Saints on a New Earth

As goodness is synonymous with God's glory, so too is holiness. The essence of the glory of the Lord is the magnificent radiance of His holiness. The Lord is a morally perfect spiritual being without sin and cannot be in the presence of sin; therefore, He is holy. What does this mean for us? It means everything! Without holiness, no man or woman claiming to be a Christian shall see the Lord when He returns.

> Follow peace with all men, *and holiness, without which no man shall see the Lord....*
>
> Hebrews 12:14

It is the responsibility of all Christians to prepare themselves for the final day. Daily repentance is necessary for all Christians because "all have sinned, and come short of the glory of God." There must be true repentance of personal sins, genuine sorrow for sinful ways in their lives, and forsaking all such sins as proof that they have genuinely repented.

Jesus shall return on clouds of great glory, and His glory is the radiance of His holiness. Without holiness, no man or woman shall see the Lord. Therefore, the Church must be holy! Our Lord Jesus Christ will present to God the Father "a glorious church, not having spot, or wrinkle, or any such thing; but that it should be holy without blemish." In other words, we must be holy.

> **Wherefore, beloved, seeing that ye look for such things, *be diligent that ye may be found of him in peace, without spot, and blameless.***
>
> 2 Peter 3:14

> **Husbands, love your wives, even as Christ also loved the church, and gave himself for it; that he might sanctify and cleanse it with the washing of water by the word, *that he might present it to himself a glorious church, not having spot, or wrinkle, or any such thing; but that it should be holy and without blemish.***
>
> Ephesians 5:25-27

In Old Covenant times, the tabernacle was the portable dwelling place of God transported by the Hebrews from the Exodus until the conquest of Canaan. It was also known as the Tent of the Congregation. God's glory sanctified the tabernacle. In the glorified, holy tabernacle, God met with the children of Israel.

And there I will meet with the children of Israel, and the tabernacle shall be sanctified by my glory.

Exodus 29:43

In the New Covenant age, Jesus Christ is our high priest and our perfect tabernacle God did not make with human hands. God meets with the children of Israel, meaning the Church, in the glorified, holy tabernacle, Jesus Christ, the resurrected Savior of the world. Apostle Peter referred to Jesus as a "living stone." Indeed, St. Peter was referencing Isaiah 28:16, in which God declares that He will "lay in Zion for a foundation a stone, a tried stone, a precious cornerstone, a sure foundation...."

The New Testament temple is not a physical building in Jerusalem constructed with expensive stones and gold. God built the new temple on a living stone, a sure foundation chosen by God. Apostle Peter's "living stone" is not a breathing rock with eyes, a mouth, and a heartbeat. The living stone is the resurrected Son of God, Jesus Christ, who is alive forever, chosen by Almighty God as the sure foundation upon which God would build a new temple constructed with "lively stones."

What or who are the lively stones? Each born-again Christian saint is a lively stone in God's new temple. God places us upon Jesus Christ, the living stone, the chief cornerstone. The entire New Testament temple is composed of living materials from the foundation to the roof. Together, Jesus and His disciples form a spiritual house, a holy priesthood, who offer spiritual sacrifices made acceptable to God by Jesus Christ. This Biblical truth is the primary evidence why Christian Zionism's quest to build a third temple in Jerusalem is blasphemous.

To whom coming, as unto a living stone, disallowed indeed
of men, *but chosen of God,* and precious, *ye also, as lively
stones, are built up a spiritual house, an holy priesthood,*
to offer up spiritual sacrifices, acceptable to God by Jesus
Christ.

1 Peter 2:4-5

Thus, the physical bodies of born again, baptized, command-
ment-keeping disciples of Jesus Christ are "lively stones" because
the Holy Spirit dwells inside them. Apostle Paul asked Christians
in Corinth if they understood that God joined their physical bodies
to Jesus' resurrected body and that He purchased them with a
costly price.

Know ye not that your bodies are the members of Christ?
shall I then take the members of Christ, and make them
the members of an harlot? God forbid. What? know ye
not that he which is joined to an harlot is one body? for
two, saith he, shall be one flesh. *But he that is joined unto
the Lord is one spirit.* Flee fornication. Every sin that a
man doeth is without the body; but he that committeth
fornication sinneth against his own body. *What? know ye
not that your body is the temple of the Holy Ghost which
is in you, which ye have of God, and ye are not your own?
For ye are bought with a price: therefore glorify God in
your body, and in your spirit, which are God's.*

1 Corinthians 6:15-20

Apostle John the Revelator heard a great voice from Heaven
proclaiming that the tabernacle of God is with men, and He shall

dwell with them and be their God. The Old Covenant's tabernacle of the congregation, the tent of meeting, was a tented palace for Israel's true king. It was a miniature Garden of Eden. The entrance faced east, and cherubim guarded it. The lampstand represented the Tree of Life, and the law was the Tree of Knowledge of Good and Evil.

The tabernacle represented God's house among His people Israel. During His earthly ministry, Jesus Christ tabernacled with God's people. He dwelt among them, and the people beheld His glory. He was and is and shall forever be full of grace and truth.

> **And the Word was made flesh, and dwelt among us, (and we beheld his glory, the glory as of the only begotten of the Father,) full of grace and truth.**
>
> **John 1:14**

In the Old Covenant age, the tabernacle was a tent where God's Spirit resided among the people of Israel. While Jesus Christ was physically on the Earth, He was the tabernacle. After Jesus ascended to Heaven, He sent the Holy Spirit on Pentecost to dwell in our physical bodies, the new temple. In the eternal age to come, something more awesome will happen! Apostle John heard "a great voice out of Heaven." The heavenly voice called upon hearers to "behold," meaning to fix their eyes with great attention to something spectacular to observe.

> **And I heard a great voice out of heaven saying, Behold, the tabernacle of God is with men, and he will dwell with them, and they shall be His people, and God himself shall be with them, and be their God.**
>
> **Revelation 21:3**

What is the astonishing thing we should behold? Almighty God will relocate His official personal address from the City of Heaven to New Jerusalem, the new Garden of Eden. The tabernacle of God will be with the saints, and Yahweh shall once again dwell in the Garden of Eden with the humans He made. No more shall there be a separation between the Creator and the saved children made in His image. They will live together in the same city. We shall be His people, and He shall be our God.

Jesus' Glory Was Made Known Through Miracles

During Jesus' earthly ministry, St. John the Apostle said the Word was made flesh and dwelt among us, and humans beheld the glory of Jesus. John described Him as "full of grace and truth."

How was Jesus' glory made known to humanity? He revealed His glory to humans through the miracles He performed. Jesus' first miracle was done for His mother when He turned average water into great wine. The miracle was the first ray of hope for humanity that emanated from the Word of God arriving on Earth in human flesh to dwell among men. The Messiah who can change water into wine can spiritually change wine into blood in the Lord's Supper. In the Old Testament, wine was a symbol of gladness. In the New Testament, wine is the emblem of our Savior's blood that He shed for the remission of sins. Thus, the new wine is an emblem of our gladness, representing God's forgiveness of our sins through the shed blood of Jesus. The choice of a wedding feast as the venue to perform His first miracle on Earth also points to the great wedding feast that God will convene when the Bridegroom is married to His bride New Jerusalem.

This beginning of miracles did Jesus in Cana of Galilee, *and manifested forth his glory*; and his disciples believed on him.

John 2:11

Each miracle manifested the glory of Jesus. People believed in Him as the Messiah. Although the miracles were stunning and impressive, the greatest manifestation of the Lord's glory was not the miracles. Then, as it still is today, His most remarkable display of glory is His love for humanity. The most outstanding display of Jesus' love for mankind was His willingness to be sacrificed on a wooden cross for the sins of the world. We see Jesus' greatest miracles in the salvation of lost souls and the transformation of their lives. He can take people out of the vilest sins and place them in His kingdom of light. Nothing compares with such miracles of grace. Yes, He can turn water into wine, but, even more incredible, Jesus can turn winos into winners. Jesus saves.

Believers glorify Jesus by living holy lives, separated from the world's filth. Righteous living and loving everybody glorify Jesus Christ and inspire sinners to believe in the name of Jesus. God's divine plan is to dwell, meaning to tabernacle, with His chosen people, the Christian saints, in New Jerusalem for eternity. If you desire to live with God in the future, you must live a holy, sanctified life now because no sinful person will be permitted to dwell in New Jerusalem. Flesh and blood cannot inherit the Kingdom of God; therefore, you must be born again by the Spirit and baptized into Christ's Church. Corrupt souls cannot inherit that which is incorruptible. The time for repentance and the embrace of holiness is before you take your last breath on Earth

313

or before the final day when Jesus returns to Earth on clouds of great glory.

Our Transformation Occurs
When We See Jesus in His Glory

St. Paul the Apostle said not every Christian shall die. There will be a chosen generation of saints who will never experience physical death and the grave. They will be the Christians living on Earth on the final day when Jesus Christ bursts into our atmosphere on clouds of glory.

When Jesus descends from Heaven to Earth, His mighty shout will awaken every dead person, saved and unsaved. He will resurrect the righteous dead to eternal life, and they shall be caught up in the air to meet Christ in the clouds. Immediately after that, the righteous saints alive on that day will also be taken up into the atmosphere to join their resurrected brethren. On the final day, the living saints on Earth will never taste death or experience time in a grave.

The Church Triumphant and the Church Militant shall be changed in the twinkling of an eye. Their mortal bodies of flesh and blood shall be exchanged for new immortal bodies that shall never age, never become sick, and never die. When does this great exchange of bodies occur? In 2 Thessalonians 1:10, Apostle Paul said it will happen when Jesus Christ "shall come to be glorified in His saints, and to be admired in all them that believe...in that day." The miraculous change will occur when we see Jesus!

However, the sight of Jesus' glory will have a radically different effect on the wicked, unbelievers, and all others who rejected Christ. They shall perish in the brilliance of His revealed glory because they will not be worthy to see God. For the unsaved, Jesus Christ shall be "revealed from heaven with His mighty angels, in flaming fire taking vengeance on them that know not God, and that obey not the gospel of our Lord Jesus Christ." (2 Thessalonians 1:7-8) The unsaved "shall be punished with everlasting destruction from the presence of the Lord, and from the glory of His power..." (2 Thessalonians 1:9)

On the final day, God will scorch the wicked with great heat, and they will blaspheme the name of God because of the many plagues upon the earth. They will stubbornly refuse to repent and give Him glory. For the wicked, the final day will be gory, not glorious.

The Son of God shall come in His glory, along with all His holy angels. He shall sit upon the throne of His glory. In the glory of His Father, Jesus shall reward every man and woman according to their works in this life on Earth. When He comes in the glory of His father, Jesus shall be ashamed of whoever was ashamed of Him and His words while living in this adulterous and sinful world.

Christian saints will be partakers of the glory that God shall reveal on the final day and obtain salvation in Christ Jesus. Apostle Paul prayed for Christians in Ephesus that "the Father of glory" would open their eyes of understanding that they would "know what is the hope of His calling, what the riches of the glory of His inheritance in the saints." "Eyes of understanding" signifies our inner man in its entirety. In short, it is our heart as it relates to spiritual perception. St. Paul meant that we must summons all our inner energy that comprises our intellect, conscience, understanding, and human affection to comprehend the depth of the rich glory we will receive from God as an inheritance at the Second Coming of Jesus

Christ. Apostle Paul desired that the Ephesian saints understand how great the fulness of this glory will be on the final day.

The Apocalypse gives us a vivid picture of life in Heaven. Every living being glorifies God. The 24 elders sing, "Thou art worthy, O Lord, to receive glory and honor and power: for thou hast created all things, and for thy pleasure they are and were created." A heavenly choir too numerous to count, ten thousand times ten thousand, and thousands of thousands, can be heard singing with a loud voice, "Worthy is the Lamb that was slain to receive power, and riches, and wisdom, and strength, and honor, and glory, and blessing." More than saints and angels will sing in New Jerusalem. When God completes the consummation of all things, every animal, bird, and fish shall also sing to glorify Jesus. The creatures will sing, "Blessing, and honor, and glory, and power, be unto him that sitteth upon the throne, and unto the Lamb for ever and ever."

The Second Coming of Jesus Christ shall be glorious on a scale that humans cannot imagine is possible. His glory is the magnificent radiance of His holiness. Only the holy shall see God and inherit the Kingdom. When we meet and see Him in the clouds of His great glory, our physical bodies shall be glorified, meaning transformed by the resurrection to be made immortal, thus suitable to dwell with God. We too shall appear with Him in glory. The spotless Church shall share in the magnificent radiance of His holiness. The head of the Church shall unite Himself with His body, the saints. And so, all Israel shall be saved.

When Christ, who is our life, shall appear, *then shall ye also appear with him in glory.*

Colossians 3:4

The Second Coming of Jesus Christ on the final day shall be:

- Singular
- Sudden and unexpected
- Atmospheric
- Visible
- Noisy
- Disruptive
- Fiery
- Glorious

CHAPTER 9

HIS SECOND COMING SHALL BE JUDGMENTAL

WHEN THE FINAL DAY arrives, God shall judge the secrets of all people. He will do it by Jesus Christ, according to His Gospel.

> **....in the day when God shall judge the secrets of men by Jesus Christ according to my gospel.**
>
> **Romans 2:16**

Jesus Christ is both the mediator of our salvation and the mediator of our judgment. God the Father has committed to Jesus Christ, the Son, the "authority to execute judgment" on the final day "because He is the Son of Man."

> **....and hath given him authority to execute judgment also, because he is the Son of man.**
>
> **John 5:27**

The judgment of all men and women who lived on Earth from the beginning of time will occur on the final day. All will stand before the Supreme Judge of the Universe. The Second Coming, the Day of the Lord, the Last Day, the Judgment Seat of Christ, and the Great White Throne of Judgment are synonymous. Together they are the final day. It all happens when Jesus returns. He will judge every human and reward them accordingly for what they rightly deserve.

For the Son of man shall come in the glory of his Father with his angels; and then he shall reward every man according to his works.

Matthew 16:27

Christian Zionist theologians and prophecy teachers spread out these events over 1,000 years. Still, almost all traditional orthodox Christian theologians and Bible scholars believe that all judgment occurs when Jesus returns. Neither theologians nor intellectuals can comprehend it because our limited carnal human minds cannot fathom the absence of time as it has existed since Creation. The same God who made time can suspend it, abolish it, or refashion it for a new age.

What is the purpose of time? We determine hours and days by the length of the Earth's rotation and years by how long it takes the Earth to complete a revolution around the Sun. A mean solar day represents the time interval when the Earth makes one complete rotation on its axis. An hour is an interval of time equal to one twenty-fourth of a mean solar day and equivalent to sixty minutes. A year represents the time it takes the Earth to complete its orbit around the Sun, meaning 365 ¼ solar days. The Earth's seasons are due to its axial tilt. The passing of seasons affects the planet's daylight hours, weather, temperature, vegetation, and soil fertility.

Time as we presently know it will cease to exist on the final day. The Sun, the Moon, and stars shall disappear. Therefore, the objects we use to measure time will vanish. How can we have hours, days, and years when the Earth, Sun, and Moon no longer exist? Undoubtedly, devotees of complicated Christian Zionist prophecy timeline charts will strenuously object to the assertion that time will cease to exist when Jesus Christ returns. Their eschatology storyline demands that God keep the Sun, Moon, and stars brightly lit for another thousand years to accommodate Greater Israel's rulership of the world, regardless of Apostle Peter's assurance that the cosmos will burn up on the day of the Lord.

It is prideful and arrogant to think that humans can reduce the incomprehensible grandness of the end of the age of humankind to fit neatly onto a prophecy timeline wall chart. The arrival and eternal presence of Jesus Christ are too much for our limited carnal minds to comprehend. God does not need nor seek permission from humans to do anything. The Creator asked Job, "Where were you when I laid the foundations of the Earth? Who has determined its measurements? To what are its foundations fastened? Or who laid its cornerstone when the morning stars sang together?"

There is an appointed time in the future that no human can avoid. God established the day. It is Judgment Day.

And the times of this ignorance God winked at; but now commandeth all men everywhere to repent: because he hath appointed a day, in the which he will judge the world

in righteousness by that man whom he hath ordained; whereof he hath given assurance unto all men, in that he hath raised him from the dead.

Acts 17:30-31

Judgment is an Unpopular Word These Day

Modern society shuns anything that sounds judgmental, but the final day will be Judgment Day. The judgment seat of Christ, a Great White Throne, the Book of Life, an examination, and verdict of every person's life on Earth, eternal life for some, and eternal damnation for others will be judgmental. Apostle Paul said, "we must all appear before the judgment seat of Christ." The definition of "must" means "to be required or compelled to, as by the use or threat of force." Attendance before the judgment seat of Christ is mandatory. Each person who ever lived shall justly receive from God appropriate rewards or punishments based on the things done while their soul dwelt in their physical body on Earth. What has your body done? The time for repentance is now.

For we must all appear before the judgment seat of Christ; that everyone may receive the things done in his body, according to that he hath done, whether it be good or bad.

2 Corinthians 5:10

In recent decades, Biblical morality in Western nations has become an outdated concept from a bygone era. Even more unpopular is the topic of the judgment of sins. Judgment has become an unfashionable word in a politically correct culture of unbridled tolerance. Talking about morality and the judgment of sins is guaranteed to reduce the number of social invitations you receive. As technology-centric societies move away from Biblical morality, the more people behave like the ancient Israelites without a king when "every man did that which was right in his own eyes." Modern sociologists call it "situational ethics." God calls it rebellion.

An unusual political movement took hold of Western nations in the early decades of the Twenty-first Century. The movement's surface is political, but beneath the surface, the movement is entirely spiritual. It is a movement of spiritual darkness. The movement's adherents despise biblical morality because they hate God. They are street thugs for the New Nimrods, breaking down and shredding society to make way for Satan's government. The movement exalts new definitions of tolerance, diversity, and inclusiveness. Their warped ideology teaches that tolerance means everybody must validate any behavior they say is acceptable, diversity means affirming mentally ill people who identify with nonexistent genders, and inclusiveness demands that sexually deviant people and gender-bending mentally disturbed people should be given political power and financial resources to advance their warped ideology.

Currently, Western nations are under siege by cultural warriors. They adhere to a Mao-like cultural revolution that angrily rejects any notion that a sinless, morally perfect God exists who will judge the lives of humans. They laugh at the Holy Bible as a moral code for humankind. They scoff at Christians who believe that Jesus Christ was resurrected from the dead and shall return in glory.

An unholy alliance of cultural communists, atheist academics, Jewish journalists, zany zealots, liberal lawyers, and deep pocket devils made sinister alliances with global corporations, think tanks, foundations, technocrats, secret societies, rogue units inside intelligence agencies, and super-rich families to reimagine society. Working together, the Devil's comrades have deliberately decimated traditional Western nations and constructed a caustic culture that viciously defames and mauls any person who dares to defy their mantra of tolerance, diversity, and inclusiveness. They seek to reimagine human society by stripping away all Biblical morality. However, their hidden goal is to reimagine humanity through genetic alterations of human DNA. The Nephilim are back in business.

Increasingly, the culture-killers bullied many churches in Western nations into tolerating an "anything goes" attitude toward doctrine, beliefs, and behavior. The rapid social acceptance of sexual sins and blatantly immoral behavior in Western nations is intimidating many sincere pastors, evangelists, and Bible teachers who know what the Word of God says about such things.

Sadly, many Christian churches in Western nations have buckled under the immense social, political, legal, and financial pressure to acquiesce to the demands of the anti-God "thought police." Consequently, many pastors privately tremble at the threat of being labeled "intolerant and judgmental" by wicked men and women who are enemies of the Cross. It should be the other way! Evil men and women should tremble because righteous men are preaching the Gospel. Because godly men and women stopped boldly preaching the Word of God in Western Christian nations, the tares now outnumber the wheat in most of those countries. Pusillanimous preaching produces disjointed disciples unable to stand upright for God in a crooked world. Fearless preaching is the only way to combat wicked weeds.

More Mockers Mean Day of Judgment is Near

Once bastions of traditional Christianity, Western nations have become hotbeds of hostility against Biblical morality and the disciples of Jesus Christ. Christians should not be surprised by the appearance of this abnormal movement that seeks to redefine society, ethics, and even humanity. The Holy Bible foretold that a particular class of people would emerge when the world quickly approached the finish line. They are called "scoffers." Scoffers arrogantly and foolishly mock, jeer, deride, scorn, and ridicule people, things, and beliefs they don't accept, like, or understand.

Apostle Peter said we must know that scoffers will appear in the last days. Their pursuit of carnal lusts will drive them. Mockingly, these last days scoffers are presently taunting Christians who are proclaiming that Jesus will return to judge all humanity. "Where is the proof that your Jesus god will return?" they arrogantly ask with derisive laughter. "The world has been the same since its creation," they arrogantly post on social media.

> **...knowing this first, that there shall come in the last days scoffers, walking after their own lusts, and saying, Where is the promise of his coming? for since the fathers fell asleep, all things continue as they were from the beginning of the creation.**
>
> **2 Peter 3:3-4**

In saying "knowing this first," Apostle Peter assured the saints the scoffers would appear in the final stage of the world's existence. Indeed, it would be a sure sign that Jesus' return is near. His emphatic statement of their future appearance educated the Church that Christians must prepare for the scoffers. Peter is saying to us today, "Trust me, saints. It's going to happen! They are coming someday! You can count on it. And when they show up in large numbers, it means we are close to the final day."

If Apostle Peter were amongst us today, the beloved saint would shout,"They're here!" The most significant populations of scoffers and mockers are in nations with the most robust Christian heritage. We should not be surprised. The Devil has worked the hardest in Christian countries to sow tares among the wheat. Satan sowed tares in Christian nations while good men and women spiritually slept. Over decades, the tares multiplied and overtook the wheat to control those nations' culture. There is no place more evident of this pattern than the United States of America. In several decades, the USA flipped from a God-fearing Christian nation to become a land of heathens, pagans, homosexuals, and communists. Satan sowed tares in America while good Christian men and women slept. They did not guard and protect the land of freedom given to their ancestors, and now have discovered that seditious termites devoured America's foundation of freedom and liberty built by the country's Founding Fathers.

Today hordes of haters arrogantly sneer in the faces of righteous men and women, warning people to repent of their sins, believe in the name of Jesus, and be baptized into the Church. They laugh at biblical prophecies of the Second Coming of Jesus. They live selfishly to satisfy their sexual lusts and carnal pleasures with no restraints of morality. They dare God to judge them.

St. Paul advised his protege Timothy to prepare the saints for vile people in the last days. He said, "in the last days perilous times shall come." The beloved apostle said people in the last days would be "lovers of their own selves, covetous, boasters, proud, blasphemers, disobedient to parents, unthankful, unholy, without natural affection, trucebreakers, false accusers, incontinent, fierce, despisers of those that are good, traitors, heady, high-minded, lovers of pleasures more than lovers of God; having a form of godliness, but denying the power thereof...." Apostle Paul advised Timothy that from such people, he should turn away.

Jesus' Words Shall Judge Sinners on the Final Day

Red-hot communists and lukewarm religionists are squeezing faithful churches from both ends. Cultural Marxists demand allegiance to their godlessness, and religious tares demand softer sermons that tolerate aberrant lifestyles. Posing as Christians, these people are fond of saying, "Jesus said He did not come to judge the world. Why are you judging people?"

Yes, Jesus said He did not come to judge the world, but that's not a complete quote, nor is it a doctrinally sound understanding of what Jesus meant. In the First Advent to humankind, Jesus' mission was to go to the Cross as the sacrificial lamb on Passover. God made a way to reconcile fallen humanity to Him; therefore, Jesus did not come to judge sinners but save them. Jesus said people must choose whether to receive or reject His words. The Word of God will judge them on the final day.

> **And if any man hear my words, and believe not, I judge him not: for I came not to judge the world, but to save the world. He that rejecteth me, and receiveth not my words, hath one that judgeth him: the word that I have spoken, *the same shall judge him in the last day.***
>
> **John 12:47-48**

In this age of grace, which is the time of God's sin amnesty, each of us judges ourselves by our response to Jesus' words. We believe and obey Him, or we disbelieve and disobey Him. Many people claim to accept Jesus' words yet disregard them. Obedience is proof of belief. There is no middle ground. Whenever people reject Jesus' words, they reject God's gracious offer of mercy and forgiveness of sins. They judge themselves as damned for eternity.

During the great expanse of time between the Cross and the Second Advent of Jesus Christ, God is saying to humanity, "According to your words, so be it." God gave humanity a choice: eternal life or eternal death. Beginning with Adam and Eve, God gave all humans free will to make choices. The Spirit of the Lord is crying out to humanity, "Choose life and live!" Jesus Christ, however, is the stumbling block to rebellious Jews and foolishness to rebellious Gentiles. They desire to choose life but stubbornly refuse to submit to the lordship of Jesus Christ. Therefore, they judge themselves to spend eternity in the lake of fire.

> **I call heaven and earth to record this day against you, that I have set before you life and death, blessing and cursing: therefore choose life, that both thou and thy seed may live...**
>
> **Deuteronomy 30:19**

You are Deciding Today Your Judgment Tomorrow

Indeed, Jesus did not come to judge people. He came to save them. His Word will do the judging on His next visit to Earth. Jesus did, however, come the first time to divide families, friends, religious institutions, cities, and nations into two groups: His disciples and His enemies. The second time He comes to Earth, the conquering King will gather all who separated themselves unto Him for discipleship. Sheep on the right, goats on the left.

You won't have a choice in deciding where you will stand before the Great Judge. The angels will assign your spot. You are choosing your future place now while living on Earth. You have free will to decide whether to be a sheep or goat. The Creator has not predestined anybody to be a goat. God desires all men and women to be saved and to come to the knowledge of the truth. He will not decide for you, but He already knows which way you will go. Therefore, you will be judged on the final day by your response to the Word of God while you lived on Earth. If you end up in the goat pen, you will have nobody to blame but yourself. Likewise, if you end up in the sheep pasture, you will have nobody to thank but Jesus!

We are unable to save ourselves from damnation in Hell. Jesus did all the work necessary for us to be saved and delivered from eternal spiritual death. When the Holy Spirit convicts us of sin and our need for salvation, we can choose to use the believing faith the Spirit bestows upon us to make the right decision to repent and believe in the name of Jesus. Sinners do not decide the day and hour when salvation comes to them, but they must act when the Holy Spirit beckons them to bow at the Cross.

God's Word will judge us on the final day; therefore, we must choose this day whether we will believe and obey Him. Believing and obeying God is what makes you a saint. Unbelief and disobedience are what make you a sinner. The choice is yours.

The Sword of Judgment

In His First Advent, Jesus did not come to bring peace on Earth. Instead, He came to send a sword to divide nations, cities, and families. Wielding His sword of the Word, Jesus drew a sharp line in society's sand and asked, "Are you with me or against me?" He is still asking the same question today.

> **Think not that I am come to send peace on earth: I came not to send peace, but a sword.**
>
> **Matthew 10:34**

> **He that is not with me is against me; and he that gathereth not with me scattereth abroad.**
>
> **Matthew 12:30**

The sword of truth divides nations, cities, families, and churches. The Word of God is an instrument of war, sharper than any two-edged sword, that pierces "even to the dividing asunder of soul and spirit, and of the joints and marrow, and is a discerner of the thoughts and intents of the heart." What is an indicator that a preacher's sermon is God-inspired? When one or more people angrily march out of the church! Fearless, uncompromised preaching of the Word of God automatically produces division, hostility, stress, and tension. Such things are not the product of the Gospel but the response from humanity's wickedness and enmity toward God's holiness.

At first glance, the angelic song heard by Bethlehem shepherds on the night Jesus was born contradicts the fiery sermons preached by Jesus as an adult. Angels hovering over Bethlehem's shepherd fields sang, "Glory to God in the highest, and on earth peace, good will toward men." Decades later, Jesus proclaimed, "Think not that I am come to send peace on earth: I came not to send peace, but a sword." How can there be both peace on Earth and a sword? Is the Bible inconsistent? Did Jesus not know God's original plan? Was Jesus radicalized in his thirties? Did He develop a bad attitude?

There is no conflict between the two statements. The angels sang correctly, and Jesus spoke truthfully. Both comments were in unison with the Heavenly Father's will. When angels sang, "peace on earth, good will toward men," they were joyfully announcing that Heaven was extending goodwill toward humankind by sending the Son of God to save their souls. Thousands of years of hostility between God and humanity was over.

Adam's sin in the Garden of Eden separated humanity from God. Beginning with the Messiah's First Advent, God made a way to be reconciled with all people. His Son is the Way. Reconciliation with God can only come through repentance of sin, belief in the name of Jesus, and baptism into the universal Church of God, which is Israel, the people of God.

Thus, angels sang over Bethlehem the good news that God had commenced the reconciliation of humanity. Three decades later, the Bethlehem babe was an adult who preached sermons filled with sharp words that demanded unwavering loyalty to Him. No longer was there talk about peace on Earth, goodwill toward men. Instead, Jesus told crowds He did not come to bring peace, but a sword!

Think not that I am come to send peace on earth: I came not to send peace, but a sword.

Matthew 10:34

He that is not with me is against me; and he that gathereth not with me scattereth abroad.

Matthew 12:30

Through the death, burial, and resurrection of Jesus Christ, Almighty God has reconciled us to Himself. Reconciliation requires the settlement of a quarrel. It also means that two or more parties have come into agreement and harmony. To be reconciled with somebody means they are no longer your enemy but restored as your friend. God desires to call every human His friend. First, however, they must be reconciled to God through faith in Jesus Christ. He is the only way to obtain reconciliation with our Heavenly Father. Sadly, pride and rebellion have prevented multitudes of sinners from reconciliation with their Maker. They foolishly preferred to burn in Hell than bow before Christ.

And all things are of God, who hath reconciled us to himself by Jesus Christ, and hath given to us the ministry of reconciliation; to wit, that God was in Christ, reconciling the world unto himself, not imputing their trespasses unto them; and hath committed unto us the word of reconciliation.

2 Corinthians 5:18-19

The Gospel of the Prince of Peace Causes Division

How ironic is it that the Prince of Peace causes commotion and division everywhere the Gospel is proclaimed? Jesus said there are two groups of people in the world: People who are with Him, and people who are against Him. Whoever is not with Jesus is automatically against Him. And whoever does not assist Jesus in gathering lost souls into His kingdom is automatically helping Satan scatter lost souls to damnation.

There's no middle ground. His demand for fidelity and loyalty are much greater than most modern Christians realize. Jesus espouses the same demand for loyalty as did his Old Testament namesake Joshua who shouted to the Hebrews to choose the god they would serve. There was no waffling in Joshua's mind. He served the God of Moses who delivered the Hebrews out of Egypt.

> **And if it seem evil unto you to serve the Lord, *choose you this day whom ye will serve;* whether the gods which *your fathers served that were on the other side of the flood,* or the gods of the Amorites, in whose land ye dwell: *but as for me and my house, we will serve the Lord.***
>
> **Joshua 24:15**

Yes, indeed, Jesus did not come the first time to judge sinners. His First Advent was to save mankind, but His Second Advent will judge mankind. Almighty God's sin amnesty expires one second before the start of the final day. There will be no thousand-year gap between God's two economies. The transition from mercy to judgment is instantaneous. Only God the Father knows when it will happen. Apostle Peter said God's patience is longsuffering because He is not willing that any soul perish, but desires that all humans come to Him in a humble spirit of repentance. However, the door to God's mercy and forgiveness, will violently slam shut on the first second of the final day, never to open again for any human pleading for Yahweh to spare them from the endless agony of Hell. Now is the accepted time. Now is the day of salvation.

As opposition to His message intensified, Jesus not only doubled down in His rhetoric, He cranked it up too. He told the people that He came to send fire upon the Earth, it was already burning! How more radically could He talk? Today, law enforcement agencies would spy on Jesus as a dangerous revolutionary. Social media platforms would ban Jesus for spewing "violent, inflammatory, hate speech" that violates their standards." His bank account would be frozen, and His assets seized on criminal charges of making terroristic threats against religious and governmental institutions.

I am come to send fire on the earth; and what will I, if it be already kindled? But I have a baptism to be baptized with; and how am I straitened till it be accomplished!

Luke 12:49-50

In the Holy Bible, fire represents adversity or persecution. It also signifies holy zeal for God. To paraphrase the Lord's remarks, Jesus said, "I came to send fire on the Earth, and oh how I wish it was already burning!" At first, His words appear to be a strange utterance from the Son of God. He said it immediately after talking about the faithful and wise servant, and the unfaithful and foolish servant. Speaking of the last days, Jesus said faithful and wise servants would be found serving "meat in due season" when the master of the house returns. The unfaithful, foolish servants will not prepare for the master's return. Such people shall be severely punished because they knew the Lord's will but did not do it.

There are instances in the Gospels when the Last Adam's sacred humanity was briefly unveiled. Jesus gave us a glimpse of his feelings, the innermost thoughts of His compassionate heart when He wished the fire was already burning on Earth. He mentioned a baptism that He had to experience, and that He was determined to carry on His ministry until that baptism was accomplished.

What was the baptism that Jesus desired? It was not a baptism of water. John the Baptist had done that in the Jordan River years earlier. It was not a baptism of the Holy Spirit. The Spirit of God had already descended upon Jesus like a dove. There was another baptism that Jesus had to experience. It was a baptism in blood, a baptism of suffering. Peering into the future, Jesus's humanity shone through His words as He contemplated the terror of the cruel crucifixion the Jews and Romans were preparing for Him. He had to get through it. As the Son of God, He could endure the Cross. As the Son of Man, Jesus dreaded the crucifixion's awful pain and agony. Yet, Jesus was determined to complete His mission.

There could be no salvation for fallen humanity if there were no resurrection. There could be no resurrection if there were not a death. There could be no death if there were not a crucifixion. There would be no crucifixion if there were not a sacrificial lamb on Passover. There would be no sacrifice if Jesus did not willingly go to Jerusalem to be killed by the Jews and Romans. It had to be done!

He longed to get it done and over with, and to unleash the holy fire of the Gospel of the Kingdom of God. His suffering on the Cross would kindle the fire that would perpetually burn around the world until He came again. Jesus also knew that the preaching of the Gospel would start the separation of goats and sheep. Nations, cities, towns, neighborhoods, and families would be split apart over their allegiance to or rejection of Him. The fiery Gospel will burn until the final day, dividing and separating people. This fire does not originate on Earth. It is a holy fire sent from Heaven!

> **Suppose ye that I am come to give peace on earth? I tell you, Nay; but rather division: for from henceforth there shall be five in one house divided, three against two, and two against three. The father shall be divided against the son, and the son against the father; the mother against the**

daughter, and the daughter against the mother; the mother-in-law against her daughter in law, and the daughter in law against her mother-in-law.

Luke 12:51-53

Trees That Don't Produce Good Fruit are Cut Down and Burned

It is a sight to behold in modern churches watching pansy preachers dance around the topic of judgment when presenting the Gospel of Christ. John the Baptist introduced Jesus as the Messiah by saying that in Jesus' hand was a fan and that He would "thoroughly purge his floor, and gather his wheat into the garner, but he will burn up the chaff with unquenchable fire." John the Baptist also warned that "every tree which bringeth not good fruit is hewn down, and cast into the fire."

Jesus went farther than John in His warnings about a coming day of judgment. The Son of God said:

- People who angrily denounce others with contemptuous, scornful, bitter words and name-calling "shall be in danger of hell fire." (Matthew 5:22)
- Every tree that does not produce fruit is cut down and cast into the fire. (Matthew 7:19)
- Tares will be gathered and burned in the fire, so it shall be at the end of this world. (Matthew 13:40)
- Angels will go forth on the day of the Lord and gather out of His Kingdom all things that offend Him and all who commit acts of iniquity. The angels will cast them into a furnace of fire where there shall be wailing and gnashing of teeth. (Matthew 13:41-42)

- If you continuously sin with your hands, it's better to cut off your hands and live in this life physically maimed than to enter with two hands into Hell where the fire shall never be quenched, and worms never die. (Mark 9:43-44)
- On the day of the Lord, fire, and brimstone from Heaven will rain upon the wicked as it did on Sodom the same day Lot fled the city. (Luke 17:29-30)
- People who do not abide in Christ are thrown away and wither. As men cast dead branches into the fire, so too will angels gather the wicked and cast them into the fire to be burned. (John 15:6)

That kind of preaching is not seeker-friendly material fit for today's religious social clubs. If Jesus were physically walking on the Earth today, many churches that nominally identify with Him would not welcome Jesus to preach from their pulpits. Likewise, Jesus would not be permitted to purchase airtime on many religious television and radio stations. Why? They would condemn His sermons as judgmental and divisive.

On the final day, Jesus will grant admission to New Jerusalem to every person who kept His commandments. They shall enter through the gates of the city because God will graciously confer upon them the right to feast on the fruit of the Tree of Life. However, He will prohibit entry to dogs, meaning vile, filthy, depraved, wicked men and women. Likewise, God will deny access to sorcerers, sexually immoral heathens, murderers, idolaters, and liars. He will permanently encase that crowd inside invisible flames of black fire.

Blessed are they that do his commandments, that they may have right to the tree of life, and may enter in through the

gates into the city. For without are dogs, and sorcerers, and whoremongers, and murderers, and idolaters, and whosoever loveth and maketh a lie.

Revelation 22:14-15

The Final Day Shall Come
When the Gospel is Preached in All the World

Jesus foreknew that the unleashed Gospel would incense the world to strike against all people who declared their allegiance to Him. Rebellious reprobates gleefully slander, revile, persecute, attack, imprison, even kill devout sanctified saints. Before the final day arrives, Christians will be persecuted and hated in every nation. Christ will save those who endure to the end.

And ye shall be hated of all men for my name's sake: but he that endureth to the end shall be saved.

Matthew 10:22

Then shall they deliver you up to be afflicted, and shall kill you: and ye shall be hated of all nations for my name's sake.

Matthew 24:9

The final day shall come when this Gospel of the Kingdom—the Gospel that causes division, strife, fire, and persecution!—shall be preached in all the world for a witness unto all nations. Jesus knew that the introduction of the New Covenant Gospel would spread like holy fire through nations. The Gospel will automatically clash with the world's love of sin wherever His disciples fulfill the Great Commission. Indeed, if there is no opposition, the true Gospel has not been preached.

And this gospel of the kingdom shall be preached in all the world for a witness unto all nations; and then shall the end come.

Matthew 24:14

"And this gospel of the kingdom shall be preached in all the world" means that the Church must proclaim wherever humans inhabit the world the message of joyful glad tidings of peace and reconciliation with Almighty God. It is "a witness unto all nations" for two reasons. Firstly, the proclamation of the Gospel of the Kingdom of God outside the boundaries of ancient Israel is evidence that God accepts as His chosen people all who repent of their sins, believe in the name of Jesus Christ, and are baptized into the Church.

Secondly, it is a witness unto all nations because it constitutes evidence in each nation's legal files in Heaven's court that God will open on Judgment Day. Jesus said His holy angels would gather all the nations before Him on that day. Jesus will instruct the separation of the inhabitants of each nation into two groups: Jesus' sheep and Satan's goats. The Great Prosecutor will question them. Each nation's legal folder will contain evidence that God's sons and daughters preached the Gospel of the Kingdom within their respective borders. Enoch, Methuselah, and Noah preached the Gospel before the Great Flood. Apostle Paul wrote that Abraham heard the Gospel preached to him.

And the scripture, foreseeing that God would justify the heathen through faith, preached before the gospel unto Abraham, saying, In thee shall all nations be blessed.

Galatians 3:8

Therefore, no unsaved human since the beginning of time will have an excuse on the final day to escape their rightful guilty verdict. They were offered mercy and forgiveness during the extended sin amnesty but rejected it when they rejected Jesus. The Judge shall swiftly render a judgment. The court's angelic bailiffs will promptly carry out the Judge's sentence upon the guilty. They shall be bundled and burned. God alone will decide the day when "this gospel of the kingdom" has done its work as "a witness unto all nations." Then shall the end come.

How long shall this final judgment take? Puny men cannot fathom God's magnificence and the greatness of His stupendous plan. When Jesus returns on the last day, time will cease to exist in its present form. Mankind's fixed measurements of time shall instantly stop. The Second Coming has no seconds. Neither is the final day a twenty-four-hour day. It will only be now! The final day's length of time will be as short or long as necessary for Almighty God to do all that His Word says will happen when Jesus Christ returns. Seconds, minutes, hours, days, months, years, and millennia will cease to exist. Apostle Peter spoke of the final day when He wrote that "one day is with the Lord as a thousand years, and a thousand years as one day."

The One who calls Himself "I Am" shall preside on a Great White Throne. Earth and Heaven will vanish from His face because there will no longer be a place for them in His new world order. Yes, God will even abolish Heaven and create a new Heaven. The Church is grossly misrepresenting the magnificent splendor of God's new works of creation on that day. The Creator will create again! The books will be opened, including the Book of Life. The sea, death, and Hell will surrender to God the dead in them. Based on the words written in those books, Christ will judge the dead according to their works in this life. Idle words spoken on Earth will be judged. The Lord will cast death and Hell into the lake of fire. Along with Hell and death will go everybody whose name Christ did not find in the Book of Life.

> **And I saw a great white throne, and him that sat on it, from whose face the earth and the heaven fled away; and there was found no place for them. And I saw the dead, small and great, stand before God; and the books were opened: and another book was opened, which is the book of life: and the dead were judged out of those things which were written in the books, according to their works. And the sea gave up the dead which were in it; and death and hell delivered up the dead which were in them: and they were judged every man according to their works. And death and hell were cast into the lake of fire. This is the second death. And whosoever was not found written in the book of life was cast into the lake of fire.**
>
> **Revelation 20:11-15**

Judge Jesus Will Preside on the Final Day

Judge Jesus will do the judging on Judgment Day. Because the Son of God is also the Son of Man, our Heavenly Father has given Jesus Christ high and sovereign power to govern all things and to sit on the Great White Throne to judge all secrets in the hearts of men and women. He shall judge us according to the truth of the Gospel. The courtroom examination will include more than our outward deeds and words. The Judge will introduce all our secret

341

and hidden thoughts, desires, and motives into our trial, both good and evil. Apostle Paul said the secrets of our heart should be made manifest "in the day when God shall judge the secrets of men by Jesus Christ" according to His Gospel. Thus, our true character shall be on display for all to see.

A final day judgment of our lives on Earth was not a new concept introduced by early Christianity. Knowledge of it has existed since the fall of Adam and Eve. King Solomon wrote about it.

For God shall bring every work into judgment, with every secret thing, whether it be good, or whether it be evil.

Ecclesiastes 12:14

Fortunately for fallen humanity, there is Good News for repentant sinners who place their faith in Jesus Christ and know they are justified because of what Jesus did for them on the Cross. If you live by faith in Jesus Christ, knowing that you are justified by Him and made righteous (meaning, in right standing with God), you will finish your journey by still having faith in King Jesus. You will stand before the judgment seat of Christ justified by His righteousness! He will not condemn you for sins committed on Earth because there is now no condemnation for those who are in Christ Jesus.

Jesus does not dole out salvation nor condemnation at His judgment seat. He made that determination while we lived on Earth based on how we responded to the Gospel. For Believers, our sins will be revealed at the judgment seat of Christ as transgressions forgiven by God, washed away by the blood of the Lamb of God. On that final day, all Christians will finally comprehend the fullness of the work of grace that Jesus did for us.

Our court file folder marked "Sins" will be empty because Jesus Christ expunged our transgressions. Expungement means the court erased criminal offenses as though they never happened. It is not probation, which means the defendant is guilty of crimes but will not justly serve an appropriate prison sentence. Expungement is much better than probation or even "not guilty." It means that in the eyes of the court, no crimes ever occurred. You will be declared sinless!

Our Works on Earth Must Pass the Test of Fire on the Final Day

It will be a different story, however, regarding the court folders marked "works." Those folders will not be empty. Our works on Earth must pass the test of fire, and our eternal rewards will depend on the fire test results.

According to the grace of God which is given unto me, as a wise master builder, I have laid the foundation, and another buildeth thereon. But let every man take heed how he buildeth thereupon. For other foundation can no man lay than that is laid, which is Jesus Christ. Now if any man build upon this foundation gold, silver, precious stones, wood, hay, stubble; every man's work shall be made manifest: for the day shall declare it, because it shall be revealed by fire; and the fire shall try every man's work of what sort it is.

1 Corinthians 3:10-13

Sins and works are two different matters. The Greek word "ergon," according to Strong's Concordance, means "work, task, employment; a deed, action; that which is wrought or made, a work." It refers to our actions and the things we did with the precious time God allotted us over our lifetime. It is a significant biblical verse about the eternal worth of our works.

God gives all humans the same amount of time: 24 hours each day. Wealthy people do not receive more time than poor people, and successful people do not have more hours each day than non-productive people. Generous people don't have more time than stingy people. Each day has 1,440 minutes. Some people consciously devote their daily allotted minutes to achieving their goals, while others waste their daily minutes on frivolous matters. Would you insert a rare gold coin into a vending machine for a candy bar or soft drink? That's what we do every time we waste a golden hour on frivolous nonsense.

The number of our works shall not be the determining factor when God tests our works by fire. Nor will it be the economic value of our works that count. The only thing that will matter on the final day shall be the eternal value of our work on Earth. Specifically, a holy fire will test the building materials we used to construct the works we built upon "this foundation." And what is this foundation? It is the "faith which was once delivered unto the saints." This foundation is the Gospel of the Kingdom.

Apostle Paul described himself as a "wise master builder" who laid the foundation. Referring to the Gospel, the apostle said every man and woman must heed how they build upon the foundation. The materials available to us to build upon the foundation of the Gospel are described symbolically as "gold, silver, precious stones, wood, hay, stubble." Three will quickly go up in smoke. Three will survive the flames, minus some dross accumulated along the way.

On the final day, all of us must watch Jesus Christ place our life's works, achievements, accomplishments, and use of the precious gift of time in His crucible. A crucible is a hollow area at the bottom of a furnace where a substance must endure extremely high temperatures. What did we do with the precious Gospel delivered once unto the saints? What materials did we use to build upon the pure foundation put in place by the apostles? Did we build structures composed of manufactured doctrines, errors, or even heresies and idolatry? The fire will reveal the components of our construction materials. Will it sizzle or shine?

Every man and woman involved in Christian ministry must daily ponder the test of fire that awaits them on the final day. What was the result of your preaching, teaching, writing, speaking, and activities in your home, church, ministry, business, and workplace? Did your words truly convince people of the necessity of repenting of their sins and following Jesus? Did your words and works make converts for Christ or recruits for your denomination? Did you persuade people to become citizens of the Kingdom or patriot activists for your nation? Did your words and actions inspire people to stand for Jesus or stand for your favorite politician? Did you seek people's votes more than their souls? What were your true motives in religious affairs? Were the things you taught and did in God's name genuine and pure? Did your lifestyle glorify God to the people you met? Did people see Jesus in you? How many lost souls were influenced by your behavior and words? Did your example inspire them to believe in the name of Jesus? Did you teach the Apostles' Doctrine or your denomination's doctrines?

When Christ tosses your works into the crucible, will they survive or go up in smoke? Apostle Paul said if our works survive the fiery test, we shall receive an eternal reward from God. Your reward will be the appropriate wages you earned. If our works burn up, our soul will be narrowly saved with great difficulty like a person who must pass through flames to escape from a burning house. However, entering the kingdom of God naked and covered in soot is preferable to entering the lake of fire clothed!

Nevertheless, many Christians will sadly leave behind a pile of ashes as a monument to their lives on Earth. Their lifetime of toil will be rendered worthless; thus, they shall receive no eternal rewards. They shall eternally pay for their mishandling of the precious things of God while on Earth because their reward will be negligible or nonexistent. The test of fire results will lock in place forever at a low level their position in the Kingdom of God. Other saints will dwell in New Jerusalem at much higher levels based on their works on Earth. The quality of your works on Earth will follow you for eternity in New Jerusalem. There will be no way to return to the old Earth to do it again and make things better the second time. The fire test will happen on the final day when Jesus Christ suddenly and unexpectedly arrives on clouds of great glory.

> If any man's work abide which he hath built thereupon, he shall receive a reward. If any man's work shall be burned, he shall suffer loss: but he himself shall be saved; yet so as by fire. Know ye not that ye are the temple of God, and that the Spirit of God dwelleth in you? If any man defile the temple of God, him shall God destroy; for the temple of God is holy, which temple ye are.
>
> **1 Corinthians 3:14-17**

Today's Religious People Behave Like Ancient Israelites

The day of the Lord is Judgment Day for every human alive and who ever lived. Why are so few professing Christians concerned about it? Fixated on the affairs of daily living, they neither contemplate giving an account of their lives nor show genuine grief over the fate of billions of lost souls on the final day. Why do they show little regard for such weighty matters? Perhaps they are not grieved by knowing that billions of souls are not ready for the final day because they, too, are not ready for it.

They are living carefree lives in the world, paying little regard to their thoughts, words, and deeds in this life. Many church members are foolishly following religious hucksters, teaching them to pursue worldly gain as the standard to measure God's blessings in their lives. Even worse, church members are divorcing their spouses, watching pornography, committing fornication or adultery, aborting babies to hide their sexual sins, stealing from their employers, swindling money from fellow church members, lying, slandering, reading horoscopes, watching movies that contain violence and nudity and occultism, getting drunk, smoking marijuana, and a host of other sinful ways. They do it because their church pastor does not preach against sin. Regardless, all will appear before the Great Judge.

Such Christian church members are no different from the ancient Israelites, who freely sinned and went to the temple to tell each other they were saved and delivered because they were God's chosen people. In the days of Jeremiah, the people of Judah greatly grieved the Lord by their sinful ways while deceiving themselves into believing they were saved because of their ethnicity. Nothing has changed over thousands of years.

The Israelites' prevalent idolatry, sexual debauchery, and dishonesty were more than the Lord could endure. He had enough of their sinful acts. God commanded Jeremiah to deliver a stern message to the Jews: Amend your ways and stop trusting in your lies. The Lord told the people to stop insulting Him by chanting "the temple of the Lord" when they entered the temple after committing vile sins in the privacy of their homes and shops. Yahweh was disgusted with their pious hypocrisy. The priests lied to the people and gave them a false sense of security. God let them know that the temple's sanctity did not guarantee them protection from His divine wrath. He would punish the guilty regardless of their temple attendance. There's no middle ground. His demand for fidelity and loyalty are much more significant than most modern Christians realize. Jesus espouses the same demand for commitment as did His Old Testament namesake Joshua who shouted to the Hebrews to choose the god they would serve. There was no waffling in Joshua's mind. He served the God of Moses, who delivered the Hebrews out of Egypt.

> And if it seem evil unto you to serve the Lord, *choose you this day whom ye will serve;* whether the gods which *your fathers served that were on the other side of the flood,* or the gods of the Amorites, in whose land ye dwell: *but as for me and my house, we will serve the Lord.*
>
> Joshua 24:15

The word that came to Jeremiah from the Lord, saying, Stand in the gate of the Lord's house, and proclaim there this word, and say, Hear the word of the Lord, all ye of Judah, that enter in at these gates to worship the Lord.

Thus saith the Lord of hosts, the God of Israel, Amend your ways and your doings, and I will cause you to dwell in this place. Trust ye not in lying words, saying, The temple of the Lord, The temple of the Lord, The temple of the Lord, are these.

Jeremiah 7:1-4

How does behavior of spiritually rebellious Jews in biblical times differ from the defiant behavior of many Christians today? Is it different from a modern-day church deacon or elder committing adultery and idolatry with his eyes by secretly watching pornography on his smartphone on Saturday night and going to church on Sunday to act religious in front of the congregation? Is it different from a Christian woman who murders the reputations of other Christians by gossiping and slandering them yet teaches a church Sunday School class about the Sermon on the Mount? Is it different from a church music director attending a Freemason lodge meeting on Tuesday night to pay homage to Baphomet, the goat god, and then leading the church worship and praise music on Wednesday night? The devious deacon, the slanderous Sunday School teacher, and Masonic music director each go to church chanting "The Church of the Lord!" while refusing to repent and turn from their wicked ways.

The Spirit of the Lord is speaking to church members worldwide to repent of their sins, turn from their wicked ways, and stop deceiving themselves by thinking they are saved when they live like the devil. They are defiling the temple of God—their physical bodies. God is calling to them to stop it now. The final day is coming! All will stand before the Great Judge.

Behold, ye trust in lying words, that cannot profit. Will ye steal, murder, and commit adultery, and swear falsely, and burn incense unto Baal, and walk after other gods whom ye know not; and come and stand before me in this house, which is called by my name, and say, We are delivered to do all these abominations?

Jeremiah 7:8-10

Consider Shiloh's Rubble

Jeremiah was a street preacher. He stood at the gate in Jerusalem, most likely the entrance to the inner court, and delivered a doozy of a sermon. It sizzled so much that King Jehoiakim sought to kill him. You know it's a good sermon when the national police launch a search for the preacher.

The fiery prophet flawlessly and fearlessly delivered the words God commanded him to speak to the people of Judah as they flocked to the city on a holy feast day to make their appearance in the temple. The Lord accused the sinful, hypocritical Jews of making the temple a den of thieves. God said, "I have seen it with my own eyes!"

Yahweh gave them an instruction to help them understand what He was saying: "Get on your donkeys and ride over to Shiloh. Look around and tell Me what you see. Try to find the town! It's not there anymore. Consider your ways!"

After the conquest of Canaan, Shiloh was for a brief time the central place of worship of Yahweh, the Holy God of Israel. The priests kept the Ark of the Covenant there. Over time, however, Shiloh lost its purity when idolatry, the kidnapping of virgin girls, and the sins of Eli and his sons spiritually defiled the city. Something happened to Shiloh. It was destroyed, perhaps by the

Philistines in 1050BC. When and how God destroyed Shiloh is not the critical thing to know. The essential lesson is this: If God destroyed Shiloh (Israel's first holy city), could not the same fate befall Jerusalem?

> **Is this house, which is called by my name, become a den of robbers in your eyes? Behold, even I have seen it, saith the Lord. But go ye now unto my place which was in Shiloh, where I set my name at the first, and see what I did to it for the wickedness of my people Israel.**
>
> **Jeremiah 7:11-12**

The people of Judah foolishly believed the temple would protect them from God, even though they profaned the temple with vile sins. Their faith was in a religious building, not the Lord. Because they believed their own lies, they told themselves that temple attendance counted more than holy living. Their worst sin was religious schizophrenia! They simultaneously worshipped idols and the Holy God of Israel! What were they thinking?

Before his temple gate sermon, Jeremiah had already told the people what God decreed for them. He cried out to the "children of Benjamin" to gather themselves "to flee out of the midst of Jerusalem." Why should they flee the holy city? Because "evil appeareth out of the north, and great destruction." God revealed to Jeremiah that a "great nation" from the north would invade Judah. The invaders were cruel and would show no mercy to the Jews as they captured the city with bows and spears. The invaders would seize their wives, houses, and fields.

Time had run out for Judah. Soon it would be "lights out" for them. Sudden and unexpected judgment would sweep them away in their sins. God repeatedly sent righteous preachers and prophets to warn them, but they stubbornly refused to repent. Often, the Jews beat or killed God's prophets. Why did they do it? They harmed the prophets because they didn't believe God would do what He threatened to do to the Jews. Therefore, God had no other option but to judge them harshly. The judgment suddenly and unexpectedly swept them away despite repeated warnings because the people chose not to listen to God's pleas for repentance. They were spiritually deaf.

> **Thus saith the Lord, Stand ye in the ways, and see, and ask for the old paths, where is the good way, and walk therein, and ye shall find rest for your souls. But they said, We will not walk therein. Also I set watchmen over you, saying, Hearken to the sound of the trumpet. But they said, We will not hearken. Therefore hear, ye nations, and know, O congregation, what is among them. Hear, O earth: behold, I will bring evil upon this people, even the fruit of their thoughts, because they have not hearkened unto my words, nor to my law, but rejected it.**
>
> **Jeremiah 6:16-19**

What happened to them? God started their mornings by speaking to them, but they would not answer him. Consequently, the Lord vowed to do to Jerusalem and the temple the same thing He did to Shiloh. God cast the Jews out of His sight. The Babylonian army invaded Jerusalem, plundered, and defiled Solomon's temple, and took the Jewish survivors to Babylon as slaves.

The Holy God of Israel is still pleading with sinners to repent. He is crying out to sinful humans in every nation today to ask for the old ways and walk in the good ways where they shall find rest for their souls. The final day is coming. God must judge unrepented sin. Now is the time of God's gracious and merciful sin amnesty. All sinners must hear His voice pleading with them to act wisely by accepting His merciful offer of forgiveness and eternal salvation.

> **Come now, and let us reason together, saith the Lord: though your sins be as scarlet, they shall be as white as snow; though they be red like crimson, they shall be as wool. If ye be willing and obedient, ye shall eat the good of the land: but if ye refuse and rebel, ye shall be devoured with the sword: for the mouth of the Lord hath spoken it.**
>
> **Isaiah 1:18-20**

Pre-Flood Preachers Warned About Judgment Day

St. Jude the Apostle gave us a glimpse into antediluvian history with a fascinating fragment of his knowledge of Enoch's prophecies about the final day. The apostles and early church fathers possessed knowledge of pre-flood prophecies that people lost over time. The Bible does not reveal to us how Jude knew these things. Perhaps he owned an authentic copy of the Book of Enoch or memorized the story handed down orally over thousands of years. It doesn't matter. What matters is that the Holy Spirit inspired Jude to write about it so that we are aware today that early Christians commonly knew the Book of Enoch.

Jude's astonishing assertion verifies that God revealed the First Advent to Adam and the Second Advent to Enoch. (Enoch was identified by Jude as "seventh from Adam," thus distinguishing him from Cain's son Enoch, who was third from Adam.) His reference to Enoch also signifies that God imparted knowledge to humanity after Adam's fall in the Garden that there would be a final day when Almighty God returns to Earth to eradicate sin from Creation and to justly judge all unrepentant sinners who joined Satan's rebellion by rejecting the lordship of Jesus Christ. Each generation of men and women have known in their hearts there is a holy Creator of the universe. People have known since the days of Adam the doctrine of a final judgment.

In the Book of Genesis, Moses told us that Enoch walked with God and was taken into Heaven; thus, his body never experienced death. Enoch was a righteous man whom God used, along with Noah, to preach repentance to the wicked population dwelling on earth after the fall of Adam and Eve. God has always had a faithful and obedient congregation of saints (true Israel, the Church) representing him on earth preaching repentance, righteousness, holiness, and the final day judgment. Such servants are present today on every continent as a witness to all nations in preparation for the last day.

Enoch, Noah's great-grandfather, looked beyond the Great Flood, which had not yet occurred. The Flood was the first world-wide judgment on sinners, yet Enoch saw the final day! According to Jude, Enoch prophesied that the Lord would come with ten thousand angels (meaning an innumerable multitude) to execute judgment upon all and convince the ungodly of their ungodly deeds and harsh, stern words. Among those mentioned are murmurers, complainers, those who seek to fulfill their lusts, people who speak boastful words, and those who desire to be admired.

And Enoch also, the seventh from Adam, prophesied of these, saying, Behold, the Lord cometh with ten thousands of his saints, to execute judgment upon all, and to convince all that are ungodly among them of all their ungodly deeds which they have ungodly committed, and of all their hard speeches which ungodly sinners have spoken against him. These are murmurers, complainers, walking after their own lusts; and their mouth speaketh great swelling words, having men's persons in admiration because of advantage.

Jude 1: 14-16

St. Jude, the servant of Jesus Christ and brother of James the Just, said God will come on the final day to "execute judgment upon all." God intends for His judgment to "convince all that are ungodly among them," meaning people who willfully commit acts they know are sinful, delight in them and purposefully persevere in committing such sins. Sinners guilty of "hard speeches" against God are blasphemers and all who mock, scoff, and ridicule the Holy Bible, God's laws and ways, righteousness, holiness, and sacred things. Such sinners are "murmurers and complainers" who are never satisfied with the blessings God has bestowed upon them. They always want more, pretentiously believe they are entitled to possess more, and continually express their discontent with their lot in life. They walk after their lusts. Their mouths speak "great swelling words," meaning they boast of themselves.

God will come to execute such people whose thoughts, words, and deeds are continually against the Lord with no fear or regret. Great shall be their eternal agony that commences on the final day. Their horror will never end when their bodies are resurrected unto death when Jesus opens every grave. Their resurrected bodies shall perpetually burn in Hell's furnace, but the flames will never eradicate them. They will suffer forever with no hope of escape. What sinful pleasure or unjust gain is worth such pain and anguish?

The Book of Enoch still accepted to this day by Ethiopia's Orthodox churches as an inspired canon written by Enoch, declares there shall be "no salvation" for "all of you sinners," but only "a curse." The righteous "elect," however, shall be blessed with "light and joy and peace." The elect "shall inherit the Earth." God will bestow wisdom upon the elect, and "they shall all live and never again sin."

The Book of Enoch's first chapter opens with a declaration that the prophecy was written to bless "the elect and righteous, who will be living in the day of tribulation, when all the wicked and godless are to be removed." Therefore, the Book of Enoch refutes the false doctrine that Christians will be raptured away and never experience the time of great tribulation. Jesus said the wicked will be taken first by the reapers. The book describes Enoch as "a righteous man, whose eyes were opened by God" to see "the vision of the Holy One in the heavens" which was revealed to him by angels. The angels told him everything, and from them, he understood what he was shown and heard was "not for this generation, but for a remote one which is to come."

What did the angels show Enoch? The pre-Flood prophet said, "the Holy Great One will come forth from His dwelling, and the eternal God will tread upon the Earth, (even) on Mount Sinai." He will "appear in the strength of His might from the heaven of heavens." When God appears on Earth again, "all shall be smitten with fear." Even the watchers (angels) "shall quake." Enoch said that "great fear and trembling shall seize" the people worldwide. High mountains will shake, and hills will be made low. Mountains and hills shall melt like wax next to a flame. Enoch prophesied that "the Earth shall be wholly rent in sunder," meaning that a massive earthquake would rip apart the planet. When the Lord returns, all the inhabitants living on Earth shall perish because "there shall be judgment on all" humankind.

Christians will experience a different outcome on that day. Enoch said, "But with the righteous He shall make peace." The Lord "will protect the elect, and mercy shall be upon them." They "shall all belong to God, and they will be prospered, and they shall all be blessed." And God "will help them all," and "light shall appear unto them." God will "make peace with them." Whether or not you accept the Book of Enoch as inspired scripture, its prophecies resemble Old Testament and New Testament scriptural themes about the final day:

God will return to Earth to judge all sin. A worldwide tremor will split the Earth, and the mountains and hills shall disappear. Angels will execute the wicked, but God's mercy will protect the elect, and His goodness will bless them. God's wrath is for the wicked, not the elect.

St. Jude told us to remember the "words which were spoken before of the apostles of our Lord Jesus Christ." In particular, he was referring to Paul and Peter, who both warned that mockers and scoffers would appear on Earth in the run-up to the final day. Such fools pursue their lusts. They mock holy things, have no fear of God, treat sacred matters with irreverence, laugh at admonitions to repent of their sins, and reject warnings that a day of judgment shall come to humanity. Likewise, they scoff at those who believe in the name of Jesus Christ to save their souls and eagerly wait for His return to Earth. Consumed and driven by their sensual lusts, such men and women separate themselves from God, His commandments, and His holy universal Church. Instead, they join themselves with Satan, his demons, and all who do works of iniquity.

They consciously choose to be damned.

But, beloved, remember ye the words which were spoken before of the apostles of our Lord Jesus Christ; how that they told you there should be mockers in the last time, who should walk after their own ungodly lusts. These be they who separate themselves, sensual, having not the Spirit.

Jude 17-19

According to St. Jude, we can lead some sinners to salvation by making a difference in their lives by showing compassion. However, others require stronger motivation to submit to Christ. For such people, we must make them fear judgment after death. We must pull them out of Hell's flames. Farmers know they must use different tools and methods to harvest various crops. Likewise, Christians need discernment to know when to use compassion or fear of judgment when sharing the Gospel with unsaved people. Isaiah said God would not break a bruised reed nor quench the smoking flax. He shall bring forth judgment unto truth. Jude said we must love some sinners into the Kingdom of God, yet we may have to scare Hell out of others to persuade them to make the right decision about their souls.

And of some have compassion, making a difference: and others save with fear, pulling them out of the fire; hating even the garment spotted by the flesh.

Jude 22-23

The final day's fire is coming, and the Church needs to get busy loving people into the Kingdom or pulling them off the road to Hell. Time is running out!

St. Jude alluded to the warnings by Apostles Paul and Peter about scoffers and mockers in the final days of the age of humankind. Peter said scoffers would come in the last days, eagerly pursuing their sensual lusts, and mockingly deride the truth that Jesus Christ is coming back to Earth. With obnoxious smirks, they ask, "Where is this Jesus you say is coming back?" They jab at Christians by saying, "Nothing has changed since the beginning of the world. Tomorrow will be the same as today." Showing no fear of Almighty God, such insolent men and women will brazenly mock devout Christians in the last days, saying, "We've heard this stuff all our lives. Now we are old, and nothing happened. I'm going to enjoy life and ignore the religious nuts." St. Peter forewarned us to be ready for them as the final day draws near.

This second epistle, beloved, I now write unto you; in both which I stir up your pure minds by way of remembrance: that ye may be mindful of the words which were spoken before by the holy prophets, and of the commandment of us the apostles of the Lord and Savior: knowing this first, that there shall come in the last days scoffers, walking after their own lusts, and saying, Where is the promise of his

coming? for since the fathers fell asleep, all things continue
as they were from the beginning of the creation.

2 Peter 3:1-4

People Who Mock the First Day
Also Mock the Final Day

The fire is coming, but the proud, haughty, and foolish people
of this world do not know it, nor do they desire to know it. Their
daily lives are controlled by their stomachs, genitals, digital devices,
and bank accounts. Suddenly and unexpectedly, the reapers shall
appear and carry them off to the lake of fire.

**And I will say to my soul, Soul, thou hast much goods laid
up for many years; take thine ease, eat, drink, and be merry.
But God said unto him, Thou fool, this night thy soul shall
be required of thee: then whose shall those things be, which
thou hast provided?**

Luke 12:19-20

According to St. Peter, lack of knowledge or awareness that
Jesus Christ will return someday will not be the chief reason people
will be deluded. Indeed, it's just the opposite! People willfully
choose to be ignorant. They claim the world has been the same
since the beginning of time. Their foolishness is the combined
product of having no fear of God, their rejection of His word, and
their denial that He is the Creator of the universe. In other words, a
growing number of people, especially in Western nations, embrace
a godless, humanistic worldview that exalts Darwinian evolution
to explain how the universe and life began.

Apostle Peter said God's spoken word created our planet, the heavens, and water. The same word that formed the universe, stars, and planets is the exact source of power that unleashed the Great Flood. Looking unto the last day of humanity, St. Peter said the present heavens and Earth are preserved now by God's same word and reserved to be consumed by fire on the day He judges wicked humans. Dissolving the universe by fire will not impose upon God an expectation that exceeds His abilities. It will demand no more effort on His part than speaking words that commenced the Great Flood.

In these last days, people brazenly deny that another global judgment will strike the world because they reject the reality of the first global judgment on sinful humanity. If they comprehended the terrible judgment rendered upon humankind by the worldwide Great Flood, they would not irreverently and callously disbelieve the Holy Bible's promise of a tremendous flaming flood of fire. Writing to the church in Rome, Paul the Apostle said that people do what they know to be wrong and avoid doing what they know to be correct. Consequently, they will not be allowed to plead ignorance as their defense on the Day of Judgment.

"For the wrath of God is revealed from heaven against all ungodliness and unrighteousness of men, who hold the truth in unrighteousness; because that which may be known of God is manifest in them; for God hath shewed it unto them. For the invisible things of him from the creation of the world are clearly seen, being understood by the things that are made, even his eternal power and Godhead; so that they are without excuse."

Romans 1:18-20

"From heaven" shows that the judgment is a divinely inflicted penalty against iniquity. "Against all ungodliness and unrighteousness" means the sentence is decreed by the Great Judge of the Universe for offenses against religion and righteousness, against Almighty God and His code of moral behavior. Most humans refuse or neglect to give God the honor, glory, and gratitude that He rightfully deserves. They worship idols or His Creation, but not the Creator.

God placed inside all humans an innate awareness of Himself. Apostle Paul said we plainly see the invisible things of God. How can you see invisible things? The "invisible things of God" refer to the attributes of the Godhead that cannot be perceived by human senses of sight, hearing, touch, smell, and taste. Neither can the invisible things of God be understood by human intellect and reasoning. Yet, Paul said the invisible is visible. From the day God made Adam and placed him in the Garden, humans have inwardly discerned the existence of their Maker.

Furthermore, Paul said humans understand the invisible things of God made possible by the things God made. Creation speaks to humankind every minute of each day: Worship the Creator! Humans can obtain some understanding of God's greatness by beholding, observing, studying, and appreciating the splendor of His Creation.

Regardless of atheists' lies, all legitimate sciences are studies of Creation. Man is still trying to figure out how the universe came into existence and continues to function with incredible precision and order. Great universities, research laboratories, and space observatories spend vast amounts of money each year to understand the universe's origin, the beginning of life, physics, biology, and genetics. European nations invested tens of billions of euros in constructing

CERN's Large Hadron Collider and announced plans to spend billions of euros on building the Future Circular Collider. Why did scientists build CERN in Switzerland? They were searching for the God particle! Known as the Higgs boson, the God particle is the elusive boson crucial to modern humanity's understanding of the structure of matter.

Many of the greatest minds on Earth nobly devote their lives to pursuing knowledge and understanding of the universe, yet steadfastly refuse to acknowledge and glorify the Creator. They proudly boast of their knowledge, not realizing they have become fools. They foolishly seek answers that omit God to exalt human intelligence. Like Nimrod, they purposely construct a Babylonian technological ziggurat to reach Heaven and overthrow God. However, their technological Tower of Babel will not survive the ferocious fire that will explode on the entire planet when Jesus returns.

God's wonderful Creation is so spectacular and beautiful that even atheists, agnostics, and idol-worshippers know in their hearts that it is too marvelous to have come into existence without a divine designer. Yet, their carnal minds stubbornly refuse to give God the glory and worship He rightfully deserves from the human creatures He made. Every sunrise and sunset and all the snow-covered mountains, rainbows, fields of wildflowers, cheerful songbirds, smiling infants, innocent kittens, deep canyons proclaim the glory of God. No excuse will prevail on the final day for people to claim they did not know God exists. Our purpose for living is to glorify God.

Hopefully, some may snap out of their delusion before they die or the Lord returns. Still, most will harden their hearts and stiffen their necks in rebellious opposition to God's sovereign rulership over their lives and the universe. Such rebels will stubbornly set their faces like flint to march to Hell proudly and defiantly. There is no hope for such fools.

> **For this they willingly are ignorant of, that by the word of God the heavens were of old, and the earth standing out of the water and in the water: whereby the world that then was, being overflowed with water, perished: but the heavens and the earth, which are now, by the same word are kept in store, reserved unto fire against the day of judgment and perdition of ungodly men.**
>
> 2 Peter 3:5-7

There is an Appointed Time
When Fire Shall destroy the Earth

Apostle Peter said Christians should not forget an important truth: There is no time in Heaven. As far as God is concerned, one day is as a thousand years, and a thousand years is as one day. He is the great I AM! Heaven does not possess, nor does it need, clocks and calendars. Time does not exist in Yahweh's dimension. God established time for us. Apostle Peter also reminded us that God isn't late fulfilling His promises. To men, it appears that God is taking a long time to fulfill Biblical prophecies, meaning the return of Jesus and the consummation of all things. Over 2,000 years have passed in human history since the ascension of Jesus, yet He has not returned to Earth. In the Parable of the Ten Virgins, the bridegroom delayed his arrival.

Likewise, the master traveled into a far country in the Parable of the Talents. The parabolic teaching is that Jesus returned to

Heaven, and God has delayed His Son's return to Earth. Why has the Second Advent been delayed? Because God is patient and merciful. He does not desire sinners to perish. Our Heavenly Father yearns to save all men and women. Therefore, He has graciously allotted time for sinners to renounce Satan and seek citizenship in the Kingdom of God. When the world enters the time of great tribulation, however, God will be compelled to put a stop date on it. Jesus said that if His Father did not shorten those days, no flesh would survive. He will end time for the sake of the saints. Despite His patience with sinful humanity, there is an appointed time when the heavens shall disappear, the elements of the universe shall melt, and the Earth shall burn up. When that appointed time arrives, time itself will disappear because humans will no longer need it.

> **But, beloved, be not ignorant of this one thing, that one day is with the Lord as a thousand years, and a thousand years as one day. The Lord is not slack concerning his promise, as some men count slackness; but is longsuffering to us-ward, not willing that any should perish, but that all should come to repentance. But the day of the Lord will come as a thief in the night; in the which the heavens shall pass away with a great noise, and the elements shall melt with fervent heat, the earth also and the works that are therein shall be burned up.**
>
> **2 Peter 3:8-10**

St. Peter the Apostle asked a penetrating question: If you understand that fire will consume everything on the final day, what kind of person should you be now in your daily living and conversations? How many people ponder this question daily as they interact with others and conduct their affairs in this world?

He said our conversation and behavior must be holy and godly. Apostle Peter further stated that Christians must look for and speed up the coming of the final day wherein a raging fire shall dissolve the heavens, and the elements of the universe shall melt with fervent heat. We base our anticipation of our Lord's Second Coming on His promise of new heavens and a new Earth where the righteous shall dwell with God forever. Seeing that we yearn for such things, St. Peter admonished the Church to be diligent that Jesus Christ shall find each of us on that day to be in peace, without spot, and blameless.

Seeing then that all these things shall be dissolved, what manner of person ought ye to be in all holy conversation and godliness, looking for and hasting unto the coming of the day of God, wherein the heavens being on fire shall be dissolved, and the elements shall melt with fervent heat? Nevertheless we, according to his promise, look for new heavens and a new earth, wherein dwelleth righteousness. Wherefore, beloved, seeing that ye look for such things, be diligent that ye may be found of him in peace, without spot, and blameless.

2 Peter 3:11-14

God's Warning to the Edomites
Who Persecute His People

Based on God's past judgment of nations, we can reasonably conclude that the final day will follow established Biblical patterns of divine actions. For example, God judged the kingdom of Idumea, also known as Edom. The Edomites were descendants of Esau, twin brother of Jacob. God changed Jacob's name to Israel, and Esau's name became Edom. God told Ezekiel that the Edomites had a "perpetual hatred" of Israel and used the sword to shed innocent blood. Therefore, a great calamity came suddenly and unexpectedly upon the Edomites.

Isaiah called all nations to come and hear, indeed let the Earth hear too, how the Lord's indignation burst upon the Edomites. If Isaiah were here today, he would post on social media this message: "Attention all nations! The Great Judge of the universe has issued a court summons. Pay attention to this warning. Almighty God shall judge every nation with the same fury He unleashed upon Edom for making war against His people."

Look around. Can you find the kingdom of Edom? It vanished! A worldwide judgment will spring upon all nations suddenly and unexpectedly on the final day. The wicked shall be executed with divine swords bathed in blood. The whole Earth shall emit a wretched stench coming from their carcasses, and their blood will melt the mountains. The Sun, Moon, and stars will disappear as violent convulsions reverberate throughout the cosmos. The heavens shall be rolled together like a parchment scroll. The sword of the Lord shall come down on all who persecuted and opposed His Son and His Church. All the inhabitants of the Earth will tremble and wail."

Come near, ye nations, to hear; and hearken, ye people: let the earth hear, and all that is therein; the world, and all things that come forth of it. For the indignation of the Lord

is upon all nations, and his fury upon all their armies: he hath utterly destroyed them, he hath delivered them to the slaughter. Their slain also shall be cast out, and their stink shall come up out of their carcasses, and the mountains shall be melted with their blood. And all the host of heaven shall be dissolved, and the heavens shall be rolled together as a scroll: and all their host shall fall down, as the leaf falleth off from the vine, and as a falling fig from the fig tree. For my sword shall be bathed in heaven: behold, it shall come down upon Idumea, and upon the people of my curse, to judgment.

Isaiah 34:1-5

The Old Testament Edomites represent the kingdom of the Son of Perdition, the enemies of the New Testament Church, faithful Israel. Isaiah prophesied that the Lord's vengeance would come in a day of global judgment and the year of recompenses for the controversy of Zion. Jeremiah prophesied that a noise would come even to the ends of the Earth, for the Lord has a controversy, a quarrel, with the nations. He will give the wicked to the sword. Hosea said the Lord has a controversy with all the land's inhabitants because there is no truth, nor mercy, or knowledge of God in the nation. Micah cried out to the mountains and the foundations of the Earth to hear the Lord's quarrel with the Jews.

Nobody can fathom the awful fury and doom that will strike the enemies of the Church of God. Her enemies shall be consumed by fire when the Lord returns to deliver the saints. However, even while persecuted, the Church must patiently wait for the glorious appearance of our blessed hope on the final day.

The King of Kings shall return to Earth because His Father has a controversy with the nations, and He's going to end it on His terms. God will not offer a negotiated settlement with rebellious humanity. Unequivocal submission will be the only option on that day when God commands every knee to bow before His victorious Son. His Second Coming will prove that Jesus is the Messiah promised to humanity since Adam's fall in the Garden of Eden, prophesied by the prophets, and proclaimed by preachers. The Ancient of Days will permanently silence all liars, deniers, scoffers, mockers, deceivers, and enemies of the Cross who opposed Jesus Christ and His Church. Heaven's court will close the books on the ancient quarrel between God and mankind. The Great Judge's judgment shall be final.

And the nations were angry, and thy wrath is come, and the time of the dead, that they should be judged, and that thou shouldest give reward unto thy servants the prophets, and to the saints, and them that fear thy name, small and great; and shouldest destroy them which destroy the earth.

Revelation 11:18

And I heard another out of the altar say, Even so, Lord God Almighty, true and righteous are thy judgments.

Revelation 16:7

The Second Coming of Jesus Christ on the final day shall be:

- Singular
- Sudden and unexpected
- Atmospheric
- Visible

- Noisy
- Disruptive
- Fiery
- Glorious
- Judgmental

CHAPTER 10

HIS SECOND COMING SHALL BE FINAL

D O YOU COMPREHEND THE finality of the final day? Final means the end, the termination of something, the conclusion. Most people cannot grasp the finality of "final." Final means it is over. Está terminado! C'est fini! Es ist vorbei! È finita! Het is gedaan! No matter the language spoken, it means the same: It is over!

Humans subconscfinal diously resist the fact that God long ago appointed a day in the future to end the universe, judge every human, and start over. St. Peter the Apostle said people are willfully ignorant of the fact that a forgotten world once existed before the Great Flood and that the heavens and the Earth are kept in store, by the same word that God spoke to send the Great Flood in the days of Noah and reserved unto fire against the day of judgment and perdition of ungodly men.

What comes to an end? Everything humans have known since the Garden of Eden. Life as humanity has known it will cease to exist the very moment Jesus Christ enters our dimension. The curtain will fall on the age of humankind, never to be reconstituted in its present state.

It will not only be the age of man that ends. The Earth, Sun, Moon, stars, indeed, the entire cosmos, shall vanish forever. Jesus' last words on the Cross were, "It is finished." Perhaps when He returns, Jesus will take a final look at His universe and declare, "It is done!"

> *And he said unto me, It is done.* **I am Alpha and Omega, the beginning and the end. I will give unto him that is athirst of the fountain of the water of life freely.**
>
> **Revelation 21:6**

Much has not been written in this book about the end of days. This book has few words about apostasy, the Antichrist, the Mark of the Beast, persecution, and tribulation. Many books could be written about each topic. Indeed, other authors have written numerous books on such topics. Often the focus of prophecy books has been on the works of the Antichrist and his dark kingdom. Many Christians devote too much attention to the Son of Perdition instead of the Son of Man. The so-called Antichrist will rule for a brief time. Jesus' kingdom shall have no end. Likewise, Christian films about the last days tend to dwell on mayhem, monsters, and meteors during the time of great tribulation.

Many Christians mistakenly confuse tribulation with wrath. Tribulation means calamity and suffering. Wrath means violent, passionate punishment. Satan's wrath will bring great tribulation upon the saints. God's wrath shall bring great tribulation upon the wicked. The saints will not be delivered from Satan's wrath until

God shortens the days for the elect's sake. The wicked will never be delivered from God's wrath. The saints will be removed from the Earth immediately before the wrath of God is poured out upon the wicked. The wicked shall be relocated too, from Earth to Hell. Satan's kingdom shall come to a sudden climactic end, but the saints' kingdom shall come to a sudden glorious beginning. Satan's future shall be perpetual torment in the everlasting lake of fire, but the saints' future shall be endless happiness in the presence of Almighty God, the Father, the Son, and the Holy Spirit.

What Remains After a Fervent Fire Melts the Elements?

What is the final day? It is the last "day of the Lord" visitation that humanity will ever receive from Heaven. It is the day when Almighty God shouts to rebellious humankind, "That is enough! I will not tolerate another day of your wickedness on the beautiful planet I created for you."

The final day is the grand finale of the age of mankind. It encompasses:

- the darkening of the cosmos
- the sign of the Lord
- the shout
- the trumpet blast
- the glorious appearing of Jesus Christ
- the opening of all graves
- the gathering and bundling of the wicked to be burned in the lake of fire
- the catching up of the saints to meet the Lord in the air

- the consummation of all things
- the rolling up of the universe as a scroll
- the gathering and separation of all humanity according to their respective nations
- the separation of all tribes and countries into groups of sheep and goats
- the Great White Throne of judgment
- the testing of the saints' works in this present life
- the creation of a new Earth and heavens
- the arrival of New Jerusalem
- the restitution of all things
- the relocation of God's home from Heaven to New Jerusalem
- the official start of eternity with God, the Father, the Son, and the Holy Spirit.

All of it happens in one day. Not a day as man measures time. God can accomplish all of it in one nanosecond of our present measurement of time. No human mind can grasp the speed at which Jesus will check off His final day to-do list. The age of grace will end suddenly. There will be no more forgiveness. Mercy will vanish, too, unneeded after the final day.

You will either be in the Kingdom of God forever or excluded from the Kingdom of God. The age of mankind on Earth will end abruptly. The final day is final.

Apostle Peter said the heavens would pass away with a great noise. What will produce a great noise? Will it be roaring flames? Will it be massive meteors exploding in the atmosphere? No, the tremendous noise shall be the ripping and tearing of the universe's fabric. Angels will be dispatched to the corners of the universe and instructed to roll up the solar systems, planets, moons, asteroids, black holes, stars, and everything else in the cosmos. Why will God destroy the universe? Because He will be finished with it. He made it. It belongs to Him. He can do anything He desires to do with it anytime He wants to do it. It is just that simple. We humans, however, don't think He would do it. God has a big surprise ahead for proud, arrogant, rebellious people. He will turn off the lights in the universe and start over.

Along with the great noise, St. Peter said the elements would melt with fervent heat. Elements refer to the material universe. The eight essential elements of the universe are hydrogen, helium, oxygen, carbon, neon, nitrogen, magnesium, and silicon. All matter will melt. Not a scintilla of an atom's skin will survive the fire. The temperature of the Sun's core is approximately twenty-seven million degrees Fahrenheit. The Heavenly fire that God will send on the final day will burn up the blazing Sun and all fire in the universe. What kind of fire consumes fire?

Melted Millennialism

The final day fire will not be kind to Millennialism. The day of the Lord will melt Millennialism. Millennialism is the doctrine that Jesus will set up a utopian kingdom in Israel. If you accept Millennialism, you believe that Jesus will give the Jews their long-desired dream of a revived Davidic empire that will extend Greater Israel to every nation in the world for one thousand years.

The doctrine was first known as chiliasm, as in kilo, meaning a thousand. The idea of some type of Millennial Kingdom has been around for many centuries. Early church fathers had differences of opinion about chiliasm. Some prominent God-fearing bishops espoused a view that Revelation 20:1-6 is a literal one-thousand-year kingdom on Earth. Chiliasm proponents included Justin Martyr and Irenaeus. Papias, Methodius, Lactantius, Theophilus, Tertullian, and Hippolytus also endorsed various versions of chiliasm. They taught that human history would last 6,000 years, followed by one-thousand years of a Messianic kingdom, and then the start of eternity. Thus, human history will last 7,000 years, and an eternal sabbath will follow.

For centuries, there was widespread opposition to chiliasm among early church bishops and elders. Eventually, bishops developed a consensus that declared chiliasm heretical. The main reason church fathers rejected the doctrine was that they saw it as a Jewish fable that restored a Jewish kingdom on Earth. Its proponents based their beliefs on nonbiblical literature, mainly Jewish rabbinical texts such as the Talmud. The Talmud says the Messiah will redeem Israel from bondage, gather the Jews to their land, build a third temple, and restore Jewish customs. Those rabbinical writings also claim that Gentiles will live in servitude to Jews during the Messianic age, and the kings of the Earth will bring expensive gifts to the Messiah in Jerusalem. The Talmud's predictions sound like modern Christian Zionism eschatology.

St. Augustine, the North African theologian, vanquished any possibility that chiliasm was a legitimate doctrine of the universal Church. His epic work was the *City of God*, a massive writing project that took a dozen years to complete. Augustine did not interpret the thousand years in Revelation 20 as a thousand-year kingdom after the Second Coming of Jesus. Instead, he said it is a figurative term representing the period between the first Advent of Jesus and the Second Advent of Jesus.

St. Augustine died in 430 AD. His interpretation of Revelation 20 was the dominant viewpoint of church bishops and theologians until the 1800s. Reformation-era church leaders also denounced chiliasm. John Calvin said the doctrine was "too childish either to need or to be worth a refutation." Martin Luther rejected chiliasm in the Augsburg Confession, which condemned the Anabaptists "who now scatter Jewish opinions that, before the resurrection of the dead, the godly shall occupy the kingdom of the world, the wicked being everywhere suppressed."

Reformers in Switzerland also rejected the doctrine. The Second Helvetic Confession reads, "We also reject the Jewish dream of a millennium, or golden age on earth, before the last judgment." Anglican Archbishop of Canterbury Thomas Cramer also condemned the Millennial Kingdom doctrine as a Jewish fable.

Millennialism was revived in the 1800s by John Nelson Darby's cult. Today's Christian Zionists, who fervently teach Darby's secret Rapture doctrine, also advocate his Millennial Kingdom doctrine. They believe Jesus will postpone the full manifestation of the Kingdom of God for a thousand years while Jews have their day in the Sun ruling the world. They also believe the Lord will postpone the Day of Judgment for a thousand years.

A deep dive into Christian Zionism reveals that they believe only Christians who go up in the air during the so-called secret Rapture will receive glorified bodies during the Millennial Kingdom. They think 144,000 Jewish male virgins will convert people to a new post-Christian religion during a seven-year time of great tribulation. They also claim that those converts will live in mortal bodies during the Millennial Kingdom, produce babies, and die. Furthermore, they believe that people born during the Millennial

Kingdom will not receive their glorified bodies until after a second resurrection of the dead at the end of the thousand years.

Could any of this science fiction theological nonsense be true? It directly contradicts the words of Jesus and the apostles who said sudden destruction would come upon the wicked and the Earth. How can fire consume the heavens and Earth if Christ establishes a kingdom on the old Earth for one thousand years?

Christian Zionists solved the problem the same way they invented the secret Rapture. They made up an explanation. They claim there is a gap between the Second Coming of Jesus and the Day of Judgment. Conveniently, the gap is one thousand years. They also teach that the Day of the Lord will last one thousand and seven years, meaning from the time of the secret rapture, the great tribulation, the Second Coming of Jesus, the Millennial Kingdom, and the Day of Judgment. Problem solved!

Did Jesus not clearly explain Himself? If you can see the Rapture pooka, you can see the thousand-year gap in the Holy Bible too. Those Christian Zionists are very imaginative. They even claim that God will not destroy the old Earth, but merely refurbish it. It is incredible what a new coat of paint will do for an old building.

Apostle Peter's second epistle, however, burns a massive hole in Millennialism. St. Peter spoke about the Second Coming of Jesus Christ and the Day of Judgment. He said the heavens and Earth that now exist are reserved for fire, kept for the day of judgment and destruction of the ungodly. St. Peter also said the sky would pass away with a loud noise, and intense heat would destroy the elements of the cosmos. Meanwhile, the Earth and the works in it will be burned up too. The Apostle said the saints are waiting for new heavens and a new Earth in which righteousness dwells.

Where is the one-thousand-year gap? Did Jesus Christ and Apostle Peter not know about the Millennial Kingdom? Or did they assume we would see the gap between the Second Coming and the Day of Judgment? And did they also think that we would not take the scriptures about God burning up the Earth and the universe with fervent heat seriously? Did they assume we understood that God would refurbish the old Earth, not create a new planet? Either Jesus and St. Peter did not clearly explain the meaning of their words, or today's Christian Zionists have believed and taught false doctrines.

A Disposable Universe

The universe has an expiration date. God created the cosmos for mankind's one-time use. When its expiration date arrives, the Creator will toss His universe into Heaven's trash bin like a used, soiled tablecloth.

Why? The explanation does not require a deeply profound theological thesis. God will throw away the existing universe because He will be finished with it. He will not need it anymore when the current universe becomes obsolete. Why would the Creator hold on to an old, worn-out universe? Should He box it up and store the old universe in Heaven's garage? He will become bored with His past work. Instead, God will be eager to move on to something new, something bigger and better.

> **For since the beginning of the world *men* have not heard, nor perceived by the ear, neither hath the eye seen, O God, beside thee, *what* he hath prepared for him that waiteth for him.**
>
> **Isaiah 64:4**

Reality will instantly change the moment Jesus arrives in man's dimension of time, space, and matter. Jesus said as the days of Noah were, so shall also the Second Coming of Jesus be. People ate and drank, married, and gave in marriage until Noah entered the ark. Suddenly the floodwaters came and washed them all away. The same thing will happen on the final day. It will be business as usual for billions of people around the world. They will go about their daily routine like every other day, not knowing it will be their last day alive on this Earth. Most of them will be bundled and burned in a nanosecond because they lived their lives without Christ. They chose to live on Earth separated from Jesus Christ. They will spend eternity in Hell forever separated from God.

Can you imagine the eerie sound of moaning that will sweep over the planet when the Sun, the Moon, and stars go dark? Suddenly the sky will change. Have you ever been in a theater or auditorium during an electrical blackout? Imagine a universal blackout! Billions of people will gasp simultaneously around the world. Fear will grip all who are outside the ecclesia of God. Joyous anticipation shall sweep over the saints who will immediately turn their eyes upward because they instantly know that their redemption is drawing nigh.

What global reaction will be evoked by the appearance of the sign of the Son of Man? The wicked shall wail, but the saints shall worship. The sign, perhaps the Cross in the sky, will produce joyful shouts of praise from the lips of saints in every nation. The victorious voices of millions of saved saints will saturate the atmosphere with universal proclamations of "King Jesus! We worship You." It will be far different for the wicked and unrepentant sinners. The sign of the Son of man in the sky will produce horrific fear and dread in their hearts and minds.

When Jesus enters our universe, He will power down the lighting. Angels will go to all solar systems, like maintenance workers going from room to room in an office building and turn off the lights in each part of the universe. They will never shine again.

When a business owner of a tall building decides to implode it to build something new on the site, the last step is the cutoff of electrical power in the building before the implosion. That's what Jesus will do when He arrives. He will cut off the electricity to the Sun, the Moon, and stars. It will happen immediately before the implosion of the universe. When the lights go out, angels will commence rolling up the universe. That's why both Old Covenant prophet Isaiah and New Covenant apostle John saw the universe dissolved and rolled up like a parchment scroll. People roll up scrolls to store or discard them. God will roll up the universe to toss it on the final day! Christians fail to consider how excited God will be on that day to throw away the old and create something new.

> **And all the host of heaven shall be dissolved, and the heavens shall be rolled together as a scroll:** and all their host shall fall down, as the leaf falleth off from the vine, and as a falling fig from the fig tree.
>
> Isaiah 34:4

> **And the heaven departed as a scroll when it is rolled together;** and every mountain and island were moved out of their places.
>
> Revelation 6:14

Isaiah said the "host of heaven" will drop like a leaf falling from the vine or a falling fig from the tree. Micah saw the Lord come forth out of His place and tread upon the high places of the

Earth, and the mountains turned molten under Him. St. John the Revelator saw every mountain and island moved out of their places when the heavens were rolled together as a scroll.

God is not obligated to request permission from humans to discard His property. He will toss planets, stars, comets, and asteroids into Heaven's dumpster. How will God do it? He created it by His spoken words, and He can abolish it by His spoken words. Perhaps God will merely inhale back into Himself the words He spoke at Creation. Somehow the present universe will cease to exist. One thing is sure. Destroying the universe will not require any heavy lifting on God's part. He will not break into a sweat doing it. God will merely speak it out of existence the same way He spoke it into reality.

Jesus Shall Kill Death

Death shall die on the final day. Jesus will bury it in the lake of fire. Old Testament prophet Isaiah prophesied that the Messiah will "swallow up death in victory." Death is the common sorrow shared by all humans, rich and poor, the powerful and weak. When death is dead, God "will wipe away tears from off all faces."

Death must die. Apostle Paul said the last enemy Christ shall destroy on the final day is death. "Then comes the end," said St. Paul. When death is dead, the Son will deliver up the kingdom to the Father. The conquering Christ will lay the spoils of His victory over Satan at the foot of the throne of Almighty God. In his first epistle to the Church in Corinth, Apostle Paul wrote, "Then cometh the end, when he shall have delivered up the kingdom to God, even the Father; when he shall have put down all rule and all authority and power."

What happens next? Get ready! Our Heavenly Father will give the Kingdom to us! Old Testament prophet Daniel saw it in a vision. He wrote, "And the kingdom and dominion, and the greatness of the kingdom under the whole heaven, shall be given to the people of the saints of the Most High, whose kingdom is an everlasting kingdom, and all dominions shall serve and obey Him." Daniel said the saints of the Most High "shall take the kingdom and possess the kingdom forever." When will these things happen? Daniel saw in the vision that the Antichrist "made war with the saints and prevailed against them." Satan's forces will succeed for a season "until the Ancient of Days" arrives, and judgment is given to the saints. Daniel saw "the time came that the saints possessed the kingdom."

Before the saints can live forever, death must die. Old Testament prophet Isaiah foretold the great resurrection of souls when the Messiah returns for His people. Isaiah prophesied that Jesus "will swallow up death in victory; and the Lord God will wipe away tears from off all faces; and the rebuke of His people shall be taken away from off all the Earth." St. Paul quoted Isaiah in his first epistle to the Church in Corinth. Apostle Paul wrote, "So when this corruptible shall have put on corruption, and this mortal shall have put on immortality, then shall be brought to pass the saying that is written, 'Death is swallowed up in victory. O death, where is thy sting? O grave, where is thy victory?'"

Referring to Satan, the Holy Bible appropriately represents death as a poisonous serpent. Death conquered the first Adam. The last Adam conquered the conqueror. The serpent's sting has been rendered harmless. By Adam, death came to humanity. By Jesus, victory over death came to humankind. All must die, as did Adam. Souls in Christ, however, shall overcome death on Resurrection Day.

By His death and resurrection, Jesus obtained a complete victory over death, not only for Himself but for all men and women who believe in His name and are baptized into His Church. They too shall be raised from the dead. His victory will swallow death forever. No saint will ever die after the final day. The last day shall be the fulfillment of Old Testament prophet Hosea's prophecy that God "will ransom them from the power of the grave" and "redeem them from death." Speaking through Hosea's lips, the Redeemer cried out, "O death, I will be thy plagues; O grave, I will be thy destruction..."

When the angel blows God's trumpet, and Jesus shouts, the bodies of the dead in Christ will come forth from their graves. They will pass through death and rise in incorruptible bodies. Immediately after that, those alive in Christ will likewise undergo an instantaneous change in their nature on the final day. It shall happen faster than a blink of an eye. The living shall see the resurrection of the dead. The risen dead shall see the transformation of the living. White garments will clothe both groups of saints. Jesus will snatch up into the air the resurrected saints and the transformed saints to meet Him in the clouds.

In his second letter to Timothy, St. Paul wrote, "but is now made manifest by the appearing of our Savior Jesus Christ, who hath abolished death, and hath brought life and immortality to light through the gospel." The Greek verb for *abolished* means "to make useless, powerless." Apostle Paul spoke of the abolishment of death as though it had already happened. St. Paul was supremely confident that the resurrection of Jesus Christ made sure the eventual elimination of death.

The Holy Bible identifies three types of death: spiritual death, physical death, and eternal death. Every kind of death is the result of sin. Each death involves separation. God never intended for death to be present on Earth. God never intended Adam and Eve to die. Neither were animals designed to experience death. The first death after Creation was spiritual death. Adam's sin separated his spirit from his Maker. The second death came to humanity when Adam's physical body died. Death separated his soul from his body. The third type of death is eternal separation from God. Eternal death shall grip the wicked on the day of the Lord and never let go.

When you were born as a baby, your body was alive, but your spirit was dead. It can only be awakened to life by repentance, faith in the name of Jesus Christ, and water baptism. That is why Jesus said you must be born again. Not a physical birth, but a spiritual birth. Death loses its grip on each man, woman, and child when they are born again.

Next comes physical death. Your body cannot live without your soul. How can it be reunited? The Resurrection! Physical death is the separation of your soul from your body. Resurrection is the reunion of your soul with your body. Death will be stingless when your body dies. Your Savior will escort you from this world to the peaceful abode where your soul will rest until the day of the Lord, when He will resurrect your dead body.

When the resurrected Savior of the world appears on the final day, His shout will open all graves. He will come with the souls of departed saints. They will reunite with their new glorified bodies that will come out of the graves. Saints alive on Earth when the Lord returns shall experience a transformation. When their eyes see Jesus in all His splendor and glory, He will glorify their bodies to be like his body.

Lastly comes eternal death. The wicked shall be resurrected unto eternal death when Jesus Christ returns. He will sentence them to eternal damnation in the lake of fire. Eternal death, however, cannot touch the saints. Eternal death shall have no power over the disciples of Christ. Sadly, the wicked shall be under its dominion forever. Eternal death is eternal separation from God.

Death is the last enemy destroyed because it is the "wages of sin." Sin came first, followed by death. Therefore, Christ must conquer sin and death in that order. Satan brought sin to man, and sin brought death. Death is the fruit of sin, the curse of the law. Physical death must continue to exist in the world until sin comes to an end. Sin will not end until Christ returns.

In the twentieth chapter of the Apocalypse, St. John saw the demise of Satan and death in his vision. Christ destroyed both of them in that order: Satan first, followed by death. It shall happen "when the thousand years are ended...." Inspired by John Nelson Darby, today's Christian Zionists place this event on their elaborate prophecy charts at one thousand years after the Second Coming of Christ. Traditional Christians interpret this scripture as meaning the day of the Lord when Jesus returns in glory. The conventional Christian interpretation is that the thousand years is a metaphor for an unknown number of years between the First Advent and Second Advent of the Lord. Thus, "when the thousand years are ended" means when Jesus Christ comes on the final day of humankind. Before the last day, Satan will be released from his pit prison and allowed to deceive the nations. Such will be the age leading up to and including the great tribulation for the saints of God.

"When the thousand years are ended," St. John saw in this vision fire come down from Heaven. "And the devil who had deceived them was thrown into the lake of fire and sulfur, where the beast and the false prophet were, and they will be tormented day and night forever and ever." What follows the imprisonment of Satan? Death is the next and last enemy to be conquered forever. St. John "saw a Great White Throne and the One who sat on it; the Earth and the heaven fled from His presence; and no place was found for them." The old Earth had disappeared in John's vision. It was Judgment Day. He "saw the dead, great and small standing before the throne." God's library was opened, including the Book of Life. "And the dead were judged according to their works, as recorded in the books."

St. John said, "the sea gave up the dead that were in it, and Death and Hades gave up the dead that were in them, and all were judged according to what they had done." Finally, Death and Hades, the abode of the dead, were thrown into the lake of fire. The lake of fire is the second death, meaning eternal death. King Jesus will throw anyone whose name is not in the Book of Life into the lake of fire.

In his vision, St. John the Revelator saw the victorious Son of God declare, "I am He who lives, though I was dead. Look! I am alive forevermore. Amen. And I have the keys of Hades and Death." In His letter to the seven churches in the Apocalypse, Jesus said, "He who has an ear, let him hear what the Spirit says to the churches. He who overcomes shall not be hurt by the second death."

The demise of death shall be final. Nobody will ever die again after the final day.

God's Love Story

A popular misconception of the Book of the Revelation of Jesus Christ, also known as the Apocalypse, is that it is a religious sci-fi book filled with scary stories about a seven-headed beast with ten horns, a dragon, and foul-mouth talking frogs. When a catastrophic storm strikes a city, typically, newspaper reports describe the storm as "apocalyptic," as though the word apocalyptic means end-of-the-world destruction. Apocalypse does not mean destruction. The original word in Greek is *apokalypsis*. It represents an unveiling, a revelation of something that God hid. The Holy Bible's Book of the Apocalypse is the revelation of Jesus Christ, the unveiling of the King and His kingdom.

People should not read the Apocalypse literally. Its pages contain imagery, figures, and symbols. Events in the Book of the Revelation of Jesus Christ should also not be viewed chronologically. Scenes in the vision change from chapter to chapter, but that does not mean the scenes follow a linear, chronological order. Likewise, readers should not interpret St. John's vision as futuristic, meaning predictions of the future. Some things in the Apocalypse have already happened, some things are happening now, and some things still must be fulfilled.

The best way to read and interpret Apostle John's vision is to see it as God's endearing love story. The Apocalypse is the unveiling of Jesus Christ, the King of Kings and Lord of Lords. It reveals God's extraordinary love of human beings and His mercy and grace to redeem them from their fall in the Garden of Eden. That's why the Bible starts in Genesis with God walking with humans in the first Garden of Eden and concludes in the Apocalypse with God walking with humans in a new Garden of Eden. The same tree of life in the Garden of Eden will also stand tall in New Jerusalem.

The Apocalypse is the Revelation of Jesus Christ, not the Revelation of Scary End Time Prophecies. It's all about Jesus! The entire Holy Bible, Old and New testaments, is about Jesus Christ. It's not about ancient Israel. It is about the Ancient of Days! It is not about circumcised Jews in the modern State of Israel. It is about all true Israelites worldwide with circumcised hearts. They are the genuine people of the promise, the called-out ones, the ecclesia, who have followed and obeyed God by faith throughout the ages since the Book of Genesis. Reading it in a literal, linear, chronological, futuristic manner blinds your eyes from beholding the beauty of God's love story.

Old Testament prophet Daniel saw the extraordinary end of the story too. Daniel saw the majestic and triumphant King Jesus Christ coming with the clouds of heaven as the Son of Man, meaning the Judge of humankind. He approached the Ancient of Days who gave His Son dominion, glory, and a kingdom that all people, nations, and languages should serve Him forever.

> **I beheld till the thrones were cast down, and the Ancient of days did sit, whose garment was white as snow, and the hair of his head like the pure wool: his throne was like the fiery flame, and his wheels as burning fire. A fiery stream issued and came forth from before him: a thousand thousands ministered unto him, and ten thousand times ten thousand stood before him: the judgment was set, and the books were opened. I beheld then because of the voice of the great words which the horn spake: I beheld**

even till the beast was slain, and his body destroyed, and given to the burning flame. As concerning the rest of the beasts, they had their dominion taken away: yet their lives were prolonged for a season and time. I saw in the night visions, and, behold, one like the Son of man came with the clouds of heaven, and came to the Ancient of days, and they brought him near before him. And there was given him dominion, and glory, and a kingdom, that all people, nations, and languages, should serve him: his dominion is an everlasting dominion, which shall not pass away, and his kingdom that which shall not be destroyed.

Daniel 7:9-14

The Day of the Lord is the final day of the long saga that began at Creation. It is about Jesus Christ:

- ushering in the finality of the end of the age of humanity
- conquering death and Hades
- making His enemies His footstool
- casting Satan into the everlasting lake of fire
- receiving His inheritance, meaning saved souls
- presenting the Kingdom back to His Heavenly Father
- the Father giving the Kingdom to the saints
- the consummation of all things
- restoring saved humanity to the Garden of Eden to dwell forever with God, the Father, the Son, and the Holy Spirit
- the creation of a new Earth
- the arrival of New Jerusalem
- the beginning of eternity.

The Creator Will Create a New Thing

The Creator of the present universe is eager to do a new thing. This wonderful "new thing" will be unprecedented in human history. It shall spring forth like fresh flowers, and the Divine Creator will bring forth a bud that will blossom with unspeakable beauty. God will make a way in the wilderness for His chosen people, the people of promise, the saints who love and obey Jesus Christ. The ecclesia has always consisted of pilgrims passing through this world looking for a city which has foundations, whose builder and maker is God. He will suddenly change their environment. He will deliver them from this old dying world and refresh them with new rivers of pure water to satisfy their thirsty souls. God promised to provide for His people in the wilderness on their journey from Babylon to Jerusalem just as He provided for the Hebrews on their way from Egypt to Canaan. We can rest assured that our Heavenly Father will give us a safe passage on our journey from Mystery Babylon to New Jerusalem.

Isaiah saw it thousands of years ago. What did he see? He saw God deliver Israel out of Babylon and bring them into Jerusalem.

> **Behold, I will do a new thing; now it shall spring forth; shall ye not know it? I will even make a way in the wilderness, and rivers in the desert.**
>
> **Isaiah 43:19**

The "new thing" started in Bethlehem with the birth of the Messiah. It blossomed at Calvary and flowed from the upper room on Pentecost. It shall come to fruition on the final day when the Creator abolishes this present world and creates a new world where

He will dwell forever with the sealed saints who believed in the name of Jesus Christ to save them from eternal damnation.

Speaking of the promised Messiah, Jeremiah asked the Israelites how long they would backslide. Speaking of the Christ Child in the Virgin Mary's undefiled womb, the prophet said the Lord had created a new thing on Earth. The "new thing" is Jesus! It's all about Jesus. Get your eyes off the State of Israel in the Last Days. Fix your eyes upon Jesus! He is the only star of the show. God's invitation is for all races, ethnicities, and tribes to join Him at His Son's spectacular wedding feast. You must, however, RSVP to the host now to confirm your seat. Walk-ins will not be permitted to enter on that glorious wedding day. Proper attire will be required.

> **How long wilt thou go about, O thou backsliding daughter? for the Lord hath created a new thing in the earth, A woman shall compass a man.**
>
> **Jeremiah 31:22**

Apostle John saw in the Patmos vision a "new heaven and a new Earth." Where were the old heaven and Earth? Where did they go? John said the first heaven and the first Earth had passed away and no longer existed. Neither did the sea remain.

> **And I saw a new heaven and a new earth: for the first heaven and the first earth were passed away; and there was no more sea.**
>
> **Revelation 21:1**

If there is a first Heaven and a first Earth, there must be another Heaven and another Earth that follows the original version. The hope of a new beginning for humanity runs throughout the Holy

Bible, from Genesis to the Apocalypse. Abraham did not yearn for a political kingdom with hundreds of square miles of physical territory under the dominion of his descendants. He sojourned, meaning he lived temporarily, in the land of promise as somebody living in a strange country and merely passing through on his way to another home. Abraham didn't build a permanent house. Instead, he lived in temporary tents. Abraham lived in the physical land God promised him, but he treated it as a strange country that wasn't his home. Why? The beloved patriarch of our faith was looking for a city whose builder and maker is God.

Abraham, who was not Jewish, yearned to live in New Jerusalem. A future Zionist political State of Israel meant nothing to Abraham. New Jerusalem is the ecclesia of God in a new and perfect state. We shall live with Abraham in New Jerusalem! It is the city he was yearning to find. He is our example of being justified by faith. Abraham will come out of his grave on the final day and excitedly shout for joy that he will finally live in New Jerusalem.

By faith he sojourned in the land of promise, as in a strange country, dwelling in tabernacles with Isaac and Jacob, the heirs with him of the same promise: for he looked for a city which hath foundations, whose builder and maker is God.

Hebrews 11:9-10

One of the keywords that run throughout the Holy Bible is "new." God frequently spoke about "new" things: a new song, new wine, a new moon, a new cart, new gate, a new thing, new fruit, new bottles, new covenant, new testament, new mercies, new heart, new spirit, new tongues, new commandments, new creature, new man, new heavens, new Earth, new Jerusalem. He loves making new things.

Our Heavenly Father always had a plan to redeem fallen humans and restore them to the Garden of Eden. The prophets foretold the double blessing God would give the saints: The Messiah and a new earthly home where they will be free to worship Christ without opposition from the Devil and rebellious sinners. Isaiah saw in his spirit the new heavens and new Earth. He said the saints would forget the old cosmos and this present life. God will forget the names of people blotted out of the Book of Life. Our Heavenly Father does not desire us to grieve throughout eternity in remembrance of our relatives and friends who did not enter the Kingdom of God but are suffering in the everlasting lake of fire.

For, behold, I create new heavens and a new earth: and the former shall not be remembered, nor come into mind.

Isaiah 65:17

New Jerusalem can only be situated on a new Earth that is under a new heaven. Life on the first day after the final day will be entirely new. Nobody can imagine what the saints will see and experience on the first day after the last day. It is incomprehensible! The first day after the final day shall bring forth God's final seat where He shall remain for eternity. We shall dwell together with Him for eternity with no separation.

But as it is written, Eye hath not seen, nor ear heard, neither have entered into the heart of man, the things which God hath prepared for them that love him.

1 Corinthians 2:9

The Restitution of All Things

This message is not a strange, new doctrine but the same message spoken by holy prophets since the fall of Adam and Eve. It is the Gospel! The Church did not start in Jerusalem on the day of Pentecost. Since the beginning of time, angels and prophets preached Jesus Christ and the restitution of all things to fallen men and women.

> *...and he shall send Jesus Christ, which before was preached unto you:* **whom the heaven must receive until the times of restitution of all things,** *which God hath spoken by the mouth of all his holy prophets since the world began.*
>
> Acts 3:20-21

"He shall send Jesus Christ," meaning the Savior who was always promised by God from the beginning of the world to save people, to redeem people, to teach people, to gather His people to Himself, to judge the world, and to punish the wicked. The Heavenly Father sent His only begotten Son to Earth to atone for humankind's sins and make way for fallen men and women to reunite with their Maker.

"Whom the heaven must receive..." means that the resurrected Savior's abode is in Heaven until the final day. Immediately after Jesus commissioned the apostles to be His witness "unto the uttermost part of the Earth," He was taken up, "and a cloud received him out of their sight."

"Whom the heaven must receive" also signifies that Jesus was exalted and clothed with glory and power when He ascended from Earth to Heaven. In His place, the Holy Spirit, our Comforter and Advocate, was sent to represent Him on Earth as the only Vicar of Christ until the Second Coming of the Lord. His duties include:

- directing and assisting the Church (ecclesia) in the great commission of preaching the Gospel of the Kingdom to all nations as a witness
- encouraging the saints
- advocating for the saints
- convicting saints of sin.

King Jesus is in Heaven now ruling the Kingdom of Heaven. The Holy Spirit is on the Earth, overseeing, as governor, the one, holy, catholic, and apostolic Church in her glorious endeavors to fulfill the Master's great commission.

"Until the times of restitution of all things" means that Jesus Christ must remain in Heaven until the final day. God's long-running controversy with the nations shall end abruptly. He will settle the score in His favor. The Great Judge will hear no appeal for another trial because His decrees are absolute and non-negotiable. Jesus shall avenge the iniquities committed against His Heavenly Father since the fall of Adam and Eve. He will judge the living and the dead and give the wicked the punishment they justly deserve. He will avenge all injustices on Earth committed since the beginning of the world. Every man and woman, great and lowly, rich and poor, famous and unknown, shall bow their knees and confess with their tongues that Jesus Christ is King of Kings and Lord of Lords.

Jesus Christ shall exalt His glorious Church. He shall heal and restore Creation to its proper order and splendor without sin and death. The victorious, triumphant conquering King Jesus will present the kingdom to Almighty God. The Father, in turn, will give the Kingdom to the saints. The restitution of all things is the completion of the work of Jesus Christ. The new Creation will have peace and order as it was at the beginning of the old creation.

You will not find a temple in New Jerusalem, nor shrines and altars. God will no longer dwell in a temple in Heaven, nor will He dwell in a temple on Earth. Almighty God and His Son shall be our temple.

And I saw no temple therein: for the Lord God Almighty and the Lamb are the temple of it.

Revelation 21:22

The Sun, Moon, and stars will reach their expiration date when they have completed their original purpose for existence. New Jerusalem will not need obsolete lighting fixtures. God's glory and Jesus' light will illuminate the grand city.

And the city had no need of the sun, neither of the moon, to shine in it: for the glory of God did lighten it, and the Lamb is the light thereof.

Revelation 21:23

The restitution of all things is beyond the comprehension of the most educated, intelligent theologians, philosophers, intellectuals, and scientists in the world. Who can imagine and describe the first day after the last day? Imagine life without sin! No devil, no temptations, no demons, no evil, no violence, no wars, no disease. No death, only life! Imagine the animal kingdom restored to its remarkable beauty: no wild beasts, no predators, no carnivores, and poisonous serpents.

It would be breathtaking and astounding if God takes us back to the original Garden of Eden. Living with God in an abundantly beautiful and peaceful garden environment, never to experience any of the troubles that have plagued humans since the fall of Adam and Eve, would be a tremendously gracious gift from our Heavenly Father. But wait, there's more! God will go beyond restoring Creation to its original state. The great Creator will create again! God promised He would do it for us. God will not remodel our present planet. He will create something wonderful and new for us.

> **Nevertheless we, according to his promise, look for new heavens and a new earth, wherein dwelleth righteousness.**
>
> **2 Peter 3:13**

> **And I saw a new heaven and a new earth: for the first heaven and the first earth were passed away; and there was no more sea.**
>
> **Revelation 21:1**

Our Heavenly Father eagerly anticipates the day when He creates something new for the children who love Him. Our finite human minds cannot comprehend the new Earth's size, form, features, and beauty. Think of wonders grander and more spectacular than Mount Everest, Victoria Falls, the Grand Canyon, Yosemite, Zhangjiajie, the Cliffs of Moher, Ha Long Bay, Niagara Falls, and the Marble Caves. It will be infinitely more beautiful than the original old Earth in its original perfect state.

> **And I saw a new heaven and a new earth: for the first heaven and the first earth were passed away; and there was no more sea. And I John saw the holy city, new Jerusalem, coming down from God out of heaven, prepared as a bride**

adorned for her husband. And I heard a great voice out of heaven saying, Behold, the tabernacle of God is with men, and he will dwell with them, and they shall be his people, and God himself shall be with them, and be their God. And God shall wipe away all tears from their eyes; and there shall be no more death, neither sorrow, nor crying, neither shall there be any more pain: for the former things are passed away. And he that sat upon the throne said, Behold, I make all things new. And he said unto me, Write: for these words are true and faithful. And he said unto me, It is done. I am Alpha and Omega, the beginning and the end. I will give unto him that is athirst of the fountain of the water of life freely. He that overcometh shall inherit all things; and I will be his God, and he shall be my son.

Revelation 21:1-7

Imagine the first day after the final day! It will be joy unspeakable and full of glory!

The Second Coming of Jesus Christ on the final day shall be:
- Singular
- Sudden and unexpected
- Atmospheric
- Visible
- Noisy
- Disruptive
- Fiery
- Glorious
- Judgmental
- Final

EPILOGUE

FRIGHTENING YOU ABOUT THE end of the world was not my motive in writing *Final Day*. Our focus must always remain fixed on the first day after the final day. The Gospel is about the Kingdom.

None of us know if we will be alive on Earth when Jesus returns. Multitudes of Christians since the Resurrection hoped they would be among the blessed generation that would be caught up into the air to meet our Lord. They entered their blissful repose without seeing the manifestation of the promise. Like Abraham, they were looking for "a city which hath foundations, whose builder and maker is God." Those saints died without receiving the promises of God. Having seen them far away and convinced the promises were true, they told everybody they were only pilgrims passing through a foreign country on their way home.

> These all died in faith, not having received the promises, but having seen them afar off, and were persuaded of them, and embraced them, and confessed that they were

strangers and pilgrims on the earth. For they that say such things declare plainly that they seek a country. And truly, if they had been mindful of that country from whence they came out, they might have had opportunity to have returned. But now they desire a better country, that is, an heavenly: wherefore God is not ashamed to be called their God: for he hath prepared for them a city.

Hebrews 11:13-16

If we die before the final day, we can rest peacefully knowing that Jesus Christ will raise us on the last day. Indeed, we shall see Jesus return to Earth because He will bring along our souls and call forth our bodies to come out of the graves to witness the glorious appearance of our blessed hope. When we see Jesus, He will change our bodies to be like Him. The Resurrection is the hope of humanity.

The Holy Bible tells the true story of a young man named Lazarus. His sisters were Martha and Mary, the same Mary who anointed Jesus with ointment and wiped His feet with her hair. Lazarus became very sick, and his sisters sent word to Jesus to come quickly to heal him. Jesus, however, waited two days. Afterward, He told his disciples that Lazarus was sleeping. They perceived He meant that Lazarus was resting. Jesus spoke plainly to them: Lazarus is dead.

By the time Jesus approached the outskirts of Bethany, Lazarus had been in the grave for four days. Neighbors, friends, and relatives tried to comfort the grieving sisters. When Jesus finally approached the town's outskirts, Martha left her house to meet Him. Mary, however, sat quietly in her home. Upon meeting Jesus, Martha wasted no time letting Him know what she thought about His delay in responding to their late brother's health crisis. She told Jesus her brother would be alive if the Lord had come to Bethany days earlier. In other words, Martha said, "Thanks a lot Jesus! Our brother is dead because you are late. We believed you could heal him, but you took your time getting here and now he's dead."

To her credit, Martha made an abrupt U-turn and corrected her speech. She wisely said, "But I know, that even now, whatsoever you will ask of God, God will give it to you." Jesus lovingly replied to His dear friend's grieving sister, "Your brother will rise again."

Unlike the Sadducees, Martha was a Jew who believed in the resurrection of the dead. She correctly answered Jesus, "I know that he shall rise again in the resurrection at the last day." Yes, Martha believed there would be a final day!

Jesus answered by speaking the most remarkable words of all time! He proclaimed, "I am the resurrection, and the life: he who believes in me, though he were dead, yet shall he live; and whosoever lives and believes in me shall never die."

He asked Martha, "Do you believe this?" Martha answered, "Yes, Lord. I believe that you are the Christ, the Son of God, which should come into the world."

Immediately, Martha went to tell Mary the good news that Jesus was calling her to meet Him. Mary bolted from the house to follow Martha. Her relatives and friends assumed Mary was going to the grave to mourn for her brother, so they accompanied her. Instead, she traveled to the place outside of town where Martha encountered Jesus.

Upon seeing Jesus, Mary fell at his feet and said, "Lord, if you had been here, my brother would not have died." Jesus was moved with compassion as He saw Mary and her friends weeping. Jesus wept too. He cried for two reasons. Firstly, Jesus compassionately empathized with the sisters' grief. He felt their pain and showed them that He hurt too. Secondly, death angered Jesus. He pitied humans who must suffer for Adam's fall in the Garden of Eden. He came to Earth to conquer death.

Mary's friends realized how much Jesus loved Lazarus. Some of the Jews, however, mockingly said Jesus could have healed Lazarus since He opened the eyes of blind men. In emotional agony, Jesus groaned as He walked toward the grave. After Lazarus died, his friends placed his body in a cave, and a stone covered the entrance. Jesus instructed the people to remove the stone. Martha exclaimed, "Jesus, my brother has been dead four days! His body stinks."

Jesus replied, "Did I not tell you that if you believed, you would see the glory of God?"

The people removed the stone from the cave. Jesus looked up to Heaven and prayed, "Father, I thank You that You have heard Me. I know that You always hear Me. But because of the people standing around, I said this, that they may believe that You sent Me."

When He finished His prayer, Jesus cried out with a loud voice, "Lazarus, come forth!"

The Bible says that the dead man came out! Grave clothes wrapped around his hands and feet, and a cloth covered his face. Jesus said to them, "Unbind him, and let him go."

What does it mean for us on the final day?

Jesus loved Lazarus as a dear friend. He truly cared about him. He wept at his grave. Yes, Jesus pitied Mary, Martha, and Lazarus' friends and relatives. More importantly, Jesus felt pity for all of humankind in bondage to death and Hades because of sin. He wept because His Father's children were marred and scarred by Satan's revenge against God. Humans suffered sickness, pain, and death because of Lucifer's hatred of God.

As the Son of Man befriended a human named Lazarus, so too has Jesus befriended every man, woman, and child who believed in His name to save their souls from damnation. Jesus Christ does not call Christians his "servants." He calls us His friends. If you are a born-again, baptized saint in Christ's Church, you are Jesus' friend. He loves you as He loved Lazarus.

> **I no longer call you servants, for a servant does not know what his master does. But I have called you friends, for everything that I have heard from My Father have I made known to you.**
>
> **John 15:15**

Almighty God never intended for people, animals, and plants to die. Initially, there was no death in the Garden of Eden. There was only life. Death was the result of Adam and Eve's disobedience to God when sin entered them. None of us can understand the sadness that God experiences every time an unsaved person dies and enters a grave.

Without Jesus Christ as their Savior, death won another victory. God never meant Creation to be that way. Satan introduced sin to humans, and sin introduced death. Everybody, including animals, has paid the price. The currency of death pays sin's salary.

At the beginning of this marvelous story, Martha expressed to Jesus her religious belief in the resurrection of the dead. She had hope that the righteous would live again after going into their graves and descending to Hades. Martha is the one who fretted about preparing dinner for a whole house of visitors when Jesus came to visit. Her sister Mary sat at Jesus' feet listening to him teach while Martha labored in the kitchen making a meal to satisfy everybody. Yet, this same Martha had hope! She believed in the resurrection of the dead.

In response, Jesus told Martha, "I am the resurrection, and the life: he that believeth in me, though he were dead, yet shall he live...." Jesus did not say, "Martha, I believe in the resurrection too." He proclaimed that He *is* the resurrection!

If you repent of your sins, believe in the name of Jesus Christ to save your soul, and a Church elder baptizes you into Christ's Church, the Lord will resurrect your dead body on the final day.

No man can come to me, except the Father which hath sent me draw him: and I will raise him up at the last day.

John 6:44

You can rest assured because Jesus is the Resurrection. Believing in His name as Savior and believing in the Resurrection is synonymous. Faith in the name of Jesus means you believe in the Resurrection. Faith in the promise of the Resurrection requires belief in the name of Jesus to save your soul from eternal damnation. The glorious resurrection of Jesus Christ is our lively hope that we too shall be resurrected on the final day.

You are a valuable member of Jesus' inheritance, which He purchased with His precious pure blood. He went to the Cross for you! You are more than a servant of God; you are a friend of God! Jesus will resurrect you on the final day because He will not lose one soul given to Him by His Heavenly Father. God sealed you with the promised Holy Spirit unto the day of redemption.

For this reason, Christians participate in the sacrament of Holy Communion, also known as the Lord's Supper and the Eucharist (thanksgiving). We spiritually eat His flesh and drink His blood in the holy meal to nourish our souls until the final day arrives. Every time we go to the Lord's Supper, we remember His promise to resurrect us on the last day.

Whoso eateth my flesh, and drinketh my blood, hath eternal life; and I will raise him up at the last day.

John 6:54

THE SIN AMNESTY

IN THIS BOOK'S INTRODUCTION, I shared the true story of how the Holy Spirit inspired me to write a book in 1998 titled *Judgment Day*. I explained that I erred by adding the year 2000 to the title and assuming the vision I received in 1998 was about anticipated chaos on December 31, 1999, caused by the anticipated Y2K computer rollover failure.

However, I must tell you something else before you close the cover of this book and put it on a shelf to collect dust. When I finished writing the last chapter of *Judgment Day 2000* in August 1998, the Holy Spirit whispered in my heart, "There is something I want you to say." I asked Him to reveal it to me. The Holy Spirit instructed me, "Tell the people that I have declared a sin amnesty."

Puzzled by the unfamiliar term, I replied, "Lord, I have never heard of a sin amnesty. What is it?" He answered my question with a question. The Holy Spirit asked me, "Son, what is an amnesty?"

I said, "Lord, that's when a government announces that it will forgive lawbreakers who voluntarily turn themselves in to law enforcement and prosecutors and admit their guilt."

Amnesty is not a pardon. It is much more and far superior. A judge grants a pardon to an individual guilty of a criminal offense. The lawbreaker was convicted of a crime and awaits sentencing for punishment. Instead, a judge or another government official pardons the lawbreaker from receiving the deserved punishment for their crime.

Nevertheless, the lawbreaker is still guilty of committing a crime. The court records the criminal's conviction. The only thing that has changed is that the court released the lawbreaker from the penalty of the offense.

Whereas courts grant pardons to individuals, governments offer amnesty to a broad population of people. An act of amnesty is extended to many people when a government recognizes that many of its citizens are guilty of committing a particular crime, such as failure to pay their taxes. Therefore, the government will announce an amnesty.

An amnesty is not open-ended. It always has a deadline. Government officials give lawbreakers a specific amount of time to admit their crimes to law enforcement or governmental agencies. Failure to meet the deadline disqualifies the lawbreaker from receiving the amnesty benefits. Sometimes governments increase penalties after the amnesty expires. Procrastinators often pay a steep price for not responding in time to the generous offer from the government.

Judges give pardons to people convicted of breaking the law. In the matter of amnesty, prosecutors never indicted, and courts never convicted the lawbreakers. The lawbreakers turned themselves into authorities before the police arrested them. Judges give pardons to convicted lawbreakers who deserved punishment, but the court showed mercy. The pardoned felon's record of offense, the conviction, and the sentencing remain on the court records forever. The court records merely show that the criminal was granted a pardon and, thus, did not serve time in prison.

Amnesty is different. The government promises not to prosecute guilty persons if they confess their crimes before the amnesty offer expires. Furthermore, the government pledges to expunge their criminal records. Expunge means to blot out; erase, or obliterate. In the eyes of law enforcement, prosecutors, and courts, the government treats the lawbreakers as though they never committed crimes.

Prosecutors also pledge never to dig up the old offenses later and indict the defendant. Therefore, the defendant is officially viewed as innocent because the government filed no charges against them.

This is the covenant that I will make with them after those days, saith the Lord, I will put my laws into their hearts, and in their minds will I write them; and their sins and iniquities will I remember no more. Now where remission of these is, there is no more offering for sin.

Hebrews 10:16-18

All humans are lawbreakers. God gave Moses the Ten Commandments engraved by His finger on stone tablets. The commandments were not new to Moses and the Hebrews because they were known for a long time. God personally wrote them in stone for the benefit of the Hebrews. Abraham lived centuries before Moses was born, but Abraham kept the commandments. How did Abraham keep the commandments if God did not reveal the commandments until the days of Moses? It verifies Enoch's claim that Pre-Flood men and women heard the Gospel. The Good News is that Jesus Christ paid our penalty for breaking God's commandments.

> ...because that Abraham obeyed my voice, and kept my charge, my commandments, my statutes, and my laws.
>
> **Genesis 26:5**

Jesus Christ, the Son of God, the Last Adam, shed His holy blood on Calvary's Cross for the remission of our sins. We commemorate His sacrifice every time we eat His flesh and drink His blood in the sacrament of the Lord's Supper, the Eucharist, our great thanksgiving feast.

> And he took the cup, and gave thanks, and gave it to them, saying, Drink ye all of it; for this is my blood of the New Testament, which is shed for many for the remission of sins.
>
> **Matthew 26:27-28**

What must we do to act upon God's offer of a sin amnesty? Repent, believe in the name of Jesus Christ, and be baptized! John the Baptist "came into all the country about Jordan, preaching the baptism of repentance for the remission of sins." In the Book of Acts, Apostle Peter proclaimed the Good News to Jerusalem's Jews. He "let all the house of Israel know assuredly, that God hath made that same Jesus, whom ye have crucified, both Lord and Christ." When the Jews heard Peter's words, conviction pricked their hearts. They asked Peter and the other apostles, "Men and brethren, what shall we do?" Then Peter gave them the divine mandate.

> ...Repent, and be baptized every one of you in the name of Jesus Christ for the remission of sins, and ye shall receive

the gift of the Holy Ghost. For the promise is unto you, and to your children, and to all that are afar off, even as many as the Lord our God shall call. And with many other words did he testify and exhort, saying, Save yourselves from this untoward generation.

Acts 2:38-40

Almighty God loves you so much that He sacrificed His only begotten Son for the remission of your sins against Him. When fallen men nailed Jesus to the Cross, God proclaimed a worldwide sin amnesty for all humans.

Almighty God threw open His loving arms to receive all who come to Him for forgiveness. He amended the qualifications for membership in His race of chosen people. He enlarged the population of Israel by accepting more than twelve tribes of Israelites. Now Israel's membership is open to all races, tribes, and ethnic groups.

The Church is obligated to inform all sinners in every nation that God offered to forgive their sins, pardon them from just punishment, and even expunge their criminal records in Heaven's court. The sin amnesty is available to every man, woman, and child in every nation and among all races of people.

God has invited all to be His chosen people. The membership terms are simple: Repent of your sins, believe in the name of Jesus Christ to save your soul and be baptized into Christ's Church in the name of the Father, the Son, and the Holy Spirit.

God will forgive any lawbreaker who turns in themselves and admits their guilt. He will expunge your criminal record, wipe clean your file in Heaven's court, and promise never to bring up your sins again.

There is, however, a deadline to accept the terms of God's sin amnesty. You must surrender to Him before you die or the sudden arrival of the final day, whichever comes first. Individually, the sin amnesty abruptly ends the moment you take your last breath on Earth. Corporately, the sin amnesty ends before the last trumpet blast, and Jesus shouts that He has arrived in the atmosphere on clouds of great glory.

Foolishly ignoring God's gracious sin amnesty will result in harsh punishment on the final day. People who ignored the amnesty had the opportunity to be forgiven but rejected or ignored the gracious offer. Woe unto them on the Day of Judgment.

If you have never confessed to Almighty God that you are a lawbreaker who deserves eternal punishment, I implore you to cry out to your Maker now and ask for forgiveness of your sins. Tell the wonderful Creator of all life that you believe in the name of Jesus Christ to save your soul. Ask Him to write your name in the Book of Life. Receive the indwelling of the Holy Spirit. Find a devout Christian pastor and ask him to baptize you in water in the name of the Father, the Son, and the Holy Spirit. Confess with your mouth to other people that Jesus Christ is your Lord and Savior. Turn from your wicked ways and live! With the Holy Spirit's help, you can live a holy and righteous life until you die or the final day arrives.

Your Heavenly Father does not desire that you spend eternity in the lake of fire. God earnestly desires to save the souls of every human.

The Lord is not slack concerning his promise, as some men count slackness; but is longsuffering to us-ward, not

willing that any should perish, but that all should come to repentance.

2 Peter 3:9

Perhaps you are a confessing Christian but are secretly trapped in sinful behavior. It could be sexual immorality such as fornication (sex between two unmarried people), adultery (sex between one or two married people), homosexuality (sex between two people of the same gender), or an addiction to pornography or drugs. Any sexual activity outside of marriage between one man and one woman is a sin. You may be addicted to alcohol, illegal drugs, pain killers, antidepressants, gambling, or other destructive behavior. You may have a physically or emotionally abusive temper that explodes on other people and damages them. Or you may be involved in financial crimes in your business or place of employment. Your lust could be for money and things. Sin comes in a wide variety of shapes, colors, and sizes. Regardless, death is the currency that pays sin's salary. Payday is coming.

Whatever is outside the commandments of God is sin, and you must repent and turn from it. Don't let your pride prevent you from admitting you have problems and need help. All of us were born into a sinful world. We are flawed creatures living in sin-prone human bodies. I tell people, "God made us with dirt and water. We are mud pies with eyes!"

The Good News is that God's grace is far greater than our sins. Father knows that we dwell in mortal bodies of human flesh that are subject to temptation and sinful thoughts and actions. We desire to obey and please Him, yet we often fail in our daily lives to be the person we hope to be for God's glory. He is not looking for ways to condemn and reject us. He gave us a solution to our dilemma. He gave us a Savior, a Savior who will save us from our sins every day.

Yes, Jesus was there on the day you asked Him to save your soul. Without Him, you could not have entered the Kingdom. His saving grace, however, did not stop on that day. It flows abundantly every minute of each day. I often say, "Grace is like gravy. It goes with everything." What troubles your soul today? Is it stress, lack of finances, marriage division, family disputes, or an unpleasant work environment? Put a heaping helping of God's grace on it, and watch how Jesus takes you through your problems. Grace is not a magic potion that makes problems disappear. It is Heaven's pain reliever. You can use it liberally.

Your Heavenly Father does not desire to punish you. He already knows the sins you've committed. He is waiting for you to admit your guilt. Stop denying the truth about your life. Don't allow your pride to prevent you from recognizing you are a sinner who deserves Hell. Admit that you've done many wrong things in your life. You have a Heavenly Father who dearly loves you and is eager to forgive you. He made a path for you to receive forgiveness and salvation. The road leads you to the Cross.

He has an even bigger surprise waiting for you. Contrary to popular religious doctrines, we will not live forever with God in Heaven. God plans to shutter and close Heaven on the final day. Papa plans to move in with His children in New Jerusalem situated on the new Earth. The Garden of Eden 2.0 is Papa's big gift to His children who love Him. He's been dreaming about it since Adam's sin compelled Him to evict humanity's first couple from the Garden of Eden lovingly made for them.

The sin amnesty is still in effect. It could expire any day. None of us know the hour the final day will arrive. Nor do we know the last second our heart will stop beating. The Holy Bible says that our lives are like a wind that passes by and never returns. Therefore, nobody should foolishly dismiss or delay their acceptance of the sin amnesty. All who put their trust in Jesus Christ shall be preserved, sealed, and saved on the final day. The Holy Spirit will seal your soul for eternity, and angels will protect you in this world.

Angels will not have a problem with mistaken identities on the final day. Each human will have a mark: the mark of the beast or the mark of Jesus Christ. The angelic reapers are well trained and proficient in distinguishing who the wheat and the tares are on the final day.

I fulfilled the Lord's instruction to tell you about the final day to the best of my human ability. Likewise, I have now told you about the sin amnesty. The ball is in your court. It's up to you to make a move. Will you move toward God or keep running away from Him?

Say this prayer aloud and mean it.

"Almighty God, I come to you as a sinner. I have violated all your commandments. I deserve punishment because I am a lawbreaker. I read that you declared a sin amnesty to forgive and expunge from your court records all the wrong things I have done, said, and thought in my life. I desire to be forgiven. Today I confess that Jesus Christ is my Savior, Messiah, and Lord. I will obey and follow Him the rest of the days of my life. Please write my name in your Book of Life. Please preserve my soul from eternal damnation. Please baptize me with your Holy Spirit. I promise to find a church pastor who will baptize me in water. And I promise to tell other sinners that I am now forgiven by faith in Jesus Christ. Thank you for forgiving my sins. Thank you for saving my soul. I pray these things in the name of Jesus Christ. Amen."

If you sincerely prayed this prayer, please tell me so I can rejoice with you. Contact me at RickWiles.com and enter your email to receive correspondence from me.

Your friend,
Richard Wiles
A wretched sinner saved by God's grace

ABOUT THE AUTHOR

Richard D. Wiles is a husband, father, and grandfather. He is also a business executive, entrepreneur, faith futurist, talk show host, news commentator, author, film producer, presbyter, and teaching elder. He married Susan Llewellyn on June 1, 1974. They have two children: Jeremy and Karissa. Presently, Richard and Susan have ten grandchildren. Karissa adopted eight children from Russia, Ukraine, and Ecuador.

Mr. Wiles was born in Western Maryland. Most of his ancestors were members of the German Reformed Church who migrated from Europe to America in the eighteenth and nineteenth centuries. They were members of a church jointly established in 1747 by German Reformed and Lutheran settlers in Western Maryland. Mr. Wiles has relatives today who are members of that same Reformed congregation, and many generations of family members were buried in the church's cemetery.

His career in the communications media industry started at age 21 in 1975 as an advertising sales representative for a radio station that reached parts of Western Maryland, south-central Pennsylvania, northeastern West Virginia, and northwestern Virginia.

In 1980, Mr. Wiles became one of the first sales professionals in the USA to sell local cable television advertising. He was an early pioneer in the cable television advertising interconnect industry. He initiated, built, and managed an advertising sales rep team that sold local and regional advertising in several Mid-Atlantic states.

In the 1980s, Mr. Wiles worked in Virginia Beach for the Christian Broadcasting Network as the national marketing manager for affiliate relations for the CBN Cable Network, which later became the Family Channel. After leaving CBN, he was a marketing manager for The Learning Channel, now TLC, in Washington, D.C. In the 1990s, he worked in Dallas-Ft. Worth for Trinity Broadcasting Network as its director of marketing.

Mr. Wiles also owned a distributorship with Success Motivation Institute, founded by Paul F. Meyer, and taught goal setting and sales management workshops for local businesses.

Richard D. Wiles was the Republican nominee for a seat in the Maryland House of Delegates in 1994. His opponent was the former Democratic Majority Leader of the House of Delegates. Few people gave him any chance of defeating the powerful state legislator, but it was the closest election in the State of Maryland in 1994. When Mr. Wiles went to bed on election night, he was trailing the incumbent by ten votes. Absentee votes decided the election, and Mr. Wiles lost by 72 votes.

The calling of God to preach the gospel first came upon Mr. Wiles in the mid-1980s when he was living in Virginia Beach, VA while working for CBN. He struggled many years to obey the assignment to deliver an unpopular message to the American people to repent of their sins. The calling of God returned even more substantial in April 1998 when he experienced a profound vision of a significant city on fire. He resigned from TBN in September 1998 and traveled throughout the USA speaking to church congregations and Bible study groups. He also appeared as a guest on numerous local Christian radio and television talk shows.

Mr. Wiles launched the *America's Hope* radio show in Dallas/ Ft. Worth in May 1999. His message was, "Jesus Christ is America's only hope." The weekday talk show was renamed *TruNews* in 2003.

In the early months, only one radio station covering north-central Texas broadcast America's Hope. Five months after the launch of America's Hope, the radio station's owner abruptly changed the station's format and canceled all paid programming. There were no time slots available on other radio stations in the DFW market, and the circumstance compelled Rick to find an alternative method to broadcasts his message of repentance. He sincerely believed the Holy Spirit instructed him to purchase time on an international shortwave radio station covering North America and Europe, stream his radio show, and circulate it online as an audio-on-demand MP3 audio file. Thus, he became a podcasting pioneer years before the invention of podcasting.

Mr. Wiles recorded over 5,000 interviews between 1999 to 2016. His guests included members of the United States Senate and House, governors, former intelligence agents including the former chief of the Russian KGB, retired U.S. generals and admirals, best-selling authors, scientists, astronauts, solar scientists, economists, billionaires, investors, financial advisors, celebrities, famous athletes, pastors, evangelists, and Bible teachers.

In 2008, Mr. Wiles' ministry sponsored a meeting of Christian pastors in Nairobi, Kenya. Five thousand pastors gathered in Nairobi's Kenyatta Convention Center to hear his message that

"Jesus Christ is Kenya's only hope." His ministry was among the first organizations to respond to Haiti's mega-earthquake on January 12, 2010. Days after the earthquake, *TruNews* airlifted tons of food, water, blankets, tents, and other goods to Port-au-Prince. *TruNews* also chartered a cargo plane in Jamaica that transported humanitarian aid to orphanages in Jacmel, Haiti. *TruNews* erected heavy-duty military-style tents to house children in numerous towns who the earthquake had orphaned. The ministry also kept the temporary orphanages well-stocked with food throughout 2010.

In early 2021, Mr. Wiles announced his desire to gradually reduce the amount of time he devotes to reporting and analyzing world news and spend more time writing books, recording audio, and video Bible lessons, and mentoring young men. He founded and launched *Godtribe*, a digital platform for young men, including social media, audio chat rooms, and educational content. In January 2022, Mr. Wiles announced he would launch the *Faith and Values* television network on broadcast television stations and online OTT platforms. He posts his Bible courses, commentaries, and other educational material online at RickWiles.com.

Mr. Wiles is the founder and pastor of Flowing Streams, an independent, nondenominational Baptist church in Vero Beach, Florida. Although he considers himself a Reformed Baptist, Rick does not affirm the doctrine of predestination. Mr. Wiles believes God desires that all humans be saved through faith in Jesus Christ. He preaches and teaches free grace, free salvation, and free will to accept or reject God's gracious offer of reconciliation and eternal life.

Flowing Streams excels at producing compelling digital media content to proclaim the Gospel message to the public. The church describes itself as a Gospel Accelerator. Mr. Wiles is the producer of two films, *Sacrificing Liberty* and the *Greatest Reset*.

Rick and Susan love dogs. They reside on a rural property in Florida's Treasure Coast, where they sit in lawn chairs and watch alligators swim by their home and big snook fish jump out of the creek.

Contact Information
To Connect With
Richard D. Wiles

I would love to receive comments from you! Please communicate with me to:

- Write an online review of final day
- Share comments about the Second Coming of Jesus
- Tell me the impact that final day had on you
- Let me know the "aha!" revelations you had while reading the book
- Tell me about your insights into the Second Coming of Jesus
- Receive my newsletter
- Receive invitations to participate with me in special online or in-person events
- Be the first to know about my next book, video, conference, or any other project.

Sign up for my free newsletter!
RickWiles.com